# Introduction to
# READERS
# THEATRE

## A Guide to Classroom Performance

## GERALD LEE RATLIFF

MERIWETHER PUBLISHING LTD.
Colorado Springs, Colorado

**Meriwether Publishing Ltd., Publisher**
P.O. Box 7710
Colorado Springs, CO 80933

**Editor: Arthur L. Zapel**
**Typesetting: Elisabeth Hendricks**
**Cover design: Janice Melvin**

© Copyright MCMXCIX Meriwether Publishing Ltd.
Printed in the United States of America
First Edition

**Library of Congress Cataloging-in-Publication Data**

Ratliff, Gerald Lee.
    Introduction to readers theatre : a guide to classroom performance / by Gerald Lee Ratliff. — 1st ed.
        p.    cm.
    Includes bibliographical references.
    ISBN 1-56608-053-3 (pbk.)
    1. Readers' theater. I. Title.
    PN2081.R4R38    1999
    808.5'4--dc21

                          99-37424
                          CIP

1   2   3   4   5   6   7   8          03   02   01   00   99

# Acknowledgements

There are a number of "special thanks" to acknowledge here as this book is given its final due and lovingly delivered to its readers. I would like to thank Arthur L. Zapel, who first inquired if I might be interested in writing a book on Readers Theatre early in the Fall of 1998 and Theodore O. Zapel who has served as editor for a number of my Meriwether Publishing projects; Melvin R. White, whose pioneer work in Readers Theatre encouraged my own more theatrical experiments in staging classroom literature; and to my current and former students at both The State University of New York, College at Potsdam and Montclair State University for their performance inspiration and risk-taking, especially Lisa Manchester, Karen Walsh, Joe Dalo, Raina Field, Melissa Pentecost, Matthew Horohoe, Jeremy Montroy, Rhiannon Kramer, Patricia Combes, John Peruzzi, JoAnne Ozark, Jill Moffett, and Elissa Levitt; and Jim Murphy, enthusiastic photographer.

# CONTENTS

**Chapter Six**
# Sample Performance Scripts ........................*119*

# Preface

Today's Readers Theatre is engaged in the exciting pursuit of a more contemporary self-definition, and some of the more theatrical trends of classroom performance are reflected in this book of basic practices and principles. The fundamental performance theory at work in each chapter discussion, selected exercises, and sample scripts is that today's Readers Theatre is concerned with a "dramatic visualization" of literary texts; and that performers should be challenged vocally as well as physically in role-playing literary character actions and attitudes.

Traditional theatre practices like complementary costumes, props, movement, scenic design, and staging are essential ingredients in today's Readers Theatre and play a major role in transforming abstract, literary images on the printed page into inventive, risk-taking approaches to contemporary classroom performance. The focus here is on translating primary Readers Theatre principles into classroom performance practices that feature performers artistically, transforming literary figures or images into flesh-and-blood character portraits and visual pictures.

It would be rather foolhardy to spell out too explicitly the potential use of this handbook in a classroom setting. The imaginative reader of any book will find the most useful purpose for it. Each reader should view the materials in this handbook in a manner that enriches and reinforces their individual style of teaching or performing. Each reader is also encouraged to take the creative liberty of adjusting the focus of chapter discussions, suggested readings, recommended assignments, sample scripts, rehearsal exercises, or supplemental lesson plans to meet the special needs of student performers.

Please keep in mind that this is a shared journey, one that welcomes fellow travelers who have a lively spirit of adventure. Although this book provides a number of useful road signs to direct traffic through selecting, analyzing, scripting, and staging literature, it is the reader who will ultimately make appropriate choices that determine the creative role of Readers Theatre in either principle or practice. I offer this work therefore, not as a reference of rules or regulations, but simply as an invitation to come along on today's Readers Theatre journey in search of a host of theatrical literary characters ripe for classroom performance.

May, 1999

Gerald Lee Ratliff
SUNY POTSDAM

Chapter One

# An Introduction to Readers Theatre
## A Primer for Performance

*"I can take any empty space and call it a bare stage. A man walks across this empty space while someone else is watching him, and this is all that is needed for an act of theatre to be engaged."*
— Peter Brook, *The Empty Space*

The faint sound of an ancient lute floats softly into a dimly-lit classroom. Chairs and desks are arranged in a neat semi-circle, and a glistening sword rests squarely in the center of a small, rectangular wooden box draped with black metallic fabric. A hush of muffled anticipation stirs the audience, who are seated facing the front of the classroom. The music slowly fades as four performers, dressed in red choir robes and carrying flashlights, enter from the hall corridor and move in a single line to the center of the performance space.

One performer cautiously steps out of the line, moves to the small wooden box, and quietly kneels as the other three performers boldly move to stools arranged in a triangle at the back of the playing area and sit. Slowly, the performer who is kneeling looks upward and then gazes into the audience. With trembling hands, the sword is lifted into the air and brandished overhead. Pain and suffering are etched on the sad face, and a cloud of despair hangs uneasily in the air. At first, the performer who is kneeling hesitates to speak and quickly turns again and speaks in a halting voice to the audience as the other three performers sing the opening lines from the poet Elizabeth Barrett Browning's "Wisdom Unapplied" in the tune of rhythm blues.

1

If I were thou who sing'st this song,
Most wise for others, and most strong
In seeing right while doing wrong,
I would not waste my cares, and choose,
As thou — to seek what thou must lose,
Such gains as perish in the use.

READER 1: Our birth is but a sleep and a forgetting:
The soul that rises with us, our life's Star,
Hath had elsewhere its setting,
And cometh from afar:
Not in entire forgetfulness,
And not in utter nakedness,
But trailing clouds of glory do we come
From God, who is our home.
*(The three seated performers, having completed the background song, rise from their stools and move forward to assume the individual roles of READER 2, READER 3, and READER 4.)*

READER 2: Heaven lies about us in our infancy!

READER 4: Shades of the prison-house begin to close
Upon the growing boy.

READER 3: But he beholds the light, and whence it flows
He sees it in his joy.

READER 4: Behold the child among his new-born blisses.

READER 3: A six years' darling of a pygmy size!

READER 2: See, where 'mid work of his own hand he lies.

READER 4: The little actor cons another part.

READER 3: Filling from time to time his humorous stage.

READER 2: As if his whole vocation were endless imitation.

READER 1: The clouds that gather round the setting sun
Do take a sober coloring from an eye
That hath kept watch o'er man's mortality.
Another race hath been, and other palms are won.
Thanks to the human heart by which we live,
Thanks to its tenderness, its joys, and fears,
To me the meanest flower that blows can give
Thoughts that do often lie too deep for tears.

2

In this simple introduction, the basic principles of Readers Theatre have begun to translate William Wordsworth's "Ode on Intimations of Immortality from Recollections of Early Childhood" from obscure words on a printed page to here-and-now theatrical actions, images, and sounds in a lively classroom performance. All of this and more is possible because the imagination of the young, eager minds has been creatively challenged. The classroom has now become an exciting performance laboratory to experiment with inventive ways of interpreting and staging literature.

## Basic Principles

One basic principle of Readers Theatre is to provide a creative stimulus for the student who may be unaccustomed to using imagination to interpret literary works in a classroom setting. Another basic principle is to promote an understanding that to see and hear literature performed in the classroom is as relevant to thoughtful educational development as it is to read literature silently. There are, of course, a number of traditional definitions of Readers Theatre that may prove valuable in transporting a literary text from the printed page to the classroom stage.

## Traditional Definitions

Traditional definitions of Readers Theatre suggest that (1) the performers of literary texts should give vivid life and meaning to the experience described by the author; (2) the audience should be stimulated to share in the intellectual or emotional content suggested in literary texts; and (3) both the performers and the audience should actively engage their imagination to awaken literary texts from their leather-bound slumber. There have also been a number of attempts to define Readers Theatre as a "group" performance that presents a literary text to an audience using selected oral interpretation techniques; or as a "chamber theatre" production that pursues the narrative elements of literature using minimal theatrical devices.

These representative definitions, initially coined by a number of academic scholars included in the "Suggested Readings" list at the end of the chapter, firmly planted the early seeds of Readers Theatre in terms of its content and form. For the most part, however, the first fruits of Readers Theatre performance and production were "staged readings" that emphasized the oral interpretation of non-dramatic literary texts presented by a small ensemble of "readers" performing multiple character roles. Today, of course, definitions are merely convenient word games we play as more non-traditional experiments in Readers Theatre continue with a lively host of new advocates and inventive performance artists.

## Working Blueprint

Now, perhaps more than ever, there is a need to promote a working blueprint for Readers Theatre classroom performance that not only recognizes the aesthetic and intellectual nature of a literary text, but also acknowledges the dramatic alliance with theatre. Whether constructed on the solid foundation of traditional theories or inspired by experimental discoveries, today's Readers Theatre cultivates the most imaginative theatrical techniques available to see, hear, and *feel* literature in classroom performance. Although there is no prescribed formula needed to give dramatic shape and substance to a literary text, the working blueprint of today's Readers Theatre is concerned with the inherent theatricality of literature; particularly the dramatic role that sights, sounds, or words can play in a scripted classroom performance.

Perhaps the best example of theatricality needed in Readers Theatre today is still to be found in the genius of William Shakespeare, whose intuitive and yet subtle use of literary as well as theatrical techniques challenged his sixteenth-century Elizabethan audience to rely on their own sense of sight and sound to clearly decipher the "spoken" words and "unspoken" actions of some of literature's most notable and yet perplexing characters. In *Hamlet* (I, ii) for example, the young prince is in a state of pitiful mourning for his father when approached by friend and fellow student, Horatio:

HAMLET:  My father — methinks I see my father.
HORATIO:  O where, my lord?
HAMLET:  In my mind's eye, Horatio.

It is here that Hamlet's words provide the most useful working blueprint needed for here-and-now Readers Theatre: it must be in the "mind's eye." Hamlet's dramatic imagination has called to mind much more than just the face of his murdered father. He can also hear his father's voice and feel his father's pain. These two essential ingredients of theatrical imagination later provoke Hamlet's plot of revenge, and immediately establish a special empathic relationship with the audience as they also become actively engaged in the stage action that follows.

If, like Hamlet, we view the dramatic imagination as a creative act that is dependent only upon the "mind's eye" to give heightened meaning to a character's actions and words, then Readers Theatre is much more than a dusty bookmobile exhibition that provides familiar access to the casual reader. To speak boldly, today's Readers Theatre moves at will through time and space to revisit the past armed with theatrical devices and techniques that give added dimension to familiar literature like Charles Dickens' *A Christmas Carol*, Robert Frost's "Mending Wall," Toni Morrison's *Beloved*, or Herman Melville's *Moby Dick*.

## Theatrical Impulse

The theatrical impulse in Readers Theatre is interested in pursuing the artistic and dramatic visualization of the actions, attitudes, and emotions of literary characters in classroom performance. The Readers Theatre theatrical impulse is also the same one shared with traditional theatre practice in terms of the focus on a written text, attention to pictorial composition, vocal and physical performance techniques that capture a three-dimensional character portrait, and the cultivation of an informed audience response to text, performance, and production.

Readers Theatre literary characters do not leap from the printed page full-blown in a detailed description of their performance intention or motivation. They emerge in infinitely subtle and frequently disguised classroom rehearsal clues that point the way to striking elements of character development generally found in traditional theatre approaches to role-playing. The classroom performance challenge is to seize these theatrical role-playing opportunities revealed in rehearsal and to fill in the tentative or incomplete literary character outline with as much inventive self-expression as possible.

The current theatrical trend in Readers Theatre signals unlimited artistic possibilities for continued experimentation in classroom performance. Discovering the theatrical impulse in literature gives heightened dramatic meaning to a literary text and personalizes classroom performance. It also suggests the need to pursue an illustrative approach in the performance of literary texts, giving theatrical life and meaning to the descriptions, dialog, and images associated with literary characters. Please review the convenient chart below that suggests additional Readers Theatre practices and principles in today's more theatrical classroom performance. (A discussion of theatrical staging in classroom performance is also included in Chapter four.)

| **Traditional Readers Theatre** | **Today's Readers Theatre** |
| --- | --- |
| Recreates literary text | Embodies literary text |
| Suggests author experience | Stages character experience |
| Depicts narrative world | Depicts here-and-now |
| Relates action | Dramatizes action |
| Intellectual visualization | Theatrical visualization |
| "Say words" | "Do actions" |
| Present tense Illusion | Living present tense |
| Focus on text | Focus on performer |
| Stage textual imagery | Stage theatrical imagery |
| Moves in narrative | Moves in playing space |
| Limited stage movement | Pictorial composition |
| Presents the character | Portrays the character |
| Adapted/compiled texts | Improvised/original texts |
| Audience observer | Audience participant |

6

| | |
|---|---|
| Literary term character | Theatrical agent character |
| Reveal character insight | Reveal character subtext |
| Linear pattern | Irregular pattern |
| Performance laboratory | Life performance |
| Printed page character | Flesh-and-blood character |
| Abstract literary images | Concrete dramatic action |
| Limited scenic elements | Multiple scenic elements |
| Analysis based | Observation based |
| "Thinking space" | "Seeing space" |

# SELECTED READERS THEATRE CONVENTIONS

There are a number of traditional Readers Theatre conventions that need to be addressed at this point, and they are presented here as general guidelines. For example, in Readers Theatre a single performer may play a number of different roles in a script. Performers may have individual lines of narration and dialog, or they may share narration and dialog with other performers. Sometimes the setting, mood, or even other characters suggested in the script may be directed into the audience to promote listener identification; and at other times performers may wear suggestive costumes or makeup to suggest a more physical presence for their literary character portraits. As you will no doubt discover in your continued reading, the immediate success of Readers Theatre in the classroom depends on the skill of the performers, the selection of evocative literature, the creative use of space, and the available rehearsal time needed to polish a production.

## Scripts

Readers Theatre performers may either hold their scripts or place them on lecterns or music stands. Although the script is usually visible in a classroom performance, it should not indicate that the emphasis is merely reading literature aloud. After all, it is a classroom *performance*; and that suggests a memorized text, performers assuming clearly-defined character roles, and the theatrical reality of believable dramatic action. If the hand-held script is an essential element of the classroom performance, and cannot be used effectively as a character hand-prop, then the use of chairs or stools may be more appropriate. Performers may also be so familiar with the scripted text that they glance down occasionally to voice parts of the text while delivering other parts from memory. If, however, the text is memorized and there is no apparent reason to focus attention on the script it should be eliminated from classroom performance. (An example of the role that a script might play as a character hand-prop may be found in the "Book Parade" exercise in Chapter Five.)

## Staging

The traditional approach to Readers Theatre classroom staging usually features performers who stand in line facing the audience, sit on stools, combine sitting and standing, or an occasional use of movement to suggest the pictorial composition of abstract images or character attitudes. Today's Readers Theatre staging, however, may include an elevated platform stage framed by a proscenium arch at one end of the classroom; or a playing space arranged in-the-round, three-quarters round, or in a semi-circle. Classroom staging may even include ramps, step-units, ladders, door frames, table tops, platforms, desks, curtains, draperies, window blinds, and painted backdrops or fabric panels that depict the locale of a literary text. (Additional opportunities to make use of "found space" or "environmental settings" are discussed in Chapter Four.)

Theatrical production elements like lighting, projections, music, sound, or special effects are now being used effectively in classroom staging to suggest the setting of a literary text; or to provide additional aural and visual commentary on the author's apparent theme. The most appropriate choice of staging should be determined by the author's apparent point of view in the scripted text, and the classroom performance space should capture the atmosphere and mood suggested in the selected literature. Some Readers Theatre classroom productions continue to emphasize minimal set pieces, a backdrop of dark drapes, and an occasional raised platform to provide a number of performance levels as an invitation to the audience to visualize the relatively bare staging area from their own scenic perspective.

The artistic line between a staging area that is "literal" or "localized" is a very fine one in a classroom production. A single white picket fence in a scripted adaptation of Mark Twain's *Huckleberry Finn* or a gnarled tree stump in Henry James' "The Beast in the Jungle" may, at first glance, represent a specific locale but does little to give substantial meaning to the complex issues of free will and fantasy addressed in literature. It is important, therefore, that classroom staging become a more intrinsic aspect of the visual presentation of literature. There are a number of specific questions about the stage setting that will need to be answered if the visual element of staging is to have dramatic impact on the classroom production.

For example, if the locale suggested in the literature is psychological how will the space of the mind be staged? The mystic experience of the persona described in William Faulkner's *As I Lay Dying* might suggest a non-literal, unidentified playing space that simply includes a sky-blue cyclorama, elevated platform, side lighting, and a series of suspended mobiles in abstract shapes that underscore the literary character's apparent mental state. On the other hand, if the locale suggested in the literature is very specific, how will the detailed location be staged? The clearly defined setting of a dining room in Lorna Dee Cervantes' "My Dinner with Your Memory," for example, indicates a large table, two chairs, wine, and a festive meal being served to underscore the literary character's emotional detachment and isolation.

Although it may be tempting in this last example to construct the literal setting suggested in the literature, there are a number of apparent problems to be considered. The basic nature of the literary character's action in the literature is sitting, eating, and reflecting on life. There is no compelling reason here to duplicate the static literary setting described in the text, even if the physical isolation of the character might be enriched by a confined playing space. There are, of course, no definitive rules that govern decision-making in Readers Theatre staging, and individual artistic choices invariably surface as the direct result of a critical analysis of the literary text and a detailed assessment of the production concept.

## Movement

The role of movement in traditional Readers Theatre was limited to concerns of efficiently managing stage traffic and providing convenient opportunities for performers to enter or exit the playing space. Today, however, movement is an essential ingredient in classroom performance and is used whenever it adds a dramatic dimension to the scripted text. When used creatively, movement may crystallize an abstract or symbolic point of view expressed by the author. For example, in T.S. Eliot's "The Hollow Men," having performers stagger forward to pronounce themselves "leaning together" or swaying "like wind in dry grass" may be effective in conveying the desolation and pessimism suggested by the author.

When clearly motivated, movement can create a theatrical sense of motion that reinforces or redirects an audience's understanding of a literary text; and it can provide an energetic tempo for the classroom performance as well. Movement is also a valuable tool to suggest changing literary character relationships or to externalize the storyline of the literature. Although it is best to encourage performers to improvise in order to discover their own patterns of physical gesture or motion, choreographed movement that reinforces the actions and the words expressed in the literature can reveal a variety of literary character attitudes and moods.

Regardless of the degree of movement suggested in the literature, there should always be a balance between movement that enhances the character experience described by the author and movement that sets the literary scene in the audience's imagination. The role of movement in classroom performance is always a relative one, but it does provide an accurate visual demonstration of the physical and psychological relationship of literary characters. It is only the impulse for extraneous or extensive movement that should be carefully avoided in classroom

10

performance. Gratuitous scene changes or aimless movement by performers soon diminishes the desired effect of directing an audience's attention to a specific locale or literary character for specific purpose. (An example of the role that movement might play in literary characterization may be found in the "Carry Your Character with You!" exercise in Chapter Five.)

## ORAL INTERPRETATION AND READERS THEATRE

Traditional oral interpretation of literature approaches to Readers Theatre appear to view classroom performance from a rhetorical perspective that shares the classical tradition of Greek persuasive public speaking or recitative reading. Although most traditional approaches emphasize the value of appreciating, recognizing, and even understanding the dramatic qualities of a literary text, there is less agreement on the classroom performance skills needed to give life and meaning to the feelings or thoughts of literary characters. For some, oral interpretation of literature remains an act of re-creation, the performer's voice and body merely convenient instruments that translate the author's printed words to an audience of listeners. Others, however, view oral interpretation of literature as a "performance art" that shares a decidedly theatrical tradition with selected acting theories like role-playing and character-building that emphasize physical as well as vocal performance techniques.

The primary differences of opinion regarding the traditional or the theatrical nature of Readers Theatre may have resulted at a time when the oral interpreter was encouraged to *present* rather than *represent* literary characters in classroom performance. In addition, the oral interpreter often carried a handheld script to interpret a number of characters in a scripted text; and appears to have also discarded character accessories like costumes, makeup, and props. Of course, all of these oral interpretation techniques were crafted to promote the aesthetic, emotional, and intellectual content of a literary text rather than its potential for theatrical performance.

11

Although oral interpretation remains an essential ingredient in Readers Theatre classroom performance, the serious study of literary texts should not be limited solely to the critical analysis of its isolated parts. Literature must be experienced in the realm of a theatrical interpretation that gives active voice and body to literary characters who might otherwise remain lifeless figures on the printed page. The classroom performance of a literary text releases imprisoned characters and sets free the imagination of performers to explore what the critic Kenneth Thorpe Rowe calls "... that theatre in our heads."

Of course, the classroom performance of literature is much more complex than just reading aloud. It is, in its most simple statement, the intuitive ability to transform a literary text into a living, breathing *presence* that speaks to the universal human condition. That is why today's Readers Theatre enthusiasts are concerned with blending the imaginative world of the literary text with their own personal world; and then sharing that kinship with other human beings. Readers Theatre now shares a more rewarding theatrical perspective and approaches literary texts from a less rigidly formulated set of classroom performance practices. The attempt to *portray* rather than *present* literary characters in performance has also encouraged a more inspired use of theatrical makeup, costumes, and hand-props to suggest the exterior texture of literary characters.

One of the final concerns of Readers Theatre performance today is still the need to observe human nature and to select those circumstances or experiences that may be incorporated into the fictional world of the literary text. That is not to imply that the Readers Theatre performer does not engage in a critical examination of the literary text; or that observation alone is the principal ingredient in a classroom performance blueprint. The important point here is to feature the *performance* of the literary text and to use personal observation to promote an authentic interpretation of literary characters. Readers Theatre as an art form depends on gifted performers who create an illusion of reality in the interpretation of literary texts; and it is personal observation that may provide the facial expression, gesture, physical posture, or vocal quality needed to give life and meaning to literary characters in classroom performance. A classroom performance of a literary text shaped in part by a performer's lived experiences or observations can also persuade an audience that what is revealed about literary characters is familiar, honest, and natural.

## Postscript

Perhaps the most exciting principle in Readers Theatre is that it challenges us to make choices. Although the literary text provides numerous signal lights that direct our traffic through an interpretation of the literature, the signposts that lead to an inspired classroom performance are often obscure and may often detour along winding or uncharted roads that do not always reach our charted destination. It is important, therefore, to be well prepared for the journey and to avoid unnecessary roadblocks.

No matter how you choose to use Readers Theatre, the fundamental principle to guide you on the journey is that the eye must be trained — in the same manner as the musician's ear must be tuned — to visualize the actions and incidents suggested in literary texts; paying special attention to the subtle nuances of character intention or motivation that might promote a theatrical here-and-now classroom performance. With the practical knowledge gained from your own discoveries on the journey, new and inventive Readers Theatre practices will no doubt emerge as well. What remains in the following chapters is to blend the theoretical principles of Readers Theatre into an individual artistic expression that serves as your own personal signature in classroom performance.

So, let's begin our Readers Theatre journey in search of a flurry of theatrical literary texts that hold promise of vivid literary characters ripe for classroom performance. It is a pleasure to serve as your traveling companion and, as the noted biographer Izaak Walton once remarked, "Good company on the journey will make the way seem shorter!"

# SUGGESTED READINGS

The following suggested readings provide a basic introduction to Readers Theatre and the oral interpretation of literature. The list of readings should also provide useful background information on selected approaches to classroom performance from both a traditional and theatrical perspective. Unfortunately many of these titles are no longer in print, but may be found in libraries.

Bacon, Wallace. *The Art of Interpretation.* New York: Holt, Rinehart and Winston, 1979.

Breen, Robert. *Chamber Theatre.* Englewood Cliffs, New Jersey: Prentice-Hall, 1978.

Brook, Peter. *The Empty Space.* New York: Avon Books, 1968.

Coger, Leslie Irene and Melvin White. *Readers Theatre Handbook.* Glenview, Illinois: Scott, Foresman, 1977.

Gamble, Teri and Michael. *Oral Interpretation: The Meaning of Self and Literature.* Skokie, Illinois: National Textbook Company, 1976.

Lee, Charlotte and Timothy Gura. *Oral Interpretation.* Boston: Houghton Mifflin, 1987.

Long, Beverly Whitaker and Mary Frances Hopkins. *An Introduction to Oral Interpretation.* Englewood Cliffs, New Jersey: Prentice-Hall, 1984.

Maclay, Joanna. *Readers Theatre: Toward a Grammar of Practice.* New York: Random House, 1971.

Pickering, Jerry. *Readers Theatre.* Encino, California: Dickenson, 1975.

Scrivner, Louise and Dan Robinette. *A Guide to Oral Interpretation.* Indianapolis, Indiana: Bobbs-Merrill Publishing, 1980.

Chapter Two
# Selecting and Analyzing Literature

*"My characters are assembled from past and present stages of civilization, bits from books and newspapers, scraps of humanity, ragged and tattered pieces of fine clothing, patched together as is the human soul."*

— August Strindberg, *Diary*

The range of literature available in Readers Theatre is dependent only on the dramatic imagination needed to visualize novels, poems, short stories, song lyrics, letters, diaries, journalistic articles, or other printed materials for theatrical classroom performance. The challenge of selecting and analyzing Readers Theatre literature is to go beyond the traditional choice of theatre playscripts and to make *any* form of literature dramatic by giving it the ingredients associated with the theatrical impulse described in Chapter One.

At first glance, the variety of Readers Theatre literature may appear to present critical artistic problems of judgment. For example, is the choice to be determined by its (1) inherent dramatic appeal, (2) suggestion of action, (3) language, and (4) literary character portraits? Or, is the choice to be determined by (1) author familiarity, (2) accessibility, (3) literary quality, and (4) theme? How, finally, do we make the difficult choices between classroom performance of such classic literature like Homer's *Iliad* or Chaucer's *The Canterbury Tales* and more contemporary literature like Audre Lord's "Black Mother Woman" or Laurence Ferlinghetti's "Underwear"?

# Initial Review

In an initial review, the task of selecting appropriate literature for classroom performance should be influenced by preliminary considerations such as the

- Degree of character action
- Quality of visual images
- Catalog of attitudes, emotions, or moods
- Nature of the language
- Sequence of events or incidents
- Potential for the theatrical impulse in performance.

In addition, the initial selection of literature should consider the skill of the performers. Literature should encourage performers to role-play literary characters, promote full use of the voice or body, and actively engage the spirit of the dramatic imagination.

The initial period of literature review is an opportunity to rely on theatre exercises or improvisational activities like those described in Viola Spolin's books about theatre games for performers to discover the subtle shades of author meaning or character subtext in the literary text. Theatre exercises or improvisational activities may even encourage performers to create their own "biographies" of incidents or events that may have happened prior to the story line described in the literature. The initial period of literature review is also an opportunity for performers to invent tentative "interior monologs" that may reveal subconscious or submerged literary character feelings or thoughts.

Some thought should be given to the educational role that Readers Theatre might play in classroom performance as well. The learning process is traditionally enriched when performers are challenged beyond some degree of their individual skills, or when they are provided challenging opportunities to cultivate imaginative "new" aural or visual skills. (An example of classroom assignments, activities, and improvisations to help cultivate performance skills may be found in the "Literature Alive" exercise in Chapter Five.)

Of course, it is important to encourage performer participation early in the initial stages of literature review to promote a relaxed classroom environment of inquiry and exploration. Including original compositions or narrative transitions, contemporary song lyrics, familiar popular culture texts, scenic design, or staging and movement suggestions that emerge from small-group or individual problem-solving assignments helps to promote an infectious classroom spirit of artistic ensemble. Active classroom participation is an excellent introduction to Readers Theatre as a means to interpret and perform literature. It also provides additional learning experiences in literary analysis, critical thinking, performance studies, and the technical demands of theatrical staging.

# Final Review

In Readers Theatre we rarely know how an audience will respond to classroom performance of a literary text until it is actually performed! But we do know some of the touchstones that indicate audience expectations and these should be considered part of the initial literature review process. The following observations indicate some of the more common expectations to address in achieving a heightened sense of audience interest in classroom performance.

- Abstract philosophical thought, introspective narrative passages, or psychological case studies all appear to distance an audience and limit possibilities for interaction.
- Presentation time of twenty-five or thirty minutes is sufficient for the classroom performance of literature.
- There are opportunities to perform fifteen-minute scripts for specific literature assignments like "Early American Romantics," "The Wild, Wild West," or "Street Talk."
- A small ensemble cast of eight performers is appropriate for most thirty-minute classroom performance scripts.
- Any number of supporting performers like narrator(s), chorus members, singers, dancers, or minor speaking roles may be added to classroom performance.
- Hosting an informal fifteen-minute "Reading Hour" with an

invited audience can feature original compositions or small-group programs like "Women on Women," "The Global Village," or "Just Friends."

The final review of appropriate performance literature is the time for intuitive artistic decision-making. Of primary importance is reviewing literature that promises to challenge performers to discover an inventive theatrical performance in the literary text. Whether as an inkling or a profound belief, the final review of literature should suggest that both performers and the text are in the *living present,* each experiencing a fleeting moment in the eternal life of bringing literature alive in classroom performance. There should be an emphasis on sharing the meaning of only a limited number of the imaginary incidents or events dramatized in the story line of the literature; and the untold lives of the literary characters should be sufficiently rich in dramatic action to encourage an emphatic response.

Today's theatrical approach to Readers Theatre continues to influence the final review of literature for classroom performance. For example, a performer's *reaction* to spoken lines of literature is now much more meaningful than the *action* of the individual performer who may be speaking. Action and reaction, of course, are nowhere more expressive than in the camera angles, fades, and pans of contemporary film practice. There is, however, a growing trend in Readers Theatre to script literature that focuses more on performers exchanging face-to-face character reactions, slides, or projections used to reveal character intention or motivation, and music to underscore the theme or apparent point of view of the author or the character in the literary text.

Sergei Eisenstein, the film director, suggests this additional dimension of film that should also be considered in a final review of potential Readers Theatre literature. In the book *Film Sense,* Eisenstein says that literary texts merit performance when they conjure up the "uncharted world" of a character's imagination or when they compel performers to "take possession" of the character's imagination as if it were his own. What is arresting for Readers Theatre in this cinematic approach to the selection of literature is

18

Eisenstein's description of the initial creative process at work in artistic decision-making:

> "What we actually do is to compel our imagination to depict for us a number of concrete pictures or situations appropriate to the text. The aggregation of the mental pictures so imagined evokes in us the required emotion, feeling, understanding, and actual experience that we are seeking or it does not."

After carefully reviewing the basic principles at work in the selection of literature, it may be necessary to pursue individual artistic instincts like Eisenstein suggests as well. The classroom rehearsal period is an excellent performance laboratory to test potential literary texts; or to experiment with a more theatrical production blueprint. The trial-and-error discoveries made in the rehearsal period, however, should not detract from the author's point of view expressed in the literary text. And there is always the cautious reminder to avoid the inevitable bundle of clichés, shop-worn theatrical tricks, or the convenient temptations that might mask an accurate and honest classroom performance of the literary text.

## ANALYSIS OF LITERATURE

The critical study of a literary text closely resembles the analysis techniques used in the English literature and theatre playscript interpretation classroom. In both of these settings, the primary objective is to jointly discover the complexities of a literary text in terms of its character, plot, structure, and theme. Although it may be difficult at first for some performers to imagine themselves in a literature classroom actively engaged in the critical study of a literary text *before* classroom performance, it is important that they approach the literary text with the same analytical discipline and dedication as the literary critic.

*First,* it is important to take notes concerning the mental, physical, and vocal qualities of literary characters. *Second,* it is important to make decisions regarding the specific goals or objectives of literary characters. *Third,* it is important to accurately define literary characters based on the author's description of their relationship with other characters in the text. *Fourth,* it is important to visualize literary characters in terms of potential theatrical accessories like costumes, makeup, or props. *Fifth,* it is important to voice literary characters in terms of the attitude, mood, and intention or motivation expressed in the literature.

# First Reading

At first, it is best to read a literary text *silently* with an ear for character interpretation and an eye for classroom performance clues. The first reading should indicate the literary character's emotional or intellectual condition and reveal the chronological or sequential events detailed in the story line. The first reading should indicate if the performer has the immediate personal association needed to effectively dramatize the literary character in a classroom performance as well. Finally, this first reading may also suggest the theatrical staging devices needed to visualize the author's point of view in an interpretation of the literary text.

For example, a first reading of Ernest Hemingway's "The Snows of Kilimanjaro" may initially suggest that the best staging device to capture the vast panorama described in the narration is to use a number of elevated platforms, ramps, and runways to depict the snow-covered, 19,710-foot high mountain in Africa; or that the most appropriate classroom performance approach to portray the rugged, brusque literary characters is to have the performers grow scraggly beards, wear thermal mountain-climbing jumpsuits, and carry a pick or shovel as suggestive hand props.

# Second Reading

A second reading of the literary text is more objective than the first, and should concentrate on the apparent *meaning* of the literature. The reading should consider the author's personal signature in terms of individual word choice, narrative description, imagery, and language of the spoken dialog. The second reading should direct attention more clearly to the author's point of view, descriptive tone, and the interpersonal relationships of the literary characters. A second reading of the literary text invariably calls the mind's eye to the theatrical staging devices that may help to visualize the characters and the setting in classroom performance. The second reading may also provide later scripting strategies for deleting or editing passages, isolating key episodes that reveal conflict, or providing useful transitions between dramatic incidents or events described in the literary text.

For example, a second reading of Ernest Hemingway's "The Snows of Kilimanjaro" now reveals that the snow-covered mountain is simply a metaphor used as a literary backdrop to frame the author's point of view. The second reading indicates that the literary characters are intent on discovering a personal code of conduct that allows them to live with a measure of dignity and grace while playing a no-win game of chance against nature. It may also be apparent in the second reading that the author's personal signature is to feature a number of character portrait vignettes to highlight the cultural and psychological meaning associated with the terms individuality, masculinity, and self-sacrifice.

The more perceptive second reading suggests that initial interpretations may have to be discarded or subtly revised. It may now be inadvisable to pursue the elaborate Mt. Kilimanjaro classroom setting of elevated platforms, ramps, and runways to depict a snow-covered mountain facade. It may now be inappropriate to direct undue attention to the petty quarrels and rash, spontaneous outbursts of individual characters. It may now be inaccurate to neglect primary focus on the heroic characters who must face inevitable defeat in their quest for a meaningful self-identity. Finally, it may now be time to give serious consideration to classroom performance and staging approaches that underline the tone of despair in the frequent jousting word play and the noticeable progression of assertive physical action and reaction exhibited by the literary characters.

# Performance Reading

A performance reading, especially in small groups, is voiced *aloud* and provides a more theatrical, three-dimensional interpretation of the literary text. Preliminary performance readings are frequent and establish the context to:

- Identify specific character action, attitude, and mood
- Discover appropriate Readers Theatre conventions to visualize the dramatic action
- Provide subtle clues for an inventive character interpretation
- Reveal the submerged intellectual, emotional, or psychological intention and motivation that prompts character reaction or responses
- Define the playing space in terms of literal or figurative setting
- Experiment with movement patterns that accurately reflect character goals and objectives
- Consider meaningful opportunities in the literary text to promote audience participation.

The polished performance reading of Ernest Hemingway's "The Snows of Kilimanjaro," for example, may reveal more clearly the shifting moods of fate that punctuate the build to a harrowing climax in the literary text. The performance reading should carefully pinpoint the specific vignettes that conceptualize the periods of tension and relaxation that surface in the author's point of view on masculinity as well. The performance reading should also have indicated the potential gestures, mannerisms, movement patterns, and vocal qualities of the primary literary characters.

Finally, the performance reading suggests that the most thought-provoking classroom setting for Ernest Hemingway's "The Snows of Kilimanjaro" may be, quite simply, black-and-white sheer curtains draped from the ceiling as a transparent, visual symbol of the icy, snow-capped mountain parable described in the literary text. (An example of imaginative activities to discover interesting characters in the analysis of literature may be found in the "Literary Character Charades" exercise in Chapter Five.)

# Literary Analysis Principles

The basic analysis principles at work in reading a literary text for critical perception rather than performance clues demand sensitivity to written images or words and familiar understanding of traditional theories peculiar to the study of literature. The literary critic's initial impression — in the mind's eye, of course — is primarily an *intellectual* response to an author's recorded experience in the literature. It is *not,* however, says Richard Palmer in *Hermeneutics,* " ... the reader who manipulates the work, for the work remains fixed; it is the reader who is changed." Perhaps a convenient starting point to consider this essential literary viewpoint on the interpretation of literature is to review the conventional system of codes a critic may use to decipher an author's apparent point of view.

Here, then, are some common strategies the literary critic employs to gain a deeper appreciation of a literary text. The critic begins with a review of the introduction to the literary text and becomes aware of any editorial or prefatory comments that may precede the literature. Of particular value is any discussion of the author's life, historical times, or literary movements that may have influenced the writing of the characters depicted. The critic is also concerned with the history of the literature in terms of its appraisal in the judgment of scholars and in the evidence of its merit as a literary text of some distinction.

For example, a critical understanding of the poet John Crowe Ransom's personal confession that the nostalgic flavor of the "old South" and the myth of religion greatly influenced his poetic vision gives added emphasis to the literary critic's interpretation of the author's elegy "Here Lies a Lady." Likewise, a precise understanding of Walt Whitman's social journey as a self-proclaimed "poet of democracy" is a prescient symbol to the literary critic's interpretation of the author's characteristic use of campaign slogans, folk narratives, and references to Abraham Lincoln in the poems "When Lilacs Last in the Dooryard Bloom'd" and "O Captain, My Captain."

The literary critic is attentive to the title or any suggestive caption that is used to introduce a literary text. Titles or captions

23

often suggest an author's thematic point of view to the critic, and give an added dimension of authenticity to the interpretation of literary characters. For example, the caption of "Tribute to Carl Solomon" in Allen Ginsberg's poem "Howl" may suggest the author's apologetic attitude to the literary critic when recalling the apocryphal history Allen Ginsberg and Carl Solomon shared when both men were patients at the Columbia (New York) Psychiatric Institute in 1949. Titles that rely on poetic images or descriptive word choices, like Lorna Cervantes' "The Body as Braille," Booker T. Washington's "Up From Slavery," or Randall Jarrell's "Thinking of the Lost World," just as frequently lead critics to suspect an implied point of view in the author's literary text.

The listing of character names may further alert the critic to an author's veiled point of view and amplify the critic's interpretation of a literary character's subtext. Adrienne Rich's use of well-known historical names like Chopin, Diderot, and Cicero in the poem "Snapshots of a Daughter-in-Law," for example, may suggest to the inquiring critic that the author is juxtaposing women with familiar male figures as an expression of adulation and praise. Likewise, Arnold Powell's use of non-descriptive character names like Alldad, Everymom, and Baby in *The Death of Everymom* may direct a critic's gaze to the author's unmistakable use of personification to suggest the loss of personal identity for the characters in the literary text.

It is also important for the literary critic to:

- Pay careful attention to unfamiliar words
- Be aware of subtle references to other literature mentioned in the text and
- Unravel the mystery of twisted sentences by looking for the subject, verb, and object of the main clause.

Here are some selected terms that may be of additional value in literary analysis.

- Look for the *persona,* or "second self," of the author through whom the story is told.

24

- Try to discover if the story is being told from an *omniscient* third-person, or from an interior first-person "I" point of view.
- Examine the *story line,* or sequence of events and incidents, to more clearly determine how place and time influence the character actions and reactions.
- Be alert to *auditory,* or sound, values suggested by the literary alliteration, assonance, consonance, or onomatopoeia.
- Review *rhythmic schemes,* or recurrent patterns of beat and stress, that identify the cadence or tempo of the character's spoken language.
- Identify the *climax,* or the highest point in the dramatic action revealed in plot, and anticipate a similar build of intensity in the classroom performance.
- Remember that most poetry is structured around a *fulcrum,* or balance point, that begins with forward-motion and then moves to counter-motion after the fulcrum.
- Pay particular attention to the *denotative,* or dictionary, meaning of words and the *connotative,* or implied, meaning of words to better understand the author's point of view.

Here are some abbreviated samples of literature that make effective use of other selected literary terms that may be of value in the critical analysis of literature. Framed in rather broad categories, these brief, concise excerpts from well-known literature indicate some of the more subtle elements of language to consider in literary analysis. It is sometimes a good idea in the initial analysis to use specific literary terms to define *who* the character is, *what* the character is doing, *where* the character is doing it, *when* the character is doing it, and *why* the character is doing it. These journalistic Five Ws should provide a composite of the character in terms of the given circumstances revealed in the literary text, and may even reveal the reasons a character acts or reacts in specific instances. The Five Ws approach to analysis may also provide preliminary classroom performance clues that recognize and later reconcile a character's behavior.

The accuracy of discovering informed responses to the questions posed by the Five Ws becomes noticeably more pronounced with more first-hand experience in the analysis of literary texts. Additional literary terms may also surface to more accurately define a character's basic intention or motivation and clarify a character's basic impulses or spontaneous outbursts. For now, however, it may give some comfort to know that David Perkins, the noted psychologist, once described the initial process of literary analysis as the " ... maddening drive to wrest order, simplicity, meaning, richness, and powerful expression from what is seemingly *chaos!*"

**Tone Color:**
The literary character's implied attitude toward the subject and toward the audience. Tone color may be serious, sober, intimate, solemn, playful, ironic, or condescending.

> "He snorted scornfully, 'Yeah, you just come from de church house on a Sunday night, but heah you is gone to work on them clothes. You ain't nothing but a hypocrite. One of them amen-corner Christians — sing, whoop, and shout, then come home and wash white folks' clothes on the Sabbath."
>
> — Zora Neale Hurston, *Sweat*

**Mood:**
The emotional attitude of the author toward the subject implied in the atmosphere of a literary text. On the subject of death, for example, John Donne in "Death, Be Not Proud" exhibits noble defiance, but Robert Frost in "Out, Out —" appears to embrace a more somber mood.

> "They listened at his heart.
> Little — less — nothing! And that ended it.
> No more to build on there, And they, since they
> Were not the dead one, turned to their affairs."
>
> — Robert Frost, "Out, Out —"

**Metaphor:**
An implied analogy, or comparison, which imaginatively

26

identifies one object with another; and invests the first object with qualities usually associated with the second.

> "That time of year thou mayst in me behold
> When yellow leaves, or none, or few, do hang
> Upon those boughs which shake against the cold;
> Bare ruined choirs where late the sweet birds sang."
> — William Shakespeare, "Sonnet 73"

**Simile:**
Comparison of two things essentially unlike using "as" or "like." The comparison is on the basis of a resemblance in at least one aspect, as John Milton suggests below in his simile of Hell (dungeon) and a furnace.

> "A dungeon horrible, on all sides round,
> As one great furnace flamed."
> — John Milton, *Paradise Lost*

**Poetic Quality:**
A term applied to prose to suggest it shares a striking similarity to poetry in terms of its evocative imagery, language, and word choice.

> "And this is how I see the East. I have seen its secret places and have looked into its very soul; but now I see it always from a small boat, a high outline of mountains, blue and afar in the morning; like a faint mist at noon; a jagged wall of purple at sunset."
> — Joseph Conrad, *Youth*

## THEATRE ANALYSIS PRINCIPLES

When considering the principles of theatre analysis for classroom performance, it is important to pursue literary texts that portray clearly-defined characters actively engaged in a theatrical sense. Dramatic characters liked Wolf Larsen in Jack London's *The*

*Call of the Wild* and Dewey in Truman Capote's *In Cold Blood,* or even less familiar characters like the inquisitive Lieutenant Hearn in Norman Mailer's *The Naked and the Dead* and the eccentric Miss Barrett in Virginia Woolf's *Flush: A Biography,* all provide many-faceted views or provoke sufficient conflict in their interaction with other characters to merit classroom performance. Classic literary figures like the wry, scheming husband in James Thurber's "The Unicorn in the Garden" and the legendary law-copyist in Herman Melville's "Bartleby, the Scrivener" also exhibit memorable shades of the theatrical impulse and offer conflicting comic or tragic conceits and entanglements that engage an audience in classroom performance.

There are a number of basic principles at work in the selection of Readers Theatre literature that should provide a more theatrical blueprint for classroom performance, and also actively engage a classroom audience.

- Literature should be sufficiently descriptive to evoke a memorable sense of time and place like Bram Stoker's *Dracula* or Mary Shelley's *Frankenstein.*
- Literature should capture the enduring spirit of a past event, living present, or wishful future like Washington Irving's *The Legend of Sleepy Hollow* or Stephen Vincent Benet's *John Brown's Body.*
- Literature should depict a rare, exotic geographical locale, intriguing foreign location, or dream world of fantasy, science fiction, and utopia like W.P. Kinsella's "Shoeless Joe Jackson Comes to Iowa" or Sherman Alexie's "The Lone Ranger and Tonto Fistfight in Heaven."

Perhaps the most desirable Readers Theatre performance principle, however, is that the literary text should exhibit a marked degree of implicit or explicit *theatrical action.* It is the principle of theatrical action that encourages performers to first envision and then to enact — in both voice and body — a character's intention or motivation as it is revealed in the literary text. Theatrical action is also the most direct means performers have to more accurately communicate the basic literary truths that have emerged in an interpretation of the literature in classroom performance. For today's Readers Theatre, there are primarily four types of theatrical action to consider in the analysis and selection of literature and they are listed below for easy reference.

| | |
|---|---|
| • Character Action | Details the individual habits or traits of character that surface from an analysis of the literary text. |
| • Instinctive Action | Spontaneous reactions or responses of the performer that emerge in classroom rehearsal as a result of the habits or traits of literary characters. |
| • Descriptive Action | Provides voice, gesture, and movement of characters from dialog or description in the literary text. |
| • Dramatic Action | Promotes conflict needed to propel characters into the series of incidents and events described in the literary text. |

Discovering well-defined literary characters that inhabit a specific place, exist in a certain time, and respond in explicit theatrical action is central to Readers Theatre classroom performance today. A good starting point to begin a preliminary performance analysis of the literary text is to determine the most appropriate *mental symbol* that accurately defines a literary character. A mental symbol

- Indicates the overarching intention or motivation of a character
- Suggests what actions the character is willing to commit in order to achieve a specific desire

- Underscores the price the character must pay to achieve that specific desire.

For example, in Percy Bysshe Shelley's short poem "Ozymandias," the king heartily solicits the admiration that is regally bestowed on respected rulers. He is even willing to invest extravagant resources to erect an elaborate memorial to his own imagined grandeur. The price he must pay for his hubris, or self-pride, however, is eternal despair; and the only lasting testament the king unearths in a lifetime pursuit of the glorious monument to himself is inevitable destruction and decay. If the performer were able to isolate the character's primary intention or motivation in "Ozymandias," the mental symbol of "wish for immortality" should subsequently stimulate the theatrical action and reaction that follows in classroom performance.

This is, of course, a performance principle of the master acting teacher Konstantin Stanislavsky, who emphasized giving character intentions and motivations a specific *name* as part of identifying basic performance objectives. In also giving a name to the literary character's primary objective, performers should be better equipped to express the mental symbol that has informed their preliminary interpretation of the literary text. Performers should also be better prepared to assume a more informed character role in classroom performance as well. Without sustained attention to a more detailed study of the four types of theatrical action in a literary text, performers may not be adequately armed with the dramatic imagination that inspires an inventive classroom performance.

It is also an important Readers Theatre principle in the initial performance analysis of literature to identify specific objects that are part of a character's real or imagined life. The genuine responses a character exhibits to specific objects described in the literary texts are a creative source of classroom improvisations that rely on hand-held scripts. Giving more significant meaning to specific objects identified in the literature:

- Personalizes character action
- Promotes awareness of character attitude

- Focuses attention on character mood
- Directs audience attention to the dramatic function of each object.

An imaginative use of specific objects detailed in the literature may also enrich a character's subtext, or the hidden meaning that exists beneath the surface of spoken lines of dialog. (An example of active word play that also promotes a literary character's subtext may be found in the "I Beg Your Pardon, What Did You Say?" exercise in Chapter Five.)

Selected examples of literary texts that establish an intimate relationship between the objects that *represent* the character and the objects that are an *extension* of the character appropriate for classroom performance might include the "letters" of Elizabeth and Robert Browning in Rudolf Besier's *The Barretts of Wimpole Street;* the "fiddle" of Fiddler Jones in Edgar Lee Masters' *Spoon River Anthology;* and the "brass balls" of Captain Queeg in Herman Wouk's *The Caine Mutiny.* Although the performer's own originality is the essential ingredient in relating any of these suggested objects to the characters they identify, when that connection is made the classroom performance is memorable in bringing literature alive!

## Postscript

The literary or performance analysis of literature should result in a Readers Theatre blueprint that addresses the complex needs of today's performers. At this point, it might be beneficial to consider a timely sample blueprint unwittingly suggested by the critic Francis Fergusson for dramatic criticism but, now, very appropriate for today's theatrical impulse in Readers Theatre. Writing in *The Idea of a Theatre,* Fergusson defines the role of analysis as a fundamental quest to discover the purpose, passion, and perception inconspicuously concealed in a literary text. Fergusson's Three P literary point of view defines *purpose* as the primary intent of a literary text; *passion* as the pain or pleasure that often results from a character's intention or motive; and *perception* as the meaningful insight gained as a result of the consequences of a character's intention or motive.

When Fergusson's theories are applied to a Readers Theatre sample blueprint for the selection and analysis of literature, the roles of purpose, passion, and perception are given added theatrical dimension. For example, if the choice is to approach a literary text like John Gardner's *Grendel* with the decided purpose of revealing the title character's subtext, then the Readers Theatre classroom performance is conceived as simple and subtle in its single-mindedness; with minimal staging and a limited number of theatrical accessories like music, projections, or sound effects to punctuate the character's hidden intention or motivation.

If the choice is to approach a literary text like Maya Angelou's *I Know Why the Caged Bird Sings* with the express passion of voicing the young character Marguerite's feelings of outrage and pain after she is raped by Mr. Freeman, then the Readers Theatre classroom performance is conceived as a more traditional oral interpretation presentation; with selective theatrical accessories, minimal movement, and emphasis on the performer's vocal qualities to carefully frame the author's apparent point of view. If, however, the choice is to approach traditional literary texts like Franz Kafka's *The Trial* or Harper Lee's *To Kill a Mockingbird* with a refreshing new *perception* that gives parabolic meaning to the trial-by-jury image suggested in each text, then the classroom performance is influenced by the theatrical impulse; with more elaborate use of theatrical accessories like the cyclorama or scrim, choreographed movement, side lighting, and scenic elements suspended above the playing space.

The Three P sample blueprint for classroom performance offers unlimited choices in selecting the most compatible Readers Theatre performance techniques available to achieve educational, instructional, or artistic objectives. At the same time, the sample blueprint affords a unique opportunity to experiment with literary texts in a classroom rehearsal setting while still in pursuit of a more personal Readers Theatre that was first suggested in Chapter One:

> "A courageous, risk-taking journey in search of inventive and incisive approaches to today's Readers Theatre performance."

It should never be enough to only prepare for the classroom performance. There must also be regularly scheduled periods of literary analysis, participatory class discussion, and small-group study projects or reading aloud activities that tune the voice, body, and mind to meet the challenges of today's Readers Theatre. Remember, as well, that no matter how valuable the preliminary selection and analysis of literature might be, it is still the classroom performance that cements the foundation building blocks of hearing and seeing Readers Theatre at work in the interpretation of a literary text that is most rewarding. Finally, today's Readers Theatre encourages the pursuit of a theatrical as well as a mind's eye approach to visualizing literary texts in classroom performance. Of course, as the talented director Michael Chekhov reminds us, the art of Readers Theatre " ... can never be properly understood without first practicing it!"

# SUGGESTED READINGS

The following suggested readings include a number of traditional or theatrical sourcebooks that may be useful in selecting and analyzing literature for Readers Theatre classroom performance. The list of basic readings should provide a solid theoretical foundation to approach the interpretation and performance of literary texts as well.

Counsell, Colin. *Signs of Performance.* New York: Routledge, 1996.

Gilbert, Carolyn. *Communicative Performance of Literature.* New York: Macmillan, 1997.

Grote, David. *Script Analysis.* Belmont, California: Wadsworth Publishing Company, 1985.

Haas, Richard. *Theatres of Interpretation.* Ann Arbor, Michigan: Roberts-Burton, Inc., 1976.

Issacharoff, Michael and Robin Jones. *Performing Texts.* Philadelphia, Pennsylvania: University of Pennsylvania Press, 1986.

Kleinau, Marion and Janet Larsen McHughes. *Theatres for Literature.* Sherman Oaks, California: Alfred, 1980.

Pelias, Ronald. The Interpretation of Aesthetic Texts. New York: St. Martin's Press, 1992.

Stern, Carol Simpson and Bruce Henderson. *Performance Texts and Contexts.* New York: Longman, 1993.

Wallis, Mick and Simon Shepherd. *Studying Plays.* New York: Oxford University Press, 1998.

Yordon, Judy. *Roles in Interpretation.* Dubuque, Iowa: Wm. C. Brown Company, 1989.

Chapter Three

# Adapting Readers Theatre Literature

*"A great part of the secret of dramatic architecture lies in 'Tension.' To maintain, heighten, suspend, and then resolve a state of tension is the main object of the writer's craft."*
— William Archer, *Playmaking*

*"O 'tis most sweet
When in the one two crafts directly meet."*
— William Shakespeare, *Hamlet*

When sufficient literature has been selected and analyzed, the next step is adapting the materials for classroom performance. Basically, adapting literary or even non-literary material for Readers Theatre depends on such external concerns as:

- Desired length of classroom performance,
- Available talent of performers,
- Limitations of playing space,
- Anticipated size of audience, and
- The occasion for which the script is being prepared.

Although there are a number of approaches to adapt Readers Theatre literature, the inherent theatrical qualities of a literary text generally shape the content and form. It is always a good idea, however, to keep in mind Aristotle's reminder in *The Poetics* that the structure of a theatrical text is, quite simply, a beginning, middle, and end.

In an analysis of traditional theatre playscripts like Henrik Ibsen's *A Doll's House* or George Bernard Shaw's *Saint Joan*, we tend to think of structure as:

- *Exposition,* or the background information needed to understand a character's action or situation
- *Rising action,* or the incidents and events that dramatically intensify a character's action and situation
- *Complication,* or the obstacles and barriers that provoke conflict and inhibit character realization of specific goals and objectives
- *Climax,* or resolution of the apparent conflict
- *Denouement,* or the French term for "unknotting" all the loose ends of the story line that follow the climax.

Keep these terms in mind in the review of approaches to adaptation that follow. A firm grasp of these mechanical elements and terms will undoubtedly give a more theatrical form and shape to classroom performance of literary texts.

# Basic Principles of Adaptation

There are four basic principles to consider in adapting literature for classroom performance.

*Deletion:* Delete action, characters, dialog, episodes, narration, subplots, and any other extraneous element that does not confuse or distort the author's apparent point of view in the literary text.

*Addition:* Add character action, narration, movement, transitions, slides, musical interludes, pantomime or any other theatrical elements that supplement the author's apparent point of view in the literary text.

*Redirection:* Redirect action, events, and episodes to focus attention on chronology or the sequential order of events  and incidents and to juxtapose inventive comparisons or to illustrate creative concepts suggested in the literary text. Although these three basic principles are also an integral part of traditional theatre's approach to adaptation, the fourth principle of *Extraction* is almost exclusively a Readers Theatre classroom performance concept. The basic principle of extraction identifies individual episodes, character speeches, rhetorical addresses, descriptive passages, group encounters, or any theatrical sequence of events that may be performed independently of the original literary text. Readers Theatre practitioners extract larger or smaller episodes, incidents, or events in a literary text to:

- Sharpen an author's apparent point of view
- Advance character development
- Promote a more perceptive audience understanding of the literary text.

## Playscripts

Playscripts are popular to adapt for Readers Theatre because they are written specifically for stage production, and they contain all of the theatrical elements necessary for classroom performance. The problem areas in adapting playscripts, however, are editing acts or scenes to a specific classroom performance time and securing author permission to make significant script changes. Although playscripts are easily translated to Readers Theatre, it may still be necessary to delete characters, lines of dialog, and stage directions. Of course, major roles in the playscript can be assigned to a single performer; minor roles can be combined into several supporting roles, single or group narrator figures can be added, and a chorus can provide additional roles for more ensemble performers.

Those who feel strongly that theatre playscripts are sacred and should not be adapted for Readers Theatre classroom performance usually avoid full-length theatre texts and concentrate on theatrical revue skits, one-act plays, short monologs, and dramatic vignettes that suggest minimal theatrical techniques. Some excellent models for this approach to Readers Theatre adaptation for classroom performance include Harold Pinter's revue sketches "The Applicant" and "Trouble in the Works," Eugene Ionesco's one-act play *The Gap*, Ntozake Shange's short dramatic monologs from the choreopoem *For Colored Girls Who Have Considered Suicide When the Rainbow Is Enuf,* and the personal vignettes written by

Christopher Durang ("The Actor's Nightmare"), Anna Deavere Smith ("Fires in the Mirror"), or Steve Martin ("Wasp").

The basic principles that follow are for those who feel just as strongly that theatre playscripts should be adapted for Readers Theatre classroom performance.

- The adaptation should accurately reveal the playwright's apparent point of view in the playscript.
- The adaptation should maintain the basic character elements of the playscript.
- The adaptation should progress from the initial incident or event to the climactic resolution of the original playscript.
- The adaptation should use a narrator figure to relate any needed description or exposition deleted from the playscript.
- The adaptation should add appropriate "spoken" transitions between episodes or events to clearly indicate the scene progression of the playscript.

In the best interest of condensation, it may be judicious to cut and edit theatre playscripts for a classroom performance time of fifty minutes. Although it is a challenge to significantly reduce the performance time of a theatre playscript, the task is made easier when the major deletions and revisions are concerned with the forward motion of the *dramatic action* rather than the individual role of characters, dialog, and scenes.

It is also a good idea to consider theatre playscripts that have concise character relationships that exhibit obvious physical action rather than those playscripts that have introspective characters that exhibit obscure intellectual discussion of abstract issues.

Finally, remember that a playscript adaptation is carefully designed to accommodate the special needs of a classroom performance; it is not a creative writing exercise to invent new characters, dialog, or events and incidents absent in the original theatre text.

# Short Stories

The short story is a convenient literary text to adapt for Readers Theatre because of its brevity, descriptive narration, and explicit characterization. There are, quite naturally, inherent problems with short stories that rely heavily on narrative description or short character exchanges of dialog. Narrative description, however, may be assigned to a narrator figure and short exchanges of dialog may be assigned to an individual student performer. A good classroom performance rule of thumb in Readers Theatre is narrative description that reflects the author's point of view is best expressed by a narrator; and  short character exchanges of dialog, especially those introduced in the narration, are best expressed by the individual performing the literary character.

Narrator figures are also a good classroom performance choice to indicate multiple scene changes or to reveal a literary character's interior feelings and thoughts. Of course, minor characters may be deleted and the Narrator used to voice the cut dialog or to describe the cut action. If the short story contains only occasional passages of character dialog, two or more narrator figures may be used to share the narrative description. Short stories may also be adapted to provide more characters by having implied thoughts, recollections, or reflections spoken by individual or small groups of performers. Short stories that share a close relationship between a narrator figure and other characters in the literary text, like Truman Capote's "A Christmas Memory," or Kurt Vonnegut's "Harrison Bergeron," are especially good choices for Readers Theatre classroom performance.

In adapting Thomas Mann's short story "Mario and the Magician," for example, the author's simultaneous use of the past and present tense in describing incidents and events is noticeably apparent. The episodes related to the present tense may be read by one narrator and those related to the past may be read by another narrator figure. In addition, the descriptive passages of short stories may also suggest a character's implicit action or explicit reaction that may be adapted to provide more meaningful insight into the author's point of view, or to provide additional ensemble roles for classroom performance. Some short stories to adapt for classroom performance might include Edgar Allan Poe's "The Tell-Tale Heart," John Steinbeck's "The Chrysanthemums," or Eudora Welty's "Why I Live at the P.O."

## Poems

Long poems that tell a story with dialog are easily adapted to Readers Theatre using a narrator and small group of performers, and they may be adapted for multiple performers to voice individual stanzas, lines of dialog, or narrative description. *Short* poems are well-suited for solo performance and provide inventive transitions to use when adapting playscripts, novels, or short stories for classroom performance. Short poems may also feature a favorite author in a "Reading Hour" performance. For example, "An Afternoon with Robert Frost" may include a number of familiar poems like "Stopping by Woods on a Snowy Evening" and "Mending Wall" as well as unfamiliar poems like "The Pasture" and "Home Burial" to dramatize the author's rural New England poetic rhythms and ordinary speech patterns.

Short poems may also provide a selected thematic motif like "Voices of Freedom" or "What Price Glory?" for ten- or fifteen-minute classroom performances. The performance potential for long or short poems presents an opportunity to suggest a theme and divide performers into small group ensembles responsible for selecting literature that represents the theme and then adapting the literature for classroom performance. It is especially important in this small-group assignment that selected short poems provide dramatic solo performance opportunities and also serve as imaginative transitions to introduce longer poems.

## Novels

The basic principles of adapting a novel are similar to those of the short story, but present special problems due to length and number of literary characters. The novel may be adapted to include only representative episodes or to focus on the "thread of action" that suggests a sequence of incidents and events that gives the story line its continuity. Performers generally portray multiple roles in the adaptation of novels and there are a series of individual narrator figures to provide the necessary transitions and descriptive narration. The considerable number of literary characters present in a novel suggests that minor figures may be deleted and a chorus or voices be assigned to perform the cut lines of dialog and description.

A preliminary adaptation of John Steinbeck's novel *Travels with Charley,* for example, may dramatize only those adventures in which the title character actively participates or those selected dramatic incidents and events that give additional meaning to the character's intention and motivation in the literary text. A narrator figure may be used to introduce each adventure, a single performer may be used to portray Charley, and group performers may be used to portray individual characters involved in each dramatic episode. It is important to remember, however, that an adaptation of selected incidents, episodes, events, or even dramatic moments should remain faithful to the author's point of view as it has been revealed in a detailed analysis of the *entire* novel.

Adapting a novel presents a number of imaginative classroom performance opportunities to feature a literary text. Narrative passages may be placed in the present tense to heighten the sense of urgency in the story line, and long, vivid passages of description may be assigned to a number of performers who voice single lines of dialog or occasionally speak in unison. Performers may also vocalize sound effects implied in the narrative or sing lines of dialog to establish the mood of the character. (An example of the properties of sound that are used in creating vocal special effects in classroom performance may be found in the "Prop Probe" exercise in Chapter Five.)

# Non-Dramatic

Although diaries, essays, letters, newspaper advertisements, song lyrics, historical documents, and slogans are generally considered "non-dramatic" literature, they are an imaginative source of theatrical materials for classroom performance. It is important, however, that non-dramatic materials:

- Exhibit a point of view
- Suggest action or the potential for conflict
- Have a bare outline of interesting characters that can be fleshed out in classroom rehearsal.

Letters and diaries arranged in chronological order to tell a story that depicts complex character relationships, or that share intimate thoughts like the letters of Oscar Wilde or Edith and Osbert Sitwell, are still traditional Readers Theatre fare. Patriotic historical documents like Davy Crockett's "Speech to the Congress" and Winston Churchill's "Address on Dunkirk," or personal essays like Boris Pasternak's "Memories" and Dr. Martin Luther King's "Letter from Birmingham Jail," are also creative examples of non-dramatic materials appropriate for classroom performance.

Adapting non-dramatic materials for Readers Theatre involves careful editing to isolate significant theatrical moments in the lives of the characters and timely transitions that punctuate the dramatic action described. The adaptation of non-dramatic materials should consider the potential for vocal and physical classroom performance as well. For example, an adaptation of Helen Keller's autobiographical description of herself in selected diaries, journals, and newspaper interviews provides a compelling Readers Theatre classroom performance blueprint of the blind humanitarian in terms of vocal quality, physical stature, colorful language, and vivid dramatic action.

# Compiled Scripts

A compiled Readers Theatre classroom performance script may be adapted from a number of literary and non-dramatic sources. Compiled scripts appear to favor letters, short poems, essays, narrative stories, and diaries. There are also opportunities to integrate song lyrics, historical documents, dramatic or humorous monologs, tributes, and epigrams in a compiled script. The compiled approach to adapting literature for Readers Theatre classroom performance is almost always an original, personal signature script that revolves around a stated theme and a theatrical *staging metaphor*.

The basic approach to compiling a Readers Theatre script for classroom performance includes the following general principles.

- The compiled script should exhibit balance in the length of each selection, topic treated, and theme.
- The compiled script should provide appropriate transitions that complement each selection and convey a sense of direction or rhythmic pacing that builds to a climax.
- The compiled script should encourage theatrical movement and staging that effectively visualizes the point of view of the classroom production metaphor.

The classroom production concept is usually a decision of the director that emerges in a critical analysis of the compiled literature and non-dramatic materials, and is an artistic expression of the theatrical treatment to be given the compiled script. For example, a director's initial classroom production concept of a compiled script entitled "Other Voices, Other Victims" might emerge as an artistic response to the stated theme "loneliness and despair" and that the staging metaphor should be "life is living in desolate, blank space." The classroom approach to production to visualize this metaphor might then include an empty playing space enclosed by a series of iron bars painted or taped on the classroom floor. Fragmented windows, door frames, oversized padlocks, and placards that read

"Hospital Zone" and "No Dumping" are suspended from the ceiling. Performers wearing black and white pajamas are shoeless. There is minimal lighting and the playing space resembles a shadowy cavern. The only recurrent sounds are the series of tape-recorded screams or sighs that periodically punctuate the classroom performance.

The compiled script of miscellaneous literature and non-dramatic materials generally begins with a narrator or an ensemble group of performers who express the stated theme in an opening narration or a "shared" selection of literature. The opening is followed by a number of incidents or events presented either as ensemble or solo performances that build in intensity to a climax. There is an unmistakably theatrical impulse in today's Readers Theatre approach to compiled scripts that include original music, pantomime, sign-language transitions, choreographed dance sequences, slides, recorded sound effects, and improvised movement. The theatrical impulse also reveals itself in today's more elaborate Readers Theatre classroom production practices that make use of complex computer graphics, rap music, strobe lights, high-tech projections, hip-hop, film sequences, circus techniques, video, and interactive audience participation.

Compiled scripts for classroom performance also present instructional tools to pursue programs that sketch composite portraits of literary periods, social movements, historical eras, and political climates as well. The range of literature and non-dramatic materials suitable for these classroom compilations actively engage performers in the study of literary texts; and may even promote new reading and research adventures that explore more contemporary literature. Recommended reference sources to consult in the initial approach to compiling a script might include the *Index to Poetry, Biography Index*, and *Speech Index*. There are also a number of suggested anthologies like the *Irish Treasury, Whitman Sampler, Black Voices, Norton's Anthology of American Literature, Norton's Anthology of Poetry, Norton's Modern Short Stories*, and *Norton's Anthology of Modern Verse* that should provide valuable sources of literature suitable for classroom performance.

# Sample Adaptation — Cyrano de Bergerac

Here is a sample adaptation of the famous "nose" speech in Edmond Rostand's delightful comedy *Cyrano de Bergerac,* which has been scripted for Readers Theatre classroom performance. Cyrano is an elegant, swashbuckling hero of gallant proportion — including an enormous nose that provokes daily ridicule! In a tirade, but also with a blend of romantic lyricism and self-mocking humor, the heroic Cyrano describes his rather large nose in a comic monolog as it appears in the original theatre playscript. When reading the following excerpt, try to discover the author's apparent point of view. Apply the preliminary skills of analysis to a studied investigation of the arrangement of incidents or events in the monolog, and begin to visualize an inventive classroom performance blueprint that might capture a creative blend of Readers Theatre performance principles and also accurately reflect the comic perspective of the literary character.

> Why, you might have said —
> Oh, a great many things! Mon dieu, why waste
> Your opportunity? For example, thus: —
> Aggressive: I sir, if that nose were mine,
> I'd have it amputated — on the spot!
> Friendly: How do you drink with such a nose?
> You ought to have a cup made specially.
> Descriptive:'Tis a rock — a crag — a cape —
> A cape? Say rather, a peninsula!
> Inquisitive: What is that receptacle —
> A razor-case or a portfolio?
> Kindly: Ah, do you love the little birds
> So much that when they come and sing to you,
> You give them this to perch on? Insolent:
> Sir, when you smoke, the neighbors must suppose
> Your chimney is on fire. Cautious: Take care —
> A weight like that might make you topheavy.
> Thoughtful: Somebody fetch my parasol —

Those delicate colors fade so in the sun!
Pedantic: Does not Aristophanes
Mention a mythologic monster called
Hippocampelephantocamelos?
Surely we have here the original!
Familiar: Well, old torchlight! Hang your hat
Over that chandelier — it hurts my eyes.
Eloquent: When it blows, the typhoon howls,
And the clouds darken. Dramatic: When it bleeds —
The Red Sea! Enterprising: What a sign
For some perfumer! Lyric: Hark — the horn
Of Roland calls to summon Charlemagne!
Simple: When do they unveil the monument?
Respectful: Sir, I recognize in you
A man of parts, a man of prominence —
Rustic: Hey? What? Call that a nose? Na, na —
I be no fool like what you think I be —
That there's a blue cucumber! Military:
Point against cavalry! Practical: Why not
A lottery with this for the grand prize?
Or — parodying Faustus in the play —
"Was this the nose that launched a thousand ships
And burned the topless towers of Ilium?"
These, my dear sir, are things you might have said
Had you some tinge of letters, or of wit
To color your discourse. But wit, — not so,
You never had an atom — and of letters,
You need but three to write you down — an Ass.

The adaptation that follows has now been scripted to feature eight performers and a Narrator. A number of lines of the original literary text were deleted, and unfamiliar words or obscure allusions were omitted for easy comprehension. The classroom performance script now features movement, stage business, and audience interaction to capture the comic spirit of the episode as the abbreviated story line builds to a more theatrical climax!)

46

*(Narrator looks into audience and stares at Reader 8. In this sequence all the Readers except Reader 8 are now wearing false clown noses.)*

Narrator:  Ah, your nose! Your nose is rather large.

Reader 8:  *(Rises from seat in audience.)* Rather.

Narrator:  *(Crosses to trunk.)* Oh, well.

Reader 8:  *(Crosses to Narrator.)* Is that all?

Narrator: Well, of course.

Reader 8:  Not so fast! You are too simple. Why, you might have said, a great many things. Why waste your opportunity? *(Leaps on top of trunk and poses with script.)* For example, thus. Aggressive.

Reader 4:  *(Crosses to trunk.)* I, sir, if that nose were mine, I'd have it amputated. On the spot.

Reader 8:  Friendly.

Reader 5:  *(Crosses to trunk.)* How do you drink with such a nose? You ought to have a cup made specially.

Reader 8:  Descriptive.

Reader 7:  *(Crosses to trunk.)* What is that receptacle? A razor case, or a portfolio?

Reader 8:  Kindly.

Reader 1:  *(Crosses to trunk.)* Ah, do you love the little birds so much that when they come and sing to you that you give them this to perch on?

Reader 8:  Insolent.

Reader 2:  Sir, when you smoke the neighbors must suppose your chimney is on fire.

Reader 8:  *(Leaps from trunk and moves into the audience for the following sequence.)* Cautious. *(Approaches a spectator.)* Take care, a weight like that might make you top heavy.
*(The Readers all move into the audience and direct their lines of dialog to selected spectators. The Narrator sits on the trunk and stares in disbelief.)*

Reader 6:  *(From Down Left)* Thoughtful. Somebody fetch me my parasol. Those delicate colors fade so in the sun.

Reader 4:  *(From Down Right)* Well, old torchlight, hang your hat over that chandelier! It hurts my eyes.

Reader 5:  *(From Down Center)* Eloquent. When it blows the typhoon howls and the clouds darken.

Reader 8:  *(From Down Right)* When it bleeds, the Red Sea.

Reader 1:  *(From Down Left)* Enterprising. What a sign for some perfumer.

Reader 3:  *(From Up Left)* Lyric. Hark, the horn of Roland calls to summon Charlemagne.

Reader 2:  *(From Center)* Simple. When do they unveil the monument?

Reader 7:  *(From Up Right)* Respectful. Sir, I recognize in you a man of parts, a man of prominence.
*(In the following sequence, Readers on the Right of the playing space indicate the specific type of nose described and the Readers on the Left side search for a corresponding type in the audience.)*

Reader 4:  Rustic.

Reader 6:  What? Call that a nose? That there's a blue cucumber.

Reader 7:  Military.

Reader 1:  Point against cavalry. *(Places nose to spectator's nose.)*

Reader 2:  Practical.

Reader 3:  Why not a lottery with this for the grand prize!

Reader 8:  *(Rushes to the playing space and leaps on trunk. The Narrator, who has fallen asleep, is startled and falls to the floor.)* Or, parodying Faustus in the play, "Was this the nose *(Poses.)* that launched a thousand ships and burned the topless towers of Ilium?" *(Readers applaud and return to the trunk. The Narrator is surrounded by the Readers and looks up at Reader 8 from the floor.)* These, my dear sir, are things you might have said had you some tinge of letters, or wit, to color your discourse. But wit, not so. you never had an atom. And of letters, you need but three to write you down.

Readers 1, 3, and 5:  A.

Readers 2, 4, and 6:  S.

All:  S.

As you experiment with your own approaches to adapt literary texts for classroom performance, remember that it is important to present the literature on its own terms. Material selected for adaptation should be condensed to meet time limitations, and there should be a specific order of incidents or events that build the script to an unmistakable climax. Be realistic about the classroom performance potential of literature, the number of performers available, and the basic information needed for an audience to make sense of the adaptation. Some practical examples of literature to adapt for an initial classroom small group performance script might include the thought-provoking Aesop fable of "The Country Mouse and the Town Mouse," the wickedly humorous "gossip scene" (I,i) in Richard Brinsley Sheridan's theatre playscript *The School for Scandal*, Sir Francis Bacon's satirical essay on education "Of Studies," and T. S. Eliot's "Gus: The Theatre Cat" or "The Love Song of J. Alfred Prufrock."

# CUTTING LITERATURE

Cutting literature in Readers Theatre is a necessary part of the artistic process of adapting literary texts for classroom performance. It is important, therefore, to think of cutting literature as the need to transfer one media (literary text) to another media (performance script), rather than as a charge to delete things to fit a specified time limit. Some literary texts like novels and theatre playscripts, of course, do lend themselves to cutting entire chapters or complete scenes. Other literary texts like short stories and narrative poems, however, may only require internal cutting of individual lines or stanzas, description, and minor characters. For today's Readers Theatre, cutting is doing whatever is needed to make a literary text function more as a classroom performance script.

# Tag Lines

While the basic guideline in cutting literature is to be accurate, appropriate, and faithful to the author's original point of view, there are some simple strategies that encourage a modest cutting without significantly altering the style and substance of the literary text as it was originally written. For example, simple tag lines like "he said" or "she said" can be eliminated when they are repetitive or simply indicate the speaker. Long, descriptive passages, incidents, or events can be deleted if the omitted sections are paraphrased or visualized in theatrical action by the narrator, other characters in the performance script, or the performers. It is often necessary to gain a benign ruthlessness in cutting literature by deleting:

- Incidental description
- Subplots
- Flashbacks
- Repetitive action
- Internal summaries
- Multiple changes of locale
- Decorative narrative description.

# Cutting Out Loud

It is important, however, to practice cutting literature *out loud* for sound appeal as well as fluency. A simple test to evaluate sound appeal and fluency is to read aloud the lines just before and just following a deletion to determine if the clarity or continuity of the dramatic action is disrupted or distorted by the deletion. If the sound sense of the cutting appears to sustain the build to a climax, mark the cuts with [brackets] in the literary text. When the preliminary cutting is complete, it is then appropriate to add transitions or narrative explanations that continue to advance the action and build the performance script to a climax.

# Cutting for Redirection

If there is any redirection, or rearrangement, of the incidents or events in the original literary text, make sure the story line also continues to build to a theatrical climax. Remember that the integration of plot, character, and thought is a key ingredient in cutting literature for classroom performance. The final cutting should strive to achieve a dynamic pattern of tension and release like that suggested by the critic William Archer in the quotation that introduces this chapter discussion.

It is this alternating tension and relaxation that promotes a rhythmic build to a performance script. So in any rearrangement or realignment of the original story line it is important not to delete important character action or staging details that might diminish the pattern of tension and release. For example, the choice to delete references to the "urban jungle" locale in Gwendolyn Brooks' poem "A Street in Bronzeville" or the tranquil historical setting in Amy Lowell's poem "Meeting-House Hill" may not sufficiently call attention to the important role that tension and release play in these environments as they shape the lives of the literary characters described in the literature.

# Cutting for Taste

Then there is the delicate matter of cutting Readers Theatre literature for taste. The role of vulgar curse words, suggestive action, "street talk," or crude references in literature is frequently a major part of a character's self-portrait in literary texts like James Baldwin's *The Fire Next Time*, Richard Wright's *Native Son*, or Philip Roth's *Portnoy's Complaint*. It is necessary, however, to be selective in deleting offensive examples of explicit language and behavior if the performers appear embarrassed by the literature or if there is a reasonable anticipation that the audience may object to insulting character language or behavior. Cutting for taste also includes deleting material that is insensitive and provocative, or that may promote cultural, ethnic, racial, or gender stereotypes. A common-sense approach to cutting for taste is to exercise good, sound judgment and delete any questionable material that has the apparent intent to be cruel, harmful, or malicious.

51

# Copyright Caution

Copyright laws exist to protect the artistic and intellectual property rights of creators of original works, and all creative works like literary texts are considered copyrighted. Although copyright laws are reasonably clear for the use of literary materials in terms of photocopying, the laws related to classroom performance of literature are not as clearly stated in terms of what is permissible and non-permissible. There are, however, a number of "fair use" exceptions for educational and instructional purposes that are important for Readers Theatre scripting and classroom performance.

In most cases, a letter of inquiry addressed to the "Permissions Department" of the publisher for the literary text is sufficient to secure information on classroom performance guidelines. It is important, nevertheless, to indicate in the letter that no admission fee is being charged and that the classroom performance is part of an instructional unit in adapting and scripting literature.

There are additional royalty complications for compiled Readers Theatre scripts intended for public performances that charge an admission fee. A growing number of author agents and permission editors consider today's Readers Theatre a formal theatrical event and may require royalty fees based on the number of public performances or the audience seating capacity. Readers Theatre scripts that feature major revisions, wholesale editing, and major realignment of the original literary text may also require special permission of the author before public performance rights are approved. It is always a good idea to read the acknowledgement page or the copyright caution notice printed in the front of the literary text by the publisher for additional information on permissions or royalties.*

---

* Contemporary Drama Service (P.O. Box 7710, Colorado Springs, CO 80933) offers a number of Readers Theatre starter packets for classroom as well as public performance that do *not* charge royalty fees. Some of the recommended scripts, adapted by Melvin R. White, include Oscar Wilde's comedy of manners theatre playscript *The Importance of Being Earnest*, and L. Frank Baum's original novel *The Wizard of Oz.* Contemporary Drama Service also offers Arnold Wengrow's theatrical adaptation of Chaucer's *The Canterbury Tales.*

# Postscript

The challenge of adapting or compiling a theatrical script from a single literary text or from numerous selections of literature can take any form to provide an artistic framework that focuses attention on classroom performance. Remember, however, that the key ingredient in adapting or compiling is the careful selection and arrangement of literature that has a theatrical impulse. As you now begin to experiment with scripting literature for classroom performance, pay particular attention to *adjectives* and *verbs*.

Active adjectives and verbs not only identify the dramatic action, but also encourage vocal and physical responses to these literary character modifiers. Being aware of adjectives and verbs when cutting or editing literature for a classroom performance can subtly underline significant intellectual, emotional, or psychological aspects of a literary character's self-portrait. Verbs are especially useful in crafting a Readers Theatre script because they encourage performers to respond to the physical movements and vocal qualities suggested in these action words. (An example of the role that performance verbs might play in literary character development may be found in the "Body Beautiful" exercise in Chapter Five.)

Careful attention to performance adjectives and verbs in the critical analysis process should also

- Alert performers to the moment-to-moment interaction of characters
- Reveal informative interpersonal relationships of characters
- Communicate the subtext of characters.

For example, selective use of expressive performance adjectives and verbs like "brick-faced smile" or "running on empty" in John Updike's novel *Rabbit, Run* provides exquisite text analysis of the author's perspective on the decay of social mores and values; and also suggests a theatrical classroom performance blueprint to visualize the intention or objective of the title character in the literary text.

The Readers Theatre discoveries made in this chapter's discussion of adapting literature should provide the basic skills needed to give fresh insight and artistic substance to classroom staging and performance clues that follow in Chapters Five and Six. Try to anticipate that discussion as part of an organic process; one that grows naturally from an introduction to Readers Theatre, selecting and analyzing literature, and adapting literature for Readers Theatre classroom performance. So, let us move along on the Readers Theatre journey with this brief motto, offered more than two thousand years ago by the Roman orator Horace, to serve as a friendly reminder to us all:

"Whatever you teach, be brief, that your reader's minds may readily comprehend and faithfully retain your words. Nothing superfluous should slip from your lips."

# SUGGESTED READINGS

The following suggested readings should provide additional information on analyzing and adapting literary texts for classroom performance. There are also a number of readings that relate to theatrical staging, production techniques, and performance approaches suitable for today's Readers Theatre.

Benedetti, Robert. *The Actor at Work.* Englewood Cliffs, New Jersey: Prentice-Hall, 1985.

Boal, Augusto. *Games for Actors and Non-Actors.* Translated by A. Jackson. London: Routledge, 1992.

Hornby, Richard. *Script into Performance.* New York: Applause Theatre Books, 1996.

Long, Beverly Whitaker, Lee Hudson and Phyllis Renstra Jeffrey. *Group Performance of Literature.* Englewood Cliffs, New Jersey: Prentice-Hall, 1977.

Marranca, Bonnie. *The Theatre of Images.* New York: Drama Book Specialists, 1997.

Mattingly, Althea and Wilma Grimes. *Interpretation: Writer, Reader and Audience.* Belmont, California: Wadsworth, 1970.

Schechner, Richard. *Performance Theory.* New York: Routledge, 1988.

Stevick, Phillip. *The Theory of the Novel.* New York: Free Press, 1967.

Thompson, David and Virginia Fredricks. *Oral Interpretation of Fiction: A Dramatic Approach.* Minneapolis, Minnesota: Burgess Publishing Company, 1964.

Yakim, Moni. *Creating a Character.* New York: Applause Theatre Books, 1995.

# Chapter Four
# Playing Space and Staging

*"I always liked the idea that [theatre] happens in three dimensions, that there is something that comes to life in space."*
— Sam Shephard, "Reflections"

To say that today's Readers Theatre comes to life in a "dramatic space" is to coin a new definition for Readers Theatre staging: literary characters inhabiting a carefully selected, well-defined spatial environment that charges every detail of their interaction with dramatic significance. The initial selection and analysis of the literature should have already called attention to the role that locale or setting plays in the literary text; and the performer should have already begun to visualize the character's attitude or behavior in that dramatic space. But, it is very important to approach the playing space used to stage literature with a certain reverence for its potential to transform abstract, literary images on the printed page into inventive, theatrical approaches to classroom performance.

Dramatic space in today's Readers Theatre is an essential staging concept because it suggests the "simultaneous behavior" of literary characters: they are not only voicing dialog or narration that interpret the literature, they are also exhibiting physical behaviors that give added dimension to an understanding of the environment in which they live. In dramatic space, each literary character present is a dynamic force; whether speaking, silent, or supporting with vocal sound effects and musical interludes. Finally, it is also in this dramatic space that literary images are artistically transformed into a flesh-and-blood character portrait for classroom performance.

# THEORIES OF PLAYING SPACE

There are a number of theatre practitioners who have influenced today's Readers Theatre approach to staging in a more dramatic playing space. The theoretical perspective of each of the theorists that follows suggests a common viewpoint that any oral interpretation of a literary text is essentially a "theatrical act." Today's Readers Theatre, of course, has embraced a number of these theories as a means to heighten the sense of theatrical reality needed to visualize a literary text. The recent Tony award-winning Broadway production of Frank Galanti's adaptation of John Steinbeck's novel *The Grapes of Wrath,* for example, offers ample evidence that Readers Theatre conventions like Off-stage focus, speaking in choral unison, and the use of minimal props can just as easily be an integral part of commercial, theatrical practices.

## Bertolt Brecht (1898-1956)

Bertolt Brecht offers some striking examples of theatrical practices that are also essential elements in today's Readers Theatre. Brecht's concepts of "epic, or concert," theatre included singing lyrical lines of dialog or narration and using choreographed movement to reveal a character's subtext. The storyteller, or narrator figure, in Brecht frequently addressed the audience directly and voiced stage directions to interpret character actions. There was an emphasis on staging that featured "verbal" scene changes, or performers indicating scene changes as part of their character role-playing. Brecht also popularized some of today's Readers Theatre staging techniques like rear-view projections, placards, and *tableaux,* or frozen performer poses, to provide a commentary on the context of an incident or event.

## Antoine Artaud (1896-1948)

Antoine Artaud and his theory of "theatre of the cruel" assaulted the audience's senses in an attempt to force them to confront their own prejudices. He rejected traditional literary texts in favor of compiled scripts that staged "lifelike events" rather than the imagined incidents or events of fictitious characters. Artaud's compiled scripts contain a number of apparently disconnected episodes that only reveal a point of view when the audience decoded the pattern of objects, gestures, signals, and signs at work in the script. At times, he experimented with the playing space and located action or characters in the audience. At other times, he redirected incidents and events or reversed time and place to tell the story line of a literary text. Artaud's most theatrical contribution to today's Readers Theatre, however, may have been his sustained experiment with "orchestrated vocal sound," or the chanting and humming intonations his performers used to create a vocal collage of overlapping sounds to set the mood or tone of a script.

## Joseph Chaikin (1935 -    )

Joseph Chaikin offers an even more compelling here-and-now invitation to the dramatic playing space. Chaikin's "open theatre" staging presents the literary text as a "scenic emblem," and encourages performers to explore the *physical* rather than *vocal* interpretation of a character. His exploration with small group or large ensemble gestures, sounds, and vocal rhythms to create mental images is especially relevant to today's Readers Theatre. Chaikin's integration of pantomime and circus techniques, like acrobatics or juggling, to physically underline spoken dialog is also a performance principle for Readers Theatre. Finally, Chaikin's use of narrative "case studies," culled from newspaper accounts and personal histories is a stimulating Readers Theatre incentive to script more flesh-and-blood original scripts that depict real human beings interacting with other human beings.

## Peter Brook (1925 -    )

Peter Brook has, perhaps, been the most influential theorist at work in twentieth-century theatre. Brook, if you recall his quotation at the beginning of Chapter One, is also interested in giving dramatic meaning to the "empty space" in theatre. His basic approach to staging is "to make the invisible visible," or to fill the empty playing space with found objects that are used in a metaphoric sense to give new and unexpected meaning to a literary text. All character actions, words, or images are simple and direct in creating the "imaginative world" of the characters. Although Brook prefers to stage traditional literary texts, he interprets them from a non-traditional perspective. His recent production of William Shakespeare's *A Midsummer Night's Dream,* for example, was staged using acrobats and gymnasts swinging on suspended trapezes. Brook's theatrical impact on today's Readers Theatre is in his improvisation of the literary text to discover shades of nuance in the author's apparent point of view.

## PLAYING SPACES

The playing spaces most conducive for Readers Theatre are essentially the same as traditional theatre. Whatever space is chosen to convey the artistic image or locale or setting, however, should be suggested in the literary text. Usually, the artistic image of locale or setting suggests an analogous space that is the most visually descriptive for staging the literature. There are, of course, no definitive rules that govern the final selection of playing space. Individual choices invariably emerge as images of locale or setting surface in the literature and the production metaphor is conceptualized.

Don't hesitate to experiment with the playing space or to visualize the literary text in a number of imaginative settings — literal or localized — that might be appropriate to stage the literature. Remember that today's Readers Theatre only comes to life in a "dramatic" space, so the spatial dimensions suggested in the literary text should indicate an appropriate staging approach for classroom performance. Here are some basic principles of playing space to consider in initial experiments with classroom staging.

(1) When staging adaptations of novels or short stories that may include multiple space locations or time spans, like J.

D. Salinger's *The Catcher in the Rye*, it is best to divide the classroom into separate playing spaces that correspond to the locale or setting described in the literary text.

(2) When staging literary texts that may include Off-stage focus to suggest a number of character placements in different locales, like Robert Louis Stevenson's *Dr. Jekyll and Mr. Hyde*, it is best not to surround the classroom playing space with a full set or large, downstage set pieces that might be distracting.

(3) When staging intimate literary texts that encourage audience interaction, like Anne Sexton's poem "Sylvia's Death," it is best to make use of vertical or asymmetrical space to help focus and frame the dramatic action.

In addition, it is important to consider how performers will move in the playing space to help establish character relationships, advance the story line, and provide visual clues to an interpretation of the author's point of view in the literature. There are a number of traditional theatre playing spaces that are viable for today's more theatrical Readers Theatre. Although not every classroom or institutional facility may be equipped to accommodate the playing spaces described below, a number of alternative choices like large, open library rooms, extended vertical corridors, museums, theatre-style lecture halls, cafeterias, art galleries, or audio-visual and media centers may provide optional venues for classroom performance.

## Arena Space

The arena, or in-the-round, playing space surrounds the dramatic action on all four sides and is especially useful to suggest character confinement or to establish intimacy with the audience. Arena staging eliminates the need for formal scenery except minimal set pieces, an occasional standing decorative unit, and a painted or carpeted floor. The open area in the middle of the arena is the playing space, and audience seating is usually bleacher-like or chairs placed on raised platforms. There is no act curtain, and screens for projections or slides may be suspended over the audience. Scene changes are made in full view of the audience by the performers. Arena staging is well-suited to compiled scripts or to adaptations of short stories like Joyce Carol Oates' "Golden Gloves" or Stephen Crane's "The Open Boat," where the performers remain in the playing space throughout the classroom performance.

## Open Space

An open, or flexible, playing is a desirable staging approach for today's Readers Theatre because it clearly defines character actions and spatial relationships. The basic arrangement of the open playing space places performers in the center of the dramatic action, as in the arena space, but provides a decorative backdrop or curtains against which the classroom performance is staged. The open space may include raised platforms, step units, or ramps to elevate performers and encourages the symbolic grouping of small groups or the entire ensemble. In addition, the open space permits different incidents or events to be performed at various locations within the playing space simultaneously. It is particularly suitable for compiled programs that feature several genres of literature or to adaptations of novels, like Charles Dickens' *Nicholas Nickleby* or Jonathan Swift's *Gulliver's Travels,* that are concerned with a title character's personal odyssey or adventure travelog of multiple events and incidents.

## Proscenium Arch Space

The proscenium arch is probably the most easily recognized architectural structure in traditional theatre practice: a raised stage framed by a proscenium arch through which the audience views the production. The proscenium arch playing space is basically a simple rectangular room in which the audience is seated on the same level facing the "picture frame" stage. The performer is usually oriented full-front, and the stage itself is rigged to accommodate curtains, drapes, and scenic units that can be hoisted above the playing space. The proscenium arch space defines the dramatic action in a very presentational manner, with the performers isolated within the framework of the arch and the audience separated at some distance in the auditorium. Although today's Readers Theatre views the proscenium arch as an interesting relic, it is an agreeable configuration to stage the adaptation of playscripts like Arthur Miller's *Death of a Salesman* or even some episodic novels like F. Scott Fitzgerald's *The Great Gatsby* that need to rely on more traditional theatrical lighting, sound, music, or other scenic devices to reveal the complex psychology of the characters.

# Thrust Space

A thrust usually arranges an audience around three, or occasionally two, sides of a raised platform in the center of the playing area. Historically, the thrust playing space appears to be reminiscent of sixteenth-century Elizabethan staging practices that placed the characters "in the midst" of the audience. The use of a raised platform thrust forward into the audience promotes a more intimate performance space, but also eliminates the use of flying scenery, drops, and curtains. Lighting instruments, however, may be placed at the side or above the playing space and set pieces or small scenic units may be shifted by the performers in full view of the audience. The thrust playing space is ideally suited to Readers Theatre classroom performances that feature continuous character action or an uninterrupted whirlwind of movement. The thrust is also appropriate for original Readers Theatre scripts that feature intricate, choreographed movement like a "dance theatre" interpretation of Langston Hughes' "The Negro Speaks of Rivers" or a Native American "ritual chanting" of short poems like Cochise's "I Am Alone" or the Chippewa song "The Sioux Women Gather Up Their Wounded."

# Space Stage

The space stage, a relatively new commercial theatre innovation, defines dramatic space in terms of lighting. To signal the beginning of an event or incident, the playing space is magically lit out of the apparent darkness; and when the event or incident concludes there is a slow fade or blackout. Size and shape of the playing area is thus defined by lighting; and the dramatic action proceeds from one event or incident to the next by illumination. A space stage concept is intriguing in today's Readers Theatre because of its potential use of the cyclorama to project images that accompany spoken dialog or narration and its ability to clearly direct audience attention to dramatic moments. The space stage also allows character action to continue without noticeable interruption. Literary texts that feature narratives rich in metaphoric or symbolic resonance, like Henry James' *Daisy Miller* or Evelyn Waugh's *The Loved One,* would be good candidates for a space stage Readers Theatre adaptation.

# Additional Playing Spaces

There is an increasing trend in today's Readers Theatre to spatially frame literature in "found" or "environmental" locations. Found space moves the literary text itself to a locale that suggests the setting described by the author. Familiar places like parks, dining halls, playgrounds, corridors, parking lots, or woodlands become playing spaces for the dramatic action described in the literature. For example, Edwin Markham's "The Man with the Hoe" is staged in an abandoned field, Edward Albee's one-act playscript *The Zoo Story* is staged in a deserted park, or Wallace Stevens' "Peter Quince at the Clavier" is staged in a music recital hall.

Environmental space embraces a large, open area with a number of separate performance "stations," or even several rooms in a building, rather than a fixed stage. There is also no fixed seating, and the audience is encouraged to move from place to place and observe multiple incidents or events being performed simultaneously. For example, a Readers Theatre production of Edgar Lee Masters' *Spoon River Anthology* is performed in the found space of a local cemetery or in the environmental space of a plaza with plaster tombstones or headstones to depict the individual life stories of such characters as "Doc Hill," "Lucinda Matlock," and "Margaret Fuller Slack." (An example of the role that found space or environmental space might play in classroom performance is included in the "Sardines Today!" exercise in Chapter Five.)

Today's most popular playing space for Readers Theatre is the practical "black box," a formless space that can be adjusted or rearranged in a number of interesting configurations. Usually a large, empty room painted black — hence its name — the black box space contains the basic elements needed to stage a literary text: minimal lighting, risers or bleachers, curtains, and openings to enter or exit the playing area. The black box can then be configured to resemble an arena, proscenium, or thrust playing space; and simply readjusted to accommodate center, corner, or an "L" playing space. The black box promotes active audience/performer interaction and is appealing for a "Reading Hour" that showcases original composition, small-group performance projects, or ten to fifteen-minute compiled scripts that feature an individual author. The black box is also an ideal space to rehearse a scripted text, experiment with metaphorical movement, or provide meaningful classroom activities for performers who may wish to direct a Readers Theatre production.

# READERS THEATRE STAGING

The primary principle of Readers Theatre staging is to direct the dramatic action and movement of the performers in relationship to the playing space. Creative staging also provides a theatrical frame of reference for the dramatic space, and stimulates the audience to understand a character's action. Staging, of course, is the most graphic medium available to visualize the analogous relationship between the dramatic space and a character's action. Today's Readers Theatre is much more influenced by the traditional theatre director's use of blocking, or pictorial composition, to create "stage pictures" that visually illustrate dramatic action.

Some Readers Theatre directors today are also interested in experimental staging approaches that lend themselves to "picturization," or detailed storytelling of a literary text, using *composition* (spatial arrangement of performers), personal *gesture* (performers moving within the playing space), and *improvisation* with character objects (props associated with characters integrated with composition and personal gesture) to suggest a theatrical interpretation of the author's apparent point of view.

As mentioned earlier in Chapter One, historical Readers Theatre approaches to staging offered performers who might stand in line facing the audience, sit on stools, combine sitting and standing, group themselves in suggestive poses, or engage in limited stage movement to represent abstract images or reflect character attitudes and moods. Performers usually remained in the playing space throughout the scripted program; and scripts were held, placed on lecterns, or blended into the performance as apparent objects that suggested the character.

Even though today's Readers Theatre has embraced a more theatrical impulse in blocking a performer's movement and focusing the dramatic action on-stage, there are a number of historical Readers Theatre staging practices that continue to serve an artistic purpose. For example, the straight-line arrangement of performers, or even chairs and stools, in staging Robert Frost's "Mending Wall" may still connote the solemnity and formality of the occasion as the author recalls it in the short poem; and using a semi-circular arrangement of chairs or stools in staging E. B. White's amusing children's story *Charlotte's Web* may still be visually effective in conveying an image of the spider's retreat!

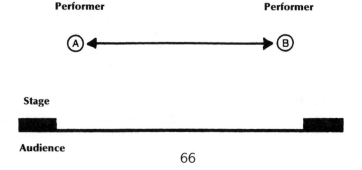

# Off-Stage Focus

Another historical staging practice that is frequently used for special effect in today's Readers Theatre is Off-stage focus, or character placement *out* of the playing space. Off-stage focus places the location of the event or incident, and of course, the characters, on a straight or angled line slightly above the heads of the audience. A performer's action, business, dialog, reaction, and sight lines are also directed slightly over the heads of the audience; intersecting at a hypothetical point in the center of the audience. As a traditional principle of Readers Theatre, the use of Off-stage focus places performers in a full-front, presentational position facing the audience; and encourages a flurry of expressive facial reactions, subtle physical movements of selected parts of the body, and a host of vocally colorful responses that appear to be directed toward the aesthetic distance of space.

**Performers**

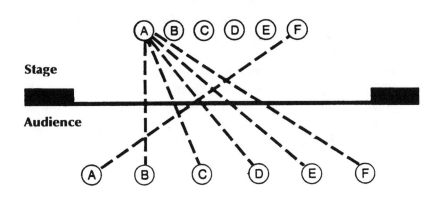

Off-stage focus, however, is still a powerful special effect in today's Readers Theatre staging. It can intensify shifting character attitudes and moods, provide a theatrical staging approach to frame dramatic moments, and visualize the abstract or symbolic intentions and motivations of a character. There are a number of potential Readers Theatre literary texts that would be enriched by the virtues of Off-stage focus, especially those that suggest exaggerated dramatic action like the title character's "suicide by decapitation" episode in Leo Tolstoy's novel *Anna Karenina* or the "blinding of horses" episode in Peter Shaffer's playscript *Equus*. (An example of Off-stage focus to promote literary character placement in the audience may be found in the "Mirror, Mirror on the Wall" exercise in Chapter Five.)

## Combined Foci

Another historical staging approach that continues to be attractive in Readers Theatre today is the use of combined foci for special effect. An interesting example of this staging approach might include a combination of foci to heighten the humor of James Thurber's comic parable "The Little Girl and the Wolf," with a Narrator placed Off-stage and the little girl and the wolf placed On-stage for the frantic chase through the deep woods to grandma's house and the climactic moment when the little girl pulls out a gun and shoots the wolf dead! There is also an opportunity to achieve a dramatic special effect in Helen Keller's autobiographical *Three Days to Live*. The combined foci staging approach here might locate two performers on opposite sides of the playing space using Off-stage focus to perform the script "reading in braille," and four performers wandering aimlessly in the center of the playing space using On-stage focus to suggest the dreadful darkness and futility of sightless existence that the author describes in the literature.

## Theatre Focus

Today's Readers Theatre is now integrating a number of traditional theatre directing approaches to more clearly identify the On-stage dramatic action of characters and to define the playing space in terms of its focus on the performers. Direct focus draws attention to the dominant performer by using an actual line in the staging of an event or incident. For example, in the blocking of a Readers Theatre episode, direct focus arranges a series of performers in a diagonal line to direct audience attention from one performer to another until it reaches the dominant performer at the apex of the line. Direct focus also makes very imaginative use of the triangle pattern in blocking and continues to emphasize the performer at the apex, whether the apex is at the side or in the center of the playing space. An excellent use of direct focus is found in the musical comedy *Hello, Dolly!* and spotlights the well-known nightclub entrance of Dolly Levi down an elaborate staircase framed by a host of singing waiters. The use of direct focus would also be an interesting Readers Theatre staging principle in an adaptation of Lewis Carroll's *Alice in Wonderland* or L. Frank Baum's *Wizard of Oz* to frame the encounters of each of these title characters.

Another traditional theatre directing approach available in staging today's Readers Theatre is the use of counter-focus. Unlike direct focus, which proceeds from point A to point B without interruption, counter-focus deliberately avoids a clearly defined point of attention and is concerned with the role of contrast in visualizing a character's reaction or response to an incident or event. For example, if all the performers but one are standing, the one seated attracts attention and is dominant in terms of visual contrast and focus. The use of counter-focus to *contrast* the performer's body position to the line of other performers is an imaginative Readers Theatre staging principle today to subtly suggest a character's subtext; and could be a perceptive interpretation approach to Walter Van Tilberg Clark's novel *The Ox-Bow Incident,* which depicts one man's struggle to resist the mob violence of a lynching, if counter-focus were used to stage the contrasting views of the individual versus the mob.

## Additional Staging Dimensions

A Readers Theatre director needs to be much more than a traffic cop charged to ticket slow-moving blocking or to patrol the right-of-way for stools and lecterns performers use in reading literary texts aloud. Like the film director, today's Readers Theatre director needs to be an artistic "image-maker" who captures and frames the enduring life spirit of a literary text in classroom performance. It is important, therefore, to learn to *see* in directing abstract images on a printed page to reveal themselves on a stage. There are a number of additional staging terms to consider and they are listed here for review. When all of these elements inform a production approach to the literary text, there should be a rewarding artistic and aesthetic classroom performance.

- Emphasis: Staging events and incidents that place special importance on specific dramatic moments.
- Balance: Spatial relationships between objects and performers in terms of number, proportion, and weight.
- Form: Shape, silhouette, and outline of the playing area and performers.
- Mass: Distribution of the number of performers and their relative spatial weight in the playing area.
- Color: Palette of hues that gives vibrant life and meaning to the costumes, lighting, props, and scenic elements.

## Complementary Staging Elements

Classroom staging may also include a number of other complementary elements like costumes, lighting, makeup, music, sound, or projections. Thomas Mann, the novelist, once remarked that drawing memorable character sketches is "... not just inventing something, but making something out of *reality*." The deeper undertones of Thomas Mann's artistic observation also appear applicable to current trends in Readers Theatre. Today's theatrical approaches to Readers Theatre recognize the intimate relationship between complementary staging elements and the visualization of literary characters; and today's classroom performers are much more eager to pursue realistic costumes and makeup in role-playing that is believable and honest. What now remains, of course, is making appropriate choices that blend these complementary staging elements and individual artistic expressions into a vivid here-and-now classroom performance.

## Costumes

Costumes, either suggestive or theatrical, are essential elements in defining character, place, and time. The difficulty when several characters are played by a single performer, however, suggests basic dress that is capable of defining a change of character by simply adding or subtracting various hats, scarves, or shawls. Today's Readers Theatre is looking for costumes that accentuate a literary character's individuality, but also subtly indicate the presence of subtext. For example, the narrator figure in Arthur Kopit's "Elegy for the House that Ruth Built" may wear the predictable New York Yankees' baseball uniform, but the numbers on the vest may be black in color and inverted to indicate the tone of lament suggested in the title of the literary text; or the ensemble performers in Charlotte Perkins Gilman's narrative "The Yellow Wallpaper" may all wear costumes that suggest a wallpaper motif in the fabric, but a closer look may indicate that each fabric is designed to reflect an individual character's attitude or mood in the literature.

## Lighting

Lighting endows an empty space with dramatic mood and focuses attention on the atmosphere of the literary text. Lighting may reveal the rhythmic nature of the story line; or selectively illuminate a character's subtext in an event or incident. Special effects like the spotlight, strobe light, or scoop may also be used effectively to highlight significant moments of narrative description. Although the facility may not be equipped to artistically conceive what the noted scenic design Adolph Appia termed "painting with light," it is still possible to achieve imaginative lighting in classroom performance. For example, merely flicking a light switch on and off during the climactic moment of Captain Ahab's fateful encounter with the whale in Herman Melville's novel *Moby Dick* continues to produce the feeling of impending doom suggested in the literary text; or the use of lighted candles in a darkened classroom during the bridal tomb episode in William Shakespeare's playscript *Romeo and Juliet* continues to evoke a solemn atmosphere of quiet resignation and heartfelt sadness for eternal "star-crossed lovers."

## Makeup

Traditional Readers Theatre values facial expression in suggesting character, so the role of makeup is usually reserved for abstract, stylized, or symbolic productions that present fantasy, make-believe worlds. Although today's Readers Theatre also shares the same basic concerns for the value of facial expression, there is a more frequent use of pancake, clown-white, or character makeup as well as assorted beards, mustaches, masks, and false hair to flesh out a literary character. The role of makeup, of course, is still an artistic choice that should be based on the production concept, but it can play a vital role in visualizing literary characters for an audience. For example, the obvious role of death-mask makeup in the "Ghost Dance Songs" of the Arapaho, or a subtle use of character makeup to accentuate the disinherited, forlorn characters in T. S. Eliot's poem "The Hollow Men," can add immeasurably to a perceptive interpretation of these literary texts.

## Music or Sound

The auditory elements of music or sound are a Reader' Theatre approach to setting the mood and creating the atmosphere in classroom performance. Music may be used as an introduction to the literary text itself or interwoven throughout the script to sustain the theme of the adaptation. Selected music may orchestrate interludes, transitions, and poignant events or incidents; or punctuate the dramatic action. The chanting, singing, or rapping of performers as they accompany themselves on musical instruments or create vocal rhythm patterns also adds theatrical impact to a classroom performance. The romantic John Keats' poem "Ode to a Nightingale," for example, lends itself nicely to the addition of a lute or lyre playing softly in the background; and Ray Bradbury's thought-provoking poem "I Sing the Body Electric" invariably achieves a heightened, new meaning for an audience when it is accompanied by the taped music of popular artists like Garth Brooks, Lauryn Hill, Madonna, Dave Matthews, Smashing Pumpkins, or the Rolling Stones!

Sound may be used to point toward scene change, call attention to shifting character attitudes or moods and dramatize a dramatic moment. Sound may also provide editorial commentary for the production concept. For example, the recorded sound of a honking horn may help to signal the change of scene from a flight of fantasy to an abrupt landing in reality for the title character in James Thurber's short story "The Secret Life of Walter Mitty"; or the recorded sound effect of an irregular, slowly-pulsing heartbeat may add psychological dimension to an interpretation of Edgar Allan Poe's story "The Tell-Tale Heart."

Performers may provide vocal orchestration of the literary text as well, creating live sounds or vocal effects that reinforce the dramatic action. For example, John Drinkwater's playscript *Abraham Lincoln* and Stephen Vincent Benet's narrative poem "John Brown's Body" may each feature performers who sing Civil War songs, voice sounds of battle, or contribute rhythmic hand-clapping and foot-marching to selected events or incidents.

## Projections

Projections, or slides, indicate scene change, locale, and setting. They may also establish attitude or mood and provide insights that clarify a character's intention or motivation. When used selectively and with discretion, projections help to identify and reinforce the production concept. For example, projections used as set pieces in Langston Hughes' poem "Downtown," with selective images of Harlem in the 1940s being revealed at dramatic moments in the narration, capture the historical spirit of the times; and also provide a critical point of reference for an audience to understand the author's point of view on social injustice. Likewise, the use of projections flashing newspaper headlines, magazine photographs, and historical documents on a screen in Peter Barnes' playscript *Auschwitz,* Robert Lowell's poem "For the Union Dead," or Megan Terry's collected narratives *Viet Rock* visually document the history of war and the horrors of man's inhumanity to man.

# Postscript

We are now at that point in our Readers Theatre journey when it is time to pause for a brief rest period before reaching the classroom performance destination. Your "memory book" of the excursion so far is probably crammed with keen observations and personal experiences that will be invaluable in classroom performance. I hope there were no detours or roadblocks along the way! Since you have been such an attentive companion, there is a very special treat of classroom performance activities and exercises waiting in Chapter Five. Just a few tidbits of thought as we now change drivers, and you follow the few remaining road signs that lead to today's Readers Theatre.

Throughout our Readers Theatre journey the artistic focus has been on the classroom performance. It is important to recognize that no two performers play the same literary character with an identical interpretation; and that no two performers sketch the same character portrait with identical information provided by an analysis of the given circumstances in a literary text. Today's Readers Theatre common sense tells us that effective role-playing of literary characters is the result of a risk-free classroom environment in which performers can experiment with a literary text to realize its performance potential.

Remember that as critical as analysis may be in the interpretation of a literary text, it is the theatrical impulse in the selection, staging, and performance of literature that indicates Readers Theatre's artistic, personal signature. Because there is no simple formula to integrate the sample activities, exercises, and scripts that follow into every classroom performance, it is important that performers take creative liberties to redefine each exercise to achieve individual self-expression. It is also important that performers be observers. They should listen to what others say; and notice how others express themselves verbally or non-verbally. These are the "hearing" and "seeing" observations that serve as authentic role models in classroom performance.

# SUGGESTED READINGS

The following suggested readings are primarily related to directing and staging for classroom performance. These suggested readings should also provide useful information on basic approaches to production, rehearsal, and theatre games that have practical value in the classroom.

Bartow, Arthur. *The Director's Voice.* New York: Theatre Communications Group, 1988.

Brockett, Oscar. *History of the Theatre.* Boston: Allyn and Bacon, 1986.

Brook, Pete. *The Empty Space.* New York: Atheneum, 1968.

Craig, David. *A Performer Prepares.* New York: Applause Theatre Books, 1996.

Dean, Alexander and Lawrence Carra. *Fundamentals of Play Direction.* New York: Holt, Rinehart, and Winston, 1989.

Hodge, Francis. *Play Directing.* Englewood Cliffs, New Jersey: Prentice Hall, 1988.

Hobgood, Burnet. *Master Teachers of Theatre.* Carbondale, Illinois: Southern Illinois University Press, 1988.

Marowitz, Charles. *Directing the Action.* New York: Applause Theatre Books, 1995.

O'Neill, R. H. and N. M. Boretz. *The Director as Artist.* New York: Holt, Rinehart, and Winston, 1987.

Spolin, Viola. *Improvisation for the Theatre.* Evanston, Illinois: Northwestern University Press, 1985.

Stanislavsky, Konstantin. *An Actor Prepares.* New York: Theatre Arts, 1936.

Chapter Five
# Classroom Performance Exercises

*"Imagination, Industry, and Intelligence — 'The Three I's' — are all indispensable to the actor, but of these three the greatest is, without any doubt, Imagination."*

— Ellen Terry, *Memoirs*

Today's Readers Theatre continues to explore imaginative approaches to classroom performance, and some of the new trends are reflected in these exercises. The traditional oral interpreter and the theatre performer both appear to be on a simultaneous journey to experiment with more theatrical approaches in classroom performance as well. David Magarshack, the noted stage director, captures the spirit of imagination needed in today's Readers Theatre in his perceptive "marriage and family" performance analogy.

Writing in *Stanislavsky on the Art of the Stage,* Magarshack suggests the birth of a literary character requires a "husband" (author) and a "wife" (actor or actress), but it is the "child" (created part) that is the unique creation. He also uses the marriage and family performance analogy to describe the mating process as one of first acquaintance, friendship, and then falling in love; with an occasional period of quarrels, differences of opinion, reconciliation, and blissful union.

The classroom performance exercises in this chapter subscribe to the "happy marriage" analogy in a series of assignments, activities, and improvisations designed to promote the theatrical union of author and performer. The primary focus, of course, is on the imaginative courtship of role-playing to effectively suggest the author's apparent point of view in classroom performance. For some, this first acquaintance with exercises may be love at first sight that reconciles initial performer anxiety. For others, however, exercises may need a longer period of friendship to become better acquainted with the theatrical impulse in today's Readers Theatre.

No matter how you choose to approach these exercises, there are still a number of practical observations to make in terms of achieving a rewarding artistic experience. It is still appropriate for performers to direct action and spoken lines of dialog to other performers if there is an intimate nature of character relationship; and performers should look for potential opportunities to interact or exchange interpersonal responses with other characters whenever possible. Remember that the goal in classroom performance is to *illustrate* the appearance of action, character, and situation with an attitude of sensitivity, conversational tone of delivery, and natural sense of movement.

The rehearsal period is the most appropriate time and place to translate these exercises into an inventive classroom performance blueprint. Reread the suggested excerpts of any distributed literature aloud several times in the rehearsal period, responding vocally and physically to the language the author uses to describe the character. The voice and body should respond simultaneously to the descriptive language as each performer considers "how" the character will act, feel, look, and sound in classroom performance. Particular attention should be given to the "choices" made in the rehearsal period to achieve the specific objective of each exercise.

Finally, practice economy and efficiency with the exercises during the rehearsal period. Concentrate on a *single* performance objective and a *selective* character portrait most appropriate to the sample literature at hand, rather than striving for a more complex character portrait that may be detailed in the complete literary text. Remember that the performer cannot include all of the information related to a character portrait in the limited time of a rehearsal period. So, practice selectivity in revealing a carefully chosen, concise character portrait that includes a single, specific unit of action to accomplish the "happy marriage" of author and performer.

# Exercise 1: Sardines Today!

**Objective:** To promote performer awareness of locale or setting that may be found in a literary text.

**Approach:** Several days before the exercise, have the performers search for suitable space that might lend itself to classroom performance. Interesting nooks or crannies might include a gallery, arched door frame, patio, balcony, or an alcove. When an imaginative space has been identified, have performers select and memorize a short poem, song lyric, or a brief prose excerpt of two or three minutes that would be appropriate to both the space and the literature.

For example, Richard Lovelace's short poem "To Althea, from Prison" is well-suited for performance in a cramped hallway, an excerpt from Ralph Ellison's novel *Invisible Man* behind a screen in a projection room, and the song lyrics to James Taylor's "Traffic Jam" in a custodian's storage closet! Review the discussion of dramatic playing space in Chapter Four and remind performers of the artistic distinction between "literal" and "localized" settings.

On the day(s) of the assignment, the class moves from playing space to playing space, and the scheduled performers share their portrayals with classmates. At the conclusion of each day's presentations, the class then reassembles for discussion and evaluation of (a) artistic choices made and (b) the role that the selected space played in the dramatic visualization of the literature.

79

**Extension:** The exercise may be extended as a small-group project, with ten to fifteen minutes of scripted literature from a single literary text or a compiled script in playing spaces suggested in the initial performances. The extended part of the exercise is also an opportunity for performers to pursue minimal costumes, props, and set pieces as well.

Literature useful for this part of the exercise might include a compiled, thematic script titled "Voices from the Grave," featuring poems like Richard Hugo's "Graves at Elkhorn," Robert Lowell's "The Quaker Graveyard in Nantucket" and Marianne Moore's "The Grave"; excerpts from William Faulkner's novel *As I Lay Dying*; and dramatic monologs from Wole Soyinka's playscript *Death and the King's Horseman.*

# Exercise 2: Zoo Story

**Objective:** To acquaint performers with alternative models for literary character role-playing and movement.

**Approach:** Begin the exercise with a review of the basic principles of movement discussed in Chapter One and the use of adjectives and verbs to identify dramatic action discussed in Chapter Three. Performers are encouraged to visit a local park, zoo, petting farm, or to observe their own pets in a natural habitat.

Each performer should compile a "Jungle Book" of observations that note peculiar habits or traits of the animal(s) observed. The detailed observation may, for example, make mention of degree of intelligence, eating habits, interpersonal skills, and movement patterns; or the observation may call attention to awareness of personality, vocal sounds, or physical appearance.

When performers conclude the period of detailed observation, summary presentations are made to the class. Performers then reduce the animal study assignment to key phrases, verbs, and adjectives that suggest an inventive portrait of an analogous character in a literary text. Examples of literature useful for this part of the exercise might include poems like Lord Byron's "She Walks in Beauty" or Edwin Arlington Robinson's "Richard Corey" and excerpts from short stories like Eudora Welty's "Petrified Man" or Isaac Bashevis Singer's "Gimpel the Fool."

Classroom performances of literary characters

should be four to five minutes and capture individuality in both movement and action. There should also be creative exhibition of the key phrases, verbs, and adjectives that define each animal study present in the classroom performance. Following the performances, class discussion should focus on the role that studied observation of animals, objects, or persons may play in suggesting incisive literary character portraits.

**Extension:** There are a number of opportunities to extend the exercise to include the ensemble performance of an adapted literary text. An adaptation of George Orwell's *Animal Farm*, Terry Siegel's satirical revue "Fun with Hamlet and hls Friends," or T. S. Eliot's *Possum Book* tales — which is the source for the long-running Broadway musical *Cats* — are imaginative choices for this part of the exercise.

Performers may also choose to do a literary analysis of the selection that follows. In this part of the exercise, particular attention should be paid to the literary terms discussed in Chapter Two, and performers should visualize the "metaphorical" movement suggested in the literary analysis of the literature.

**The Tiger**
by William Blake

Tiger, tiger, burning bright
In the forests of the night,
What immortal hand or eye
Could frame thy fearful symmetry?

In what distant deeps or skies
Burnt the fire of thine eyes?
On what wings dare he aspire?
What the hand dare seize the fire?

And what shoulder and what art
Could twist the sinews of thy heart?
And, when thy heart began to beat,
What dread hand and what dread feet?

What the hammer? What the chain?
In what furnace was thy brain?
What the anvil? What dread grasp
Dare its deadly terrors clasp?

When the stars threw down their spears
And water'd heaven with their tears,
Did He smile His work to see?
Did He who made the lamb make thee?

Tiger, tiger, burning bright
In the forest of the night,
What immortal hand or eye
Dare frame thy fearful symmetry?

# Exercise 3: The Body Beautiful!

**Objective:** To encourage performers to physicalize a literary text in terms of specific body reactions or responses.

**Approach:** Divide the class into small groups of four. Label each small group with a humorous name that corresponds to a specific part of the body. For example, The Crazy Legs, Pin Heads, Lazy Feet, Fickle Fingers, or Sleepy Arms.

Review the importance of using all parts of the body to physicalize reactions or responses of literary characters in classroom performance. Call performers of each small group to the front of the class, and voice specific reactions or responses that suggest bodily movement. Ask the performers to respond to the suggested activities using their respective label. For example, the "Sleepy Arms" small group may be asked to respond to physical activities like "slowly yawning," "anxious stretching," and "nervous scratching." The "Crazy Legs," however, may be asked to respond to physical action words like "running," "jumping," and "skipping."

In the class discussion that follows each small group's effort to overtly physicalize bodily actions, performers should recall the active degrees of tension or relaxation involved in the previous reactions or responses. Care should be taken to point out that physicalization of a literary character's overt reaction or response must be as authentic as "real" body motions involved in similar bodily movement.

Conclude the exercise by presenting each small group with individual prose or poetry selections of literature. The small groups chart the specific images, phrases, or words that suggest physical activity in the literature, and rehearse a classroom performance that includes vocal as well as physical reactions or responses.

The "body" of literature available for this part of the exercise may include Dr. Seuss' madcap description of the "harrowing flight" of *The Grinch Who Stole Christmas,* Kate Chopin's description of "combating the elements" in "The Storm," and Laurence Ferlinghetti's description of "moving body parts" in "Underwear." It may also be a good idea to include an excerpt from Ernest Hemingway's "The Snows of Kilimanjaro," discussed in Chapter Two, to help physicalize the "jousting" wordplay of the literary characters.

**Extension:** This exercise lends itself to a nice extension when combined with Exercise 9, titled "Move, But Stand Still!" to draw performance comparisons with the traditional Readers Theatre principle of confining physical action to a more limited space. There is also an opportunity to physicalize the character reactions and responses in Samuel Beckett's pantomime titled "Act Without Words," which is included as a sample performance script in Chapter Six.

Finally, Beckett's pantomime lends itself to an ensemble classroom production with the addition of music, sound effects, multiple performers, and a number of narrator figures voicing stage directions; or it can be the central focus of a compiled script of other literature that revolves around the title "Act Without Words."

85

# Exercise 4: Living Pictures

**Objective:** To promote an understanding of how improvisation may reveal four types of theatrical action for classroom performance.

**Approach:** Begin the exercise with a review of the four types of theatrical action discussed in Chapter Two.

Select a number of historical paintings and character portraits or more contemporary photographs of small groups of people involved in an action. Representative samples should convey a sense of character attitude, place, and time. The samples should also suggest an imaginative story line in the group composition.

Sources may include Honoré Daumier's caricatures, sober peasants of Pieter Brueghel, Michelangelo's "The Pieta," Jean Fouquet's "The Martyrdom of St. Apollonia," Aubrey Beardsley prints, or classical Greek vase paintings of the fifth century B.C.

Distribute the samples to equal numbers of performers, so that small groups are working with the same number of characters depicted in the samples. Each performer in a small group selects an individual character to analyze. The first part of the exercise is concerned with *character* action, detailing the imagined habits or traits of the character suggested in the sample.

The second part of the exercise is the improvisation. each small group of performers assumes the pose of their selected characters in the sample. The imaginative analysis of character action may have already indicated the dominant relationships, so the improvisation begins with the most visually prominent character in the sample initiating the first character action or the first line of improvisational dialog.

The small-group improvisation should clarify the setting or locale, reveal distinct character relationships, and provide an interesting story line for the sample. Remember, however, that the small-group improvisation is focused on *instinctive* action, exhibiting the spontaneous reaction or response of each performer to the imagined habits or traits of the sample character.

Following each small-group improvisation, there is active discussion. The class should evaluate character actions that have been clearly visualized in each performer's spontaneous reaction or response. The class discussion may also suggest a promising *dramatic* action, or conflict, for the particular group of characters depicted in each sample.

The third part of the exercise is an improvisation of *descriptive* action, providing voice, gesture, and movement to portray individual characters in the sample. Each small group assumes the pose of the initial improvisation, and performers now enact their individual character's apparent intention or motivation in the sample as it has been informed by class discussion.

**Extension:** The exercise may be extended to a critical analysis and improvisation of selected events or incidents in a specific literary text. Appropriate examples of literary texts that exhibit the four types of theatrical action may include Robert Benchley's comic snapshots of "Family Life in America," Dylan Thomas' composite portrait of community in "Under Milk Wood," Germaine Greer's finely etched sketches of "The Stereotypes," and the photographic characters in Sandra Cisneros' "The House on Mango Street."

The "Living Pictures" composed by performers in the extended exercise may be based on historical paintings, portraits, and contemporary photographs; or may emerge as *tableaux,* the frozen poses suggested by Bertolt Brecht in Chapter Four, based on an analysis of the literary text. As an added dimension, costumes and musical interludes that encourage performers to engage in movement may also be added to the small-group improvisations.

# Exercise 5: Dress-Up Day!

**Objective:** To present performers with an opportunity to explore the role of costumes and hand-props in classroom performance.

**Approach:** Divide the class into small groups of seven and distribute the following adaptation of Jacques' speech in William Shakespeare's *As You Like It.*

Performers determine the character role they would like to perform in the adaptation, and are given the following instructions: Bring to class (1) a costume piece like hat, scarf, skirt, or vest and (2) a hand-prop like eyeglasses, a briefcase, gavel, or baby rattle that defines each chosen character.

Set aside rehearsal time so each small group may memorize the literature, determine the playing space, and experiment with staging. If possible, place small groups in different rehearsal spaces to reduce possible temptations to duplicate or imitate. Following the classroom performances, there should be comparative discussion that focuses on performer choices of costume piece and hand-prop to clearly define characters.

# William Shakespeare's *As You Like It* (II, vii)

Narrator:  All the world's a stage
  And all the men and women merely players:
  They have their exits and their entrances,
  And one man in his time plays many parts,
  His acts being seven ages.
Performer 1:  At first, the infant,
  Mewling and puking in the nurse's arms.
Performer 2:  Then the whining schoolboy,
  With his satchel and shining morning face,
  Creeping like snail unwillingly to school.
Performer 3:  And then the lover,
  Sighing like furnace, with a woeful ballad
  Made to his mistress' eyebrow.
Performer 4:  Then a soldier,
  Full of strange oaths, and bearded like the pard,
  Jealous in honour, sudden, and quick in quarrel,
  Seeking the bubble reputation even in the cannon's mouth.
Performer 5:  And then the justice,
  In fair round belly with good capon lin'd,
  With eyes severe and beard of formal cut,
  Full of wise saws and modern instances.
Narrator:  And so he plays his part.
Performer 6:  The sixth age shifts
  Into the lean and slipper'd pantaloon,
  With spectacles on nose and pouch on side,
  His youthful hose, well sav'd, a world too wide
  For his shrunk shank; and his big manly voice,
  Turning again toward childish treble, pipes
  And whistles in his sound.

Narrator:  Last scene of all,

Performer 3:  That ends this strange eventful history,

Performer 5:  Is second childishness

Performer 1:  And mere oblivion.

Performer 6:  Sans teeth,

Performer 4:  Sans eyes,

Performer 2:  Sans taste,

Narrator:  Sans everything.

**Extension:** This exercise may be extended to supplement an assignment in adapting literature for classroom performance. Present each small group with the following selection from William Shakespeare's "advice to the players" in *Hamlet*.

Instruct each small group to adapt the literature for seven performers, including a narrator figure. The performers cut and edit, assign individual *and* group lines, explore staging, select costume pieces and hand-props to define the individual character in the new adaptation. Set aside class rehearsal time in separate spaces. On the scheduled day of classroom performances, invite parents, friends, and other classmates to the presentation of *both* adaptations from Shakespeare's *As You Like It* and *Hamlet*.

91

# William Shakespeare's *Hamlet* (III, ii)

Speak the speech, I pray you, as I pronounced it to you, trippingly on the tongue. But if you mouth it, as many of your players do, I had as lief the town-crier spoke my lines. Nor do not saw the air too much with your hand, thus, but use all gently; for in the very torrent, tempest, and, as I may say, whirlwind of your passion, you must acquire and beget a temperance that may give it smoothness. O, it offends me to the soul to hear a robustious periwig-patted ham tear a passion to tatters, to very rags, to split the ears of the groundlings, who for the most part are capable of nothing but inexplicable dumb-shows and noise. I would have such a fellow whipped for o'erdoing Termagant; it out-herods Herod. Pray you, avoid it.

Be not too tame neither, but let your own discretion be your tutor. Suit the action to the word, the word to the action; with this special observance, that you do not overstep the modesty of nature; for any thing so o'erdone is from the purpose of acting, whose end, both at the first and now, was and is, to hold, as 'twere, the mirror up to nature; to show virtue her own feature, scorn her own image, and the very age and body of the time his form and pressure. Now this overdone, or come tardy off, though it makes the unskillful laugh, cannot but make the judicious grieve; the censure of the which one must, in your allowance, o'erweigh a whole theatre of others. O, there be players that I have seen play — and heard others praise, and that highly — not to speak profanely, that, either having th' accent of Christians, not the gait of Christian, pagan, nor man, have so strutted and bellowed that I thought some of Nature's journeymen had made men, and not made them well, they imitated humanity so abominably.

O, reform it altogether. And let those that play your clowns speak no more than is set down for them; for there be of them that will themselves laugh, to set on some quantity of barren spectators to laugh too, though in the meantime some necessary question of the play is to be considered. That's villainous, and shows a most pitiful ambition in the fool that uses it. Go, make you ready!

# Exercise 6: Book Parade

**Objective:** To familiarize performers with use of the hand-held book, manuscript, and bound script to suggest an object or character attitude.

**Approach:** Begin the exercise with a discussion of the creative potential to use the script as a character prop or to visualize action described in the literature. Select several performers and ask them to move to the front of the classroom.

Present each performer with a book, vinyl folder, or bound script to hold. Call out specific locales like church, hospital, kitchen, restaurant, or nursery and ask performers to use their hand-held manuscripts to suggest the desired locale.

Performers may respond, for example, by holding the book toward the audience in a horizontal manner to suggest the tray of a restaurant server; or by cuddling the vinyl folder to suggest the teddy bear of a nursery. The important principle in this part of the exercise is that the suggested object and character attitude or mood be clearly defined.

Next, select several more students and ask them to move to the front of the classroom. Call out specific character occupations like farmer, bank teller, policeman, entertainer, or construction worker, and ask performers to use their hand-held manuscripts to suggest the desired occupation.

Performers may respond, for example, by "hoeing" with the book to suggest a farmer, "directing traffic" with the manuscript to suggest a policeman, or

93

"singing" with the bound script as a microphone to suggest an entertainer. The important principle in this part of the exercise is that performers begin to extend visual images of character in the creative use of a hand-held script.

Now, select several more performers and ask them to move to the front of the classroom. Call out specific attitudes or moods like anger, glee, despair, joy, or loneliness and ask performers to use their hand-held manuscripts to suggest the desired attitude or mood.

Performers may respond, for example, by caressing vinyl folders to suggest glee and joy or covering their faces to suggest despair and loneliness. The important principle in this part of the exercise is that performers reflect character attitudes or moods in the manner in which the book, vinyl folder, or bound script is held.

**Extension:** When performers are aware of the creative role a hand-held manuscript may play in classroom performance, present one brief selection of poetry or prose as a two- or three-minute assignment for future classroom performance. The sample literature should contain a definite locale, occupation, and character attitude or mood. Performers present the literature individually, using a hand-held script whenever appropriate to clearly define the locale, occupation, and attitude or mood of the literary character.

The use of one brief selection of poetry or prose should promote interesting discussion of individual performer choices in hand-held script technique.

This part of the exercise may also be extended to include small-group classroom performances of compiled scripts as well. Examples useful for any part of this exercise may include Carol Schacter's "Miss Kindergarten America," Robert Frost's "The Wood-Pile," Ann Sexton's "Lobster," Emily Dickinson's "This Is My Letter to the World," or e.e. cummings' "in Just —."

# Exercise 7: I Beg Your Pardon, What Did You Say?

**Objective:** To promote an awareness of the active word play at work in revealing a literary character's subtext.

**Approach:** Begin the exercise by providing the performers with individual copies of the selection shown below. Performers voice the word "No" to achieve the desired meaning indicated in parentheses. Using the vocal variables of pitch, rate, and volume, the "No" list is then performed in groups of two in front of the class.

| | | |
|---|---|---|
| (A) | No? | (I beg your pardon, what did you say?) |
| (B) | No. | (I don't understand what you mean!) |
| (A) | No! | (You can't mean that, can you?) |
| (B) | No? | (Well, if that's the way you feel.) |
| (A) | No. | (We'll see about that soon enough!) |
| (B) | No! | (Does this mean it's over for us?) |
| (A) | No? | (You weren't with someone else?) |
| (B) | No. | (How dare you even think that!) |
| (A) | No? | (You were with someone else!) |
| (B) | No. | (You really must be kidding.) |
| (A) | No! | (Why don't you get a life!) |
| (B) | No? | (I could be persuaded.) |
| (A) | No. | (Are you positive?) |
| (B) | No! | (I beg your pardon, what did you say?) |

Please have the performers engage in word play in the following manner: (A) voices the first "No" to achieve its desired meaning, and (B) responds with the second "No" to achieve its desired meaning. The word play continues as the performers alternate lines to achieve the desired meaning of each "No."

**Extension:** The exercise may be extended as a companion to Exercise 15, titled "Mirror, Mirror on the Wall," to introduce the principle of Off-stage focus. For this part of the exercise, place performers in small groups of three or four. Then present each group with short cuttings of several playscripts or novels with three or four literary characters involved in conversation that suggests a subtext to their relationship. Using pitch, rate, and volume, performers voice the implied interaction that exists beneath the surface of spoken language in staged classroom performances.

If Off-stage focus is an additional dimension in the extended exercise, review the basic principles of staging and the diagram of character placement in Chapter Four. All performer action, business, dialog, reaction, and sight lines should be directed slightly over the heads of the audience.

Examples of short cuttings useful for this exercise include the "Pledge of Allegiance" scene in Aristophanes' *Lysistrata*, the "unmasking of the guilty" episode in Nathaniel Hawthorne's *The Scarlet Letter*, the "Pyramus and Thisby" scene in William Shakespeare's *A Midsummer Night's Dream*, the "gathering the harvest" episode in Pearl S. Buck's *The Good Earth*, and the "Gentleman Caller" scene in Tennessee Williams' *The Glass Menagerie*.

# Exercise 8: Prop Probe

**Objective:** To explore the properties of sound and the role that "vocal" special effects might play in the interpretation of a literary text.

**Approach:** Stockpile a variety of hand-held items capable of conducting the sounds of the human voice. Examples might include cardboard tubes, garden hoses, soda cans, plastic jugs, mouth mufflers, combs, vacuum cleaner attachments, scuba masks, and glass containers.

Begin the exercise by having the performers present their found objects individually to the class. Each performer uses the found object as a mouthpiece to produce an interesting sound. Present each performer with a familiar line of verse, prose phrase, or witty quotation to voice with the found object. (Sources might include *Bartlett's Familiar Quotations*, book titles, song lyrics, television programs, or well-known quotations from William Shakespeare, Abraham Lincoln, and Benjamin Franklin.)

For example, the familiar line of verse may be William Shakespeare's "Come what come may, Time and the hour runs through the roughest day." (*Macbeth*, I, iii); the prose phrase may be Mark Twain's humorous suggestion that " ... familiarity breeds contempt, and children"; and the witty quotation may be Oscar Wilde's "I can resist everything except temptation." (*Lady Windemere's Fan*, I, i)

After the performers have been given individual

opportunities to demonstrate a found object and to voice a familiar line of verse, prose phrase, or witty quotation, repeat the exercise without the found object. Each performer is encouraged to duplicate the sound produced by the found object with the natural voice; and to create as many "vocal" sound effects as possible. Following the presentations, there should be discussion and evaluation of Antoine Artaud's suggestion in Chapter Four that "orchestrated vocal sound" is an essential ingredient in setting the mood or tone of a script.

**Extension:** The exercise may be extended as a small-group project with a sound analysis of the following selection of literature by an anonymous Texan who is visiting England for the first time. Follow the guidelines for reading literature at least three times as discussed in Chapter One, and focus on the final performance reading to add appropriate vocal special effects that may complement the excerpt that follows.

From "A Texan's Visit to England"

It is as dark as the inside of a cow here in the city of Cambridge. The fog comes up from the fens, they say — the fens that the Romans were building a road across two thousand years ago. But the dark never gets heavy enough to keep people inside. I step out on the street and, except in the puddle of light made by my own flashlight, I can distinguish nothing.

But it is not lights or absence of lights in the darkness that strikes one! It is the sounds from human feet and human voices. Especially feet. Boots, boots, boots, marching all together. I linger to let five or six voices and pairs of feet pass me. They are out in the middle of the narrow street, keeping step and keeping time. The voices and the firm but lightsome foot-plantings are of young women. They are singing a song with sadness in it — the only kind of love songs that ever were or ever will be beautiful. From the step, step, step, and from half a glimpse of a swinging arm as the voices pass me, I know that they belong to military women. There are other foot sounds without voices. Many of them. Some timid and groping, most of them direct. There are voices now and then that seem to be without feet. The Americans sometimes have louder voices, not always. Passing the mouth of a side street, I hear down it in the direction of the Red Lion, not far from the Blue Bear, "Where the Deer and the Antelope Play."

With the vocal orchestration discoveries made in this part of the exercise, the performers may now turn their attention to creating live sounds in a number of literary texts suggested in Chapter Four. For example, with the experience gained in this exercise it would now be appropriate to create live sounds or vocal special effects that reinforce the dramatic action of excerpts from John Drinkwater's playscript *Abraham Lincoln* or Stephen Vincent Benet's narrative poem "John Brown's Body." In these literary texts, however, the performers should also consider singing Civil War songs, voicing sounds of battle, and contributing rhythmic hand-clapping and foot-marching to the selected events or incidents.

# Exercise 9: Move, But Stand Still!

**Objective:** To develop awareness of the subtle degree of movement needed to confine character action to a limited playing space.

**Approach:** Select three performers and direct them to respond to the sample narrative scenario that follows. Performers are encouraged to react with complete freedom of movement in the first part of the exercise. Other narratives that may stimulate movement such as running, skipping, or falling like Albert Camus' *The Stranger*, Henry David Thoreau's *Walden*, or Elizabeth Bishop's "At the Fishhouses" are also appropriate.

Sample Narrative Scenario

Imagine a hot, dusty day in a late afternoon in July. *(Performers begin to suggest perspiration.)* You are walking down a dusty, dirty road in the middle of secluded woodlands. *(Performers walk around the classroom, coughing and wheezing.)* The air is hot and the glazing sun beats down on your bare head. *(Performers suggest the increasing heat and wipe their foreheads.)* Suddenly, you see a pond at the edge of the bumpy road! *(The performers halt and direct focus to the imaginary pond.)*

Rush toward the pond eagerly! *(Performers dash to the imaginary pond.)* Climb the high wooden fence that encloses it! *(Performers climb nearby chairs.)* Take off your shoes and stick your aching toes into the cool, refreshing water. *(Performers sit, remove their shoes, and enjoy the coolness of the water.)* Without warning, a passing farmer shouts "Hey, you! You're trespassing! Get out of there!" *(Performers are startled, but quickly gather up their shoes and scramble away in different directions.)*

Now, review the role that a more subtle degree of movement may play to suggest overt character action using "Off-stage" focus. Continue the exercise by asking each performer to hold a book, vinyl folder, or bound manuscript to re-enact the physical responses previously experienced in the same sample narrative scenario.

In this part of the exercise, however, performers should place the scene Off-stage, and use the hand-held script to suggest character action or movement. The farmer and his dialog also needs to be placed Off-stage, and any suggestive movement is limited to a confined playing space.

**Extension:** This exercise lends itself quite well to an introduction of third-person narrative. Extend the exercise by asking performers who have observed the first part of the exercise to come forward and serve as narrator figures. Each narrator figure voices individual recollections, narration, lines of dialog, and description of character action as it has been observed.

The exercise may also be extended to include a character's physical response to an attitude or mood. Present performers with excerpts of literature like Adrienne Rich's poem "I Am in Danger — Sir —," Edgar Lee Masters' dramatic monolog of "Mrs. Williams" in *Spoon River Anthology*, or the chilling narrative of Anne Sexton's poem "Unknown Girl in the Maternity Ward." Ask performers to combine subtle facial expressions, vocal qualities, and physical responses to suggest each character's attitude or mood in the selected literature.

# Exercise 10: The Touch/Tell Box

**Objective:** To acquaint performers with the use of hand-props to define literary characters.

**Approach:** Surprise performers by unveiling the Touch/Tell Box, a brightly decorated cardboard container used to store hand-props like mirrors, fans, eyeglasses, costume jewelry, walking sticks, watches, or snuff boxes that might define literary characters.

Spend some time discussing the potential role of hand-props that may have helped to define familiar characters studied previously in class. Promote an awareness of hand-props that "represent" or are an "extension" of character as discussed in Chapter Two. Following the discussion, each performer approaches the Touch/Tell Box and reaches inside to select a hand-prop at random.

Present a number of short poems, song lyrics, letters, historical documents, or dramatic monologs that contain literary characters in need of definition. Instruct performers to integrate their selected hand-prop, whenever appropriate, in classroom performance of the distributed literature. Performers should also be prepared to tell whether the hand-prop represents the characters or is an extension of the character.

Examples of literature that feature hand-props to define characters may include the "dagger" of the title character in William Shakespeare's playscript *Macbeth*, the "shaded eyeglasses" of Helen Keller in her autobiographical *Three Days to Live*, the "quill pen" of the author in John Keats' "A Love Letter,"

104

the "stump cigar" of Winston Churchill in his "Address on Dunkirk," or the "rosary beads" of Sister Agnes in John Pielmeier's playscript *Agnes of God.*

**Extension:** The exercise may be extended when performers select other literature that features a hand-prop or an object to define a character. In this part of the exercise, encourage performers to wear a suggestive costume that also helps to define the selected character. On the day(s) set aside for classroom presentation, each performer should introduce a well-defined character in terms of the action, costume, dialog, and hand-prop suggested in the literature.

# Exercise 11: The Music Scene

**Objective:** To acquaint performers with the use of music in character development.

**Approach:** Begin the assignment with a brief review of the role of music in suggesting character development. Ask for examples of recent films that use music to produce an emotional response in a selected scene or to establish the mood of an incident or event. Remind performers that music also creates a feeling of historical place and time.

Tape record a variety of musical excerpts that may include classical, waltz, popular, country-and-western, folk ballad, rock, jazz, heavy metal, tango, and blues. Work in small groups of five or six, and have each group move to the taped music in front of the classroom. There should be a noticeable difference in the movement style to the tempo and rhythm of the lyric classical, repetitive sway of the folk ballad, free and easy flow of jazz, and the staccato of rock or heavy metal.

After each small group has completed the movement to taped music, repeat the exercise *without* music. Ask individual performers to choose a simple physical activity like lacing a shoe, setting a table, reading a newspaper, or shopping in two different kinds of music. Remind performers that the choice of music should dictate the degree of tension or relaxation in the movement, but there should be *no* dancing to the imaginary music when performing the simple physical activity.

**Extension:** Extend the exercise with an assignment that each performer select a three-minute poem or prose excerpt of literature for classroom performance. Each performer should focus on using musical tempo and rhythm to define character action in the incident or event suggested in the literary text. Some external character elements like a gesture, habit, peculiar mannerism, or walk may also merge in this musical interpretation.

There are a number of literary texts that may provide a stimulus for this part of the extended exercise. If possible, consider the progressive physical activity of the title character in Ernest Hemingway's short novel *The Old Man and the Sea,* the adolescent prancing action in Gwendolyn Brooks' short poem "We Real Cool," the frantic sewer chase action in Alexander Dumas' classic novel *Les Miserables,* and the awkward gawky action of the youthful hero in Richard Bach's narrative *Jonathan Livingston Seagull.*

# Exercise 12: Carry Your Character With You!

**Objective:** To develop an awareness of the role of movement and physical action in defining literary characters.

**Approach:** Select thirteen, or twenty-six, performers at random and assign them letters of the alphabet. Present the performers with the following poem by an anonymous author of the seventeenth century titled "A Was an Archer."

Begin the exercise by clarifying any unclear words so performers understand the selected phrase for each letter of the alphabet. Each performer approaches the playing space individually in alphabetical order.

In the playing space, performers strike a pose that suggests the physical action indicated, voice the phrase, and then follow through with movement that visually defines the literary character. Finally, each performer freezes in the movement that completes the character's physical action.

For example, performer A may enter the playing space very cautiously as if stalking some invisible prey, spy the unsuspecting foe, slowly draw an imaginary bow, and release the arrow after voicing the line associated with the alphabet character. The frozen movement is the performer's feet apart, hands relaxed, and shoulders slightly tensed, having released the arrow.

The remaining performers repeat the process striking a pose, voicing the phrase, and following through with movement until all the letters of the alphabet have been formed. The frozen character sketches scattered across the playing space in suggestive postures of physical action now offer vivid testimony to the Readers Theatre maxim, "Carry your character with you!"

From "A Was an Archer"

A   was an archer, and shot at a frog.
B   was a blind man, and led by a dog.
C   was a cutpurse, and lived in disgrace.
D   was a drunkard, and had a red face.
E   was an eater, a glutton was he.
F   was a fighter, and fought with a flea.
G   was a giant, and pulled down a house.
H   was a hunter, and hunted a mouse.
I   was an ill man, and hated by all.
J   was a jackass, locked in its stall.
K   was a knave, and he robbed great and small.
L   was a liar, and told many lies.
M   was a madman, and beat out his eyes.
N   was a nobleman, nobly born.
O   was an ostler, and stole horses' corn.
P   was a peddler, and sold many pins.
Q   was a quarreller, and broke both his shins.
R   was a rogue, and ran about town.
S   was a sailor, and knavishly bent.
T   was a tailor, and man of renown.
U   was a usurer, took ten percent.
V   was a viper, serpent-like.
W   was a writer, and money he earned.
X   was a Xenophon, prudent and learn'd.
Y   was a yeoman, and worked with his hands.
Z   was one Zeno the Great, but he's dead.

**Extension:** The exercise may also be extended to include a creative writing or critical thinking assignment. Each performer selects a favorite letter of the alphabet and writes a brief phrase that accurately describes a more contemporary figure.

For example, letters of the alphabet may identify figures like B (Batman), G (Garth Brooks), M (Madonna), O (Oprah), or X (Malcolm X). Phrases that identify the figures may include "Batman was a hero, pow! Wow!," "Garth was a singer, country and cute," "Madonna was a star, tinsel and tune," "Oprah was a host, talk and tell," or "Malcolm was a leader, shot in hate."

The contemporary alphabet characters are also presented in classroom performance as each performer recites the brief phrase, strikes a representative pose, and then follows through with an appropriate action or improvised movement that suggests the contemporary figures. In the class discussion that follows, performance comparisons should be drawn between role-playing literary characters and contemporary figures.

# Exercise 13: Literary Character Charades: See, Show, and Speak

**Objective:** To provide inventive opportunities for performers to discover metaphors for classroom performance.

**Approach:** Distribute to each performer a short poem, excerpt of prose, or dramatic monolog that provides one three-dimensional character suitable for a three- or four-minute solo classroom performance. Instruct performers to analyze their individual selection and determine the character's attitude, intention, or motivation in the literature.

Performers are then to observe with a critical, discerning eye the physical and vocal habits or traits of those with whom they may come in contact in the next five days. Those observed might include parents, friends, public figures, local citizens, casual acquaintances, trade persons, or even strangers.

Following the period of detailed observation, each performer isolates the appropriate gesture, mannerism, movement pattern, and vocal quality of those observed which most accurately reflects the literary character's attitude, intention, or motivation revealed in an analysis of the literature.

The personal signature of each performer in this part of the exercise is to discover in both the analysis and the observation a performance metaphor, or implied comparison, between the literary character and something else inventive; and then to integrate those complementary features in classroom performance.

111

**Extension:** The exercise may be extended to include a second classroom performance of metaphors based solely on a critical analysis of selected literature. In the extended part of the exercise, there is *no* observation of others, and performers rely on theatrical self-expression to draw imaginative comparisons between a literary character and something else inventive.

For example, a critical analysis of the character Leah in Joyce Carol Oates' narrative *Bellfleur* might suggest the performance metaphor of an ostrich or the character Miss Williams in Paule Marshall's short story "Brooklyn" as a stalking leopard on the prowl. Other literary characters to consider include Herbert in Robert Anderson's *You Know I Can't Hear You When the Water's Running* as a knight errant, Minnie in William Faulkner's "Dry September" as an uncurried horse awaiting death, and Perry in Truman Capote's *In Cold Blood* as an animal walking wounded.

# Exercise 14: Empty Space

**Objective:** To familiarize performers with movement patterns in staging that fill the empty playing space.

**Approach:** Begin the exercise by dividing performers into small groups of four. There should be a narrator figure and three performers in each small group. Select a literary text that suggests a number of settings or locales. Have each small group cut or edit the literature to accommodate a narrator figure, three performers, and possibilities for movement.

At first, each small group fills the empty playing space with geometrical patterns like a circle, star, triangle, and square. Then each small group improvises inventive movement patterns that locate events or incidents suggested in an analysis of the literature. Performers may, for example, move to the periphery of the empty playing space to locate a specific event or move right and left of center to locate a specific incident.

After the empty playing space has been filled with a number of inventive movement patterns, each small group stages the literary text distributed. The narrator figure and three performers may use geometrical movement patterns, inventive movement patterns that emerge in improvisation, or spontaneous movement patterns that surface in the performance of the selected literature.

A number of movement patterns need to be explored in this part of the exercise. The narrator figure and performers should pay particular attention to *character movement* that indicates attitude, intention, or motivation and relationship to other characters; and *story line movement* that indicates action and locale or setting. There is also a need to explore *mood movement* that indicates a character's emotional or mental state in each event or incident described in the literature.

Conclude the exercise by placing stage pieces like lecterns, stools, or small scenic units in the empty playing space. Each small group performs the literary text again using geometrical, inventive, and spontaneous movement patterns, but also makes appropriate adjustments to accommodate the additional stage pieces.

**Extension:** The exercise may be extended as a small group assignment in stage blocking. Each small group selects a sample classroom performance script included in Chapter Six and fills the empty playing space with movement and scenic units to create imaginative stage pictures which visualize the selected literature.

In the extended part of the exercise small groups should also review the stage composition elements like emphasis, balance, form, mass, and color discussed in Chapter Four. Literature appropriate for any part of this exercise may include John Dos Passos' trilogy *U.S.A.*, Lord Byron's "Childe Harold's Pilgrimage," Eleanor Farjeon's "Hannibal Crosses the Alps," or Roald Dahl's *James and the Giant Peach*.

# Exercise 15: Mirror, Mirror on the Wall

**Objective:** To develop an awareness of Off-stage focus and the placement of character and physical action in the audience.

**Approach:** Begin the exercise with a review of the basic principles of Off-stage focus discussed in Chapter Four.

Select a literary text that contains both dialog and physical action. For each character represented in the literature, place a full-length mirror on the wall at the back of the classroom. If full-length mirrors or rooms with wall-to-wall mirrors are not available, the exercise may be directed toward each performer's body response and facial expression as it is revealed in Off-stage focus.

Performers On-stage should establish a relationship with characters Off-stage in an initial series of conversational chats and improvised vocal or physical exchanges that establish specific Off-stage placement. It is very important in this part of the exercise for performers to indicate the point of intersection to which dialog and physical action is to be directed when addressing or responding to characters placed Off-stage.

At first, there is informal voicing of the selected literature so performers feel comfortable with the convention of addressing or responding to someone standing next to them as if they were located at the back of the classroom, slightly above the heads of the audience. Remind performers that all responses to the dialog and physical action of the characters is within a very confined space On-stage.

115

Re-read the selected literature a number of times, exploring vocal and physical qualities that distinguish one character from another. Encourage performers to pay special attention to adjectives and verbs that may help to visualize individual characters in performance. With each re-reading, the basic principles of Off-stage focus in character placement and lines of intersection are polished and refined.

When performers are confident and precise in Off-stage focus, the mirrors are removed and the selected literature performed. Follow the performance with classroom discussion that focuses on noticeable differences in staging techniques with mirrors and without. There should also be evaluation of performance approaches in executing dialog and physical action using Off-stage rather than On-stage focus.

**Extension:** The exercise can be extended to include a combination of On-stage and Off-stage foci, or to stage character subtext using the theatrical convention of an aside. Sample literature useful for the extended part of the exercise may include the tea scene between Gwendolyn and Cecily in Oscar Wilde's *The Importance of Being Earnest,* the seduction scene of Abbie and Eben in Eugene O'Neill's *Desire Under the Elms*, the alien sightings of Trudy in Jane Wagner's *Search for Signs of Intelligent Life in the Universe*, the true confessions of the title characters in J.D. Salinger's *Franny and Zoey,* or the confrontation scenes of Clay and Lula in Amiri Baraka's *Dutchman.*

# SUGGESTED READINGS

The following suggested readings are directed toward classroom performance and rehearsal techniques that focus on the performer's voice and body. These suggested readings should provide basic principles of vocal and physical qualities that help to frame a Readers Theatre production.

Anderson, Virgil. *Training the Speaking Voice.* New York: Oxford University Press, 1961.

Barton, Robert. *Styles for Actors.* Mountain View, California: Mayfield Publishing Company, 1988.

Berry, Cicely. *The Actor and the Text.* New York: Applause Theatre Books, 1996.

Carnicle, Sharon Marie. *The Theatrical Instinct.* New York: Praeger Press, 1995.

Crannell, Kenneth. *Voice and Articulation.* Belmont, California: Wadsworth, 1991.

Downs, David. *The Actor's Eye: Seeing and Being Seen.* New York: Applause Theatre Books, 1997.

Heinig, Ruth Beall. *Creative Drama for the Classroom Teacher.* Englewood Cliffs, New Jersey: Prentice-Hall, 1988.

McGaw, Charles and Larry Clark. *Acting Is Believing.* New York: Holt, Rinehart and Winston, 1987.

Owen, Mack. *The Stages of Acting.* New York: Harper Collins Publishers, 1993.

Siks, Geraldine Brain. *Drama with Children.* New York: Harper & Row, 1983.

Way, Brian. *Development Through Drama.* Atlantic Highlands, New Jersey: Humanities Press, 1967.

Wells, Lynne K. *The Articulate Voice.* Scottsdale, Arizona: Gorsuch-Scarisbrick, 1989.

# Chapter Six
# Sample Performance Scripts

*"Love the art in yourself, not yourself in the art.*

.  .  .  .  .

*And let those who cannot sense the magic threshold of the stage not presume to cross it."*

— Stanislavsky

Throughout this book the focus has been on the theatrical impulse of today's Readers Theatre. The pattern of chapter organization, supplemented with experiments and exercises, has been presented as a kind of working blueprint for imaginative exploration and study. Of course, no simple formula yet exists to translate basic Readers Theatre theories into every classroom performance assignment. It is even more important, therefore, to now invite inventive departures from these basic theories whenever it stimulates the creative talents of all the participants.

The following sample scripts should challenge performers to make those inventive choices that give vivid life and meaning to Readers Theatre in classroom performance. Each sample script is designed to address physical and vocal problem areas and to promote flesh-and-blood character portraits. There are also a number of sample adaptations that should help performers familiarize themselves with basic Readers Theatre elements like blocking, scripting, and staging.

Although there are character interpretation clues indicated in the brief introduction to each sample script, individual performers should already have a clear set of performance objectives in mind from an analysis of the selected literature. Remember, however, that it is still important to read the complete literary text whenever possible; and to approach classroom exercises or performance experiments in a disciplined period of rehearsal that is comfortable, risk-free, and suitable for an individual style of self-expression.

Begin your study of the sample scripts slowly, exploring the first series of abbreviated literature to discover an original characterization or a fresh, imaginative interpretation. Then proceed to the more complex sample scripts that follow. Frequent analysis, rehearsal, and repetition of the exercises included in Chapter Five should help you meet the performance expectations of these sample scripts, and also encourage you to trust your own performance instincts.

Finally, as you become better acquainted with today's Readers Theatre principles, don't forget to include observation in the classroom performance blueprint. Alertness to interesting "here-and-now" role models, awareness of simple, universal truths, and sensitivity to everyday incidents or events may just provide that believable, honest character portrait you've been sketching from an analysis of the literature. The "performance sense" you develop in observation should speed you on your Readers Theatre journey with a truly theatrical impulse. Bon voyage!

# from "An Encounter With an Interviewer" by Mark Twain

American humorist Mark Twain (Samuel L. Clemens) casts a piercing eye on human nature and reveals a penetrating wit that continues to provoke thoughtful humor even today. In the following "Two By Two Twain" sketches, the author's use of tall tales and folklore quickly becomes apparent in character attitude and colloquial language. Performers should integrate these "folksy" elements in both character movement and staging, perhaps using period nineteenth-century set pieces and authentic music to capture the spirit of Twain's historical time. There are also opportunities here to promote active audience interaction or participation with the performers.

## Cast of Characters

### Narrator
*An effective storyteller, man or woman*

### Twain
*An affable man, middle-aged or older*

### Young Man
*Described by Mark Twain as
a "… nervous, dapper, 'peart' young man"*

## Setting
All that is necessary, two chairs placed Down Center, on which, and around which, the two men in the cast may sit and leave as their emotions dictate, in the main to provide some variety in the stage picture. This conversation, as that is what it actually is, may be given as a period piece, approximately in 1873, with Twain

and the interviewer in period costume and makeup (pictures of Twain are readily available for makeup purposes), but this is not necessary. However, if it is done as a period production, the chairs should be roughly of the same age. No special lighting or setting is needed.

NARRATOR: The interview is much in evidence these days, not only on local and national television, but in magazines and newspapers. We see it often on "60 Minutes," on "20/20," on Barbara Walters Specials, on the "Today Show," and in such publications as *Esquire, NewsWeek* and *Playboy.* The interview in its various forms is a staple of journalism today. But it is not new. Samuel L. Clemens, better known as Mark Twain, satirized the interview in his essay, "An Encounter With An Interviewer." He wrote:

TWAIN: *(To the audience)* The nervous, dapper, "peart" young man took the chair I offered him, and said he was connected with the *Daily Thunderstorm,* and added:

YOUNG MAN: *(Hereafter YM; nervously)* Hoping it's no harm, I've come to interview you. *(Taking the seat offered him)*

TWAIN: Come to what?

YM: *Interview* you.

TWAIN: Ah! I see. Yes — yes. Ym! Yes — yes. *(To audience)* I was not feeling bright that morning. Indeed, my powers seemed a bit under a cloud. So I went to the bookcase, and when I had been looking for six or seven minutes, I found I was obliged to refer to the young man. I said: "How do you spell it?"

YM: Spell what?

TWAIN: Interview.

YM: Oh, my goodness! What do you want to spell it for?

TWAIN: I don't want to spell it; I want to see what it means.

YM: Well, this is astonishing, I must say. I can tell you what it means, if you — if you —

TWAIN: Oh, all right! That will answer, and much obliged to you, too.

YM: In, *in*, ter, *ter*, inter —

122

TWAIN: Then you spell it with an "I"?

YM: Why, certainly!

TWAIN: Oh, that is what took me so long.

YM: Why, my *dear* sir, what did you propose to spell it with?

TWAIN: Well, I — I — hardly know. I had the Unabridged, and I was ciphering around in the back end, hoping I might tree her among pictures. But it's a very old edition.

YM: Why, my friend, they wouldn't have a *picture* of it in even the latest e— my dear sir, I beg your pardon, I mean no harm in the world, but you do not look as — as — intelligent as I had expected you would. No harm — I mean no harm at all.

TWAIN: Oh, don't mention it! It has often been said, and by people who would not flatter and who could have no inducement to flatter, that I am quite remarkable in that way. Yes — yes; they always speak of it with rapture.

YM: *(Nonplussed)* I can easily imagine it. But about this interview. You know it is the custom, now, to interview any man who has become notorious.

TWAIN: Indeed? I had not heard of it before. It must be very interesting. What do you do with it?

YM: *(Increasingly upset)* Ah, well — well — well — this is disheartening. It *ought* to be done with a club in some instances; but customarily it consists in. the interviewer asking questions and the interviewed answering them. It is all the rage now. Will you let me ask you certain questions calculated to bring out the salient points of your public and private history?

TWAIN: *(Warmly)* Oh, with pleasure — with pleasure. I have a very bad memory, but I hope you will not mind that. That is to say, it is an irregular memory — singularly irregular. Sometimes it goes in a gallop, and then again it will be as much as a fortnight passing a given point. This is a great grief to me.

YM: Oh, it is no matter, so you will try to do the best you can.

TWAIN: I will. I will put my whole mind to it.

YM: *(A bit relieved)* Thanks. Are you ready to begin? *(Stands.)*

123

TWAIN: *(Sits, pulling himself together, physically.)* Ready.

YM: How old are you?

TWAIN: Nineteen, in June.

YM: *(Astonished)* Indeed. I would have taken you to be thirty-five or six. Where were you born?

TWAIN: In Missouri.

YM: When did you start to write?

TWAIN: In 1836.

YM: Why, how could that be, if you are only nineteen now?

TWAIN: *(Puzzled)* I don't know. It does seem curious, somehow.

YM: It does, indeed. UH — tell me. Whom do you consider the most remarkable man you ever met?

TWAIN: Aaron Burr.

YM: But you never could have met Aaron Burr, if you are only nineteen years —

TWAIN: *(Faking some slight irritation)* Now, if you know more about me that I do, what do you ask me for? *(Stands to cross to YOUNG MAN.)*

YM: *(Perplexed)* Well, it was only a suggestion; nothing more. How did you happen to meet Burr?

TWAIN: Well, I happened to be at his funeral one day, and he asked me to make less noise, and —

YM: But, good heavens! If you were at his funeral, he must have been dead, and if he was dead how could he care whether you made a noise or not?

TWAIN: I don't know. He was always a particular kind of a man that way.

YM: Still, I don't understand it at all. You say he spoke to you, and that he was dead.

TWAIN: I didn't say he was dead.

YM: But wasn't he dead?

TWAIN: Well, some said he was, some said he wasn't.

YM: What did you think?

TWAIN: Oh, it was none of my business! It wasn't any of my funeral.

YM: Did you — *(Giving up)* However, we can never get this matter straight. Let me ask you something else. What was the date of your birth?

TWAIN: Monday, October 31, 1693.

YM: What? 1693? Impossible! That would make you a hundred and eighty years old. It's an awful discrepancy. How do you account for that?

TWAIN: I don't account for it at all.

YM: But you said at first you were only nineteen and now you make yourself out to be one hundred and eighty. It's an awful discrepancy.

TWAIN: *(Moving to the YOUNG MAN)* Why, have you noticed that? *(Shaking hands)* Many a time it has seemed to me like a discrepancy, but somehow I couldn't make up my mind. How quick you notice a thing!

YM: Thank you for the compliment, as far as it goes. Had you, or have you, any brothers or sisters?

TWAIN: Eh! I — I — I — think so — yes — but I don't remember.

YM: Well, that is the most extraordinary statement I ever heard.

TWAIN: Why, what makes you think that?

YM: How could I think otherwise? Why, look here! Who is this a picture of on the wall? *(Focuses on an imaginary picture on the fourth wall, toward the audience.)* Isn't that a brother of yours?

TWAIN: *(Focusing his eyes on the same spot on the fourth wall as the YOUNG MAN)* Oh, yes, yes yes! Now you remind me of it; that was a brother of mine. That's William — Bill we called him. Poor old Bill!

YM: Why? Is he dead, then?

TWAIN: Ah! Well, I suppose so. We never could tell. There was a great mystery about it.

YM: That is sad, very sad. He disappeared, then?

TWAIN: *(Hesitatingly)* Well, yes, in a sort of general way. We buried him.

YM: *(Astonished)* Buried him! Buried him, without knowing whether he was dead or not?

TWAIN: Oh, no! Not that. He was dead enough.

YM:  Well, I confess that I can't understand this. If you buried him, and you knew he was dead —

TWAIN:  No, no! We only *thought* he was.

YM:  Oh, I see! He came to life again?

TWAIN:  I bet he didn't.

YM:  *(Almost hysterical)* Well, I never heard anything like this. *Somebody* was dead. *Somebody* was buried. Now, where was the mystery?

TWAIN:  That's just it! That's it exactly. You see, we were twins — defunct and I — and we got mixed in the bathtub when we were only two weeks old, and one of us was drowned. But we didn't know which. Some think it was Bill. Some think it was me.

YM:  *(Astonished)* Well, that is remarkable. What do you think?

TWAIN:  Goodness knows! I would give whole worlds to know. This solemn, this awful mystery has cast a gloom over my whole life. *(Looks about, assumes a* sotto voce *voice quality.)* But I will tell you a secret now, which I have never revealed to any creature before. One of us had a peculiar mark — a large mole on the back of his left hand; that was *me.* That child was the one that was drowned!

YM:  Very well, then, I don't see that there is any mystery about it, after all.

TWAIN:  You don't? Well, I do. Anyway, I don't see how they could ever have been such a blundering lot as to go and bury the wrong child. But, 'sh! — don't mention it where the family can hear of it. Heaven knows they have heart-breaking troubles enough without adding this.

YM:  *(Decides it is time to beat a retreat.)* Well, I believe I've got material enough for the present, and I am very much obliged to you for the pains you have taken. But I was a good deal interested in that account of Aaron Burr's funeral. Would you mind telling me what particular circumstance it was that made you think Burr was such a remarkable man?

TWAIN:  Oh! It was a mere trifle! Not one man in fifty would have noticed it at all. When the sermon was over, and the

126

procession all ready to start for the cemetery, and the body all arranged nice in the hearse, he said he wanted to take a last look at the scenery, and so he got up and rode with the driver. *(The YOUNG MAN registers astonishment; then, realizing he has been "taken" by the humorist TWAIN, stalks off in anger and frustration. TWAIN turns to the audience, with a twinkle of pleasure in his eye, and says to them:)* Then the young man reverently withdrew. He was very pleasant company, and I was sorry to see him go. *(With a slight audience bow, TWAIN turns and walks off, too.)*

# from "Adam's Diary" and "Eve's Diary" by Mark Twain

The second "Two by Two Twain" sketch features excerpts from the author's separately published diaries of Adam and Eve, juxtaposed here to reveal the characters' conflicting first impression and later intimate desire of each other. Although both characters are writing entries in their respective diaries, staging should not simply limit the performers to lecterns and stools. There are performance opportunities for subtle, choreographed movement and additional vocal sound effects. It is important, however, to clearly indicate an imaginative locale or setting that suggests the Garden of Eden.

EVE: *Saturday.* I am almost a whole day old now. I arrived yesterday. It must be so, for if there was a day-before-yesterday, I was not there when it happened; or I should remember it. It could be, of course, that it did happen and I was not noticing. It will be best to start right now, and not let the record get confused; for some instinct tells me that these details are going to be important to the historian some day.

ADAM: *Monday.* The new creature with the long hair is a good deal in the way. It is always hanging around and following me

127

about. I am not used to company, and wish it would stay with the other animals. Cloudy today; think we shall have rain ... *We?* Where did I get that word? ... I remember now — the new creature uses it.

EVE: *Tuesday.* I followed the other Experiment around, yesterday afternoon, to see what it might be for, if I could. But I was not able to make out. I think it is a man. I had never seen a man, but it looked like one. It has frowsy hair and blue eyes, and looks like a reptile. It has no hips; it tapers like a carrot; when it stands, it spreads itself apart like a derrick; maybe it is architecture. I was afraid of it at first, and started to run every time it turned around. I thought it was going to chase me, but by-and-by I found it was only trying to get away. So after that I was not timid any more, but tracked it along, several hours, about twenty yards behind; which made it nervous and unhappy. At last it was a good deal worried and climbed a tree. I waited a while, then gave it up and went home.

ADAM: *Sunday.* This day is getting to be more and more trying. It was selected and set apart as a day of rest. I already had six of them per week, before. This morning found the new creature trying to clod apples out of that forbidden tree.

EVE: *Tuesday.* It is up in the tree again. Resting, apparently. It looks to me like a creature that is more interested in resting than in anything else. It has low tastes ... and is not kind. It had crept down from the tree and was trying to catch the little speckled fishes that play in the pool. I had to clod it to make it go up the tree again and let them alone. One of the clods took it back of the ear, and it used language. I did not understand the words, but they seemed expressive. When I found I could talk I felt a new interest in it, for I love to talk, all day, and in my sleep, too; and I am very interesting, but if I had another to talk to I could be twice as interesting, and would never stop.

ADAM: *Wednesday.* I wish it would not talk; it is always talking right at my shoulder, right at my ear, and I am used only to sounds that are more or less distant from me. Been examining the great waterfall ... The new creature calls it Niagara Falls — why, I am sure I do not know. Says it looks like Niagara Falls. I get no chance to name anything myself. The new creature names everything that comes along, before I can get in a protest. And always the same pretext is offered — it *looks* like the thing. There is the dodo, for instance. Says the moment one looks at it one sees at a glance that it "looks like a Dodo." It will have to keep that name, no doubt. Dodo! It looks no more like a dodo than I do!

EVE: *Next Week Sunday.* All week I tagged around after him and tried to get acquainted. I had to do the talking, because he was shy, but I didn't mind it. He seemed pleased to have me around, and I used the sociable "we" a good deal because it seemed to flatter him to be included. He does not try to avoid me as much, which is a good sign. During the last day or two I have taken all the work of naming off his hands for he has no gift in that line.

ADAM: *Wednesday.* Built me a shelter against the rain, but could not have it to myself in peace. The new creature intruded. When I tried to put it out, it shed water out of the holes it looks with and wiped it away with the back of its paws; and made a noise such as some of the other animals make when they are in distress. I wish it would not talk; it is always talking. And the new creature eats too much fruit. We are going to run short. "We" again — that is its word; mine, too, now, from hearing it so much.

EVE: *Wednesday.* I tried to get him some of those apples, but I cannot learn to throw straight. I failed, but I think the good intention pleased him. They are forbidden, and he says I will come to harm.

ADAM: *Thursday.* It told me it was made out of a rib taken from my body. This is at least doubtful, if not more than that. I have not missed any rib ...

EVE: *Monday.* This morning I told him my name, hoping it would interest him. But he did not care for it. It is strange. If he should tell me his name, I would care.

ADAM: *Monday.* Its name is Eve. Says this word is to call it by when I want it to come. Says it is not an It; it is a She.

EVE: *Tuesday.* He took no interest in my name. I tried to hide my disappointment, but I suppose I did not succeed. I went away and sat on the mossbank with my feet in the water.

ADAM: *Sunday.* Pulled through.

EVE: *Tuesday.* All morning I was at work improving the estate. I purposely kept away from him in the hope that he would get lonely and come. But he did not. I shall talk with the snake. He is very kindly disposed ...

ADAM: *Friday.* She has taken up with a snake now. The other animals are glad, for she is always experimenting with them and bothering them; and I am glad because the snake talks, and this enables me to get a rest. She is always beseeching me to stop going over the falls. What harm does it do? Says it makes her shudder. I wonder why. I went over the falls in a barrel — not satisfactory to her. Went over in a tub — still not satisfactory. Swam the whirlpool and the rapids in a fig-leaf suit. It got much damaged. I am too much hampered here. What I need is a change of scene.

EVE: *Sunday.* It is pleasant again, now, and I am happy; but those were heavy days. I do not think of them when I can help it.

ADAM: *Wednesday.* I escaped last night and rode a horse all night as fast as he could go; hoping to clear out of the park and hide in some other country before the trouble should begin. But is was not to be. About an hour after sunup, as I was riding through a flowery plain where thousands of animals were grazing, all of a sudden they broke into a tempest of frightful noises; and in one moment the plain was in a frantic commotion, and every beast was destroying its neighbor. I knew what it meant — Eve had eaten that fruit, and death was come into the world. I found this place, outside the park, and was fairly comfortable for a few days ... but she found me out. I was not sorry she came, for there are but meagre pickings here; and she had brought me some of those apples. I was obliged to eat them, I was so hungry. She came curtained in boughs and bunches of leaves; and when I snatched them away and asked her what she meant by such nonsense, she tittered and blushed. She said I myself would soon know why it was thus. This was correct. I laid down the apple, half-eaten — certainly the best one I ever saw, considering the lateness of the season — and arrayed myself in the discarded boughs and branches. I ordered her to go and get some more and not make such a spectacle of herself. Afterward, we crept down to where the wild-beast battle had been, and collected some skins. I made her patch together a couple of suits proper for public presentation. They are uncomfortable, it is true, but stylish; and that is the main point about clothes. I find she is a good deal of a companion. I see I should be lonesome and depressed without her. Another thing, she says it is ordered that we work for our living hereafter. She will be useful. I will superintend!

EVE: *Friday.* I tried once more to persuade him to stop going over the falls. That was because the fire which I had discovered had revealed to me a new passion — quite new, and distinctly different from love, grief, and those others which I had already discovered — fear.

ADAM: *Friday.* Perhaps I ought to remember that she is a very young girl and make allowances. She is all interest, eagerness, vivacity; and the world is to her a charm, a wonder, a mystery, a joy. And she is color-mad: brown rocks, yellow sand, gray moss, green foliage, blue sky, the pearl of the dawn — none of them is of any practical value, so far as I can see; but because they have color and majesty that is enough for her, and she loses her mind over them. If she could but quiet down and keep still a couple minutes at a time, I think I could enjoy looking at her. Indeed, I am sure I could. Once, when she was standing marble-white and sun-drenched on a boulder, with her head

131

tilted back and her hand shading her eyes, I recognized that she was beautiful.

EVE: *Friday, Six Months Later.* Tuesday — Wednesday — Thursday — and today; all without seeing him. It is a long time to be alone. But he will come back soon.

ADAM: *Next Year. Monday.* We have named it Cain. She caught it while I was away trapping on the North Shore of the Erie. It resembles us in some ways, and may be a close relation. That is what she thinks, but this is an error, in my judgment. The difference in size warrants that it is a different and new kind of animal — a fish, perhaps; though when I put it in the water to see, it sank; and she plunged in and snatched it out before there was an opportunity to determine the matter. *Wednesday.* It isn't a fish. It makes curious noises when not satisfied, and says "goo goo" when it is. It is not one of us, for it doesn't walk. *Three Months Later.* I sleep but little. It has ceased lying around, and goes about on its four legs now. Yet it differs from the other four-legged animals in that its front legs are unusually short; consequently causing the main part of the person to stick up uncomfortably high in the air, and this is not attractive. *Three Months Later.* The Kangaroo still continues to grow. It has fur on his head now; except that it is much finer and softer, and instead of being black it's red. *Five Months Later.* The Bear has learned to paddle around all by itself on its hind legs; and says "poppa" and "momma!" It is certainly a new species. I will go off on a far expedition among the forests of the north and make an exhaustive search. There must certainly be another one somewhere, and this one will be less dangerous when it has company of its own species. In my judgment, it is either an enigma or some kind of bug. *Three Months Later.* It has been a weary hunt, and I have had no success. In the meantime, without stirring from the home estate she has caught another one! I never saw such luck. This new one is as ugly now as the old one was at first; has the same sulphur and raw meat complexion and

132

the same singular head without any fur on it ... She calls it Able. *Ten Years Later.* They are *boys*! We found it out long ago. It was their coming in that small shape that puzzled us. There are some girls now. Abel is a good boy, but if Cain had stayed a bear it would have improved him.

EVE: *Five Years Later. After the Fall.* When I look back, the Garden is a dream. It was beautiful, enchantingly beautiful; and now it is lost, and I shall not see it any more. The garden is lost, but I have *him.* He loves me as well as he can. I love him with all the strength of my passionate nature. If I ask myself why I love him, I find I do not know. I love certain birds because of their song; but I do not love Adam on account of his singing — no, it is not that. The more he sings, the more I do not get reconciled to it! It is not on account of his gracious and considerate ways and his delicacy that I love him. No, he has lacks in these regards; but he is well enough, and is improving. It is not on account of his chivalry that I love him — no, it is not that. He told on me, but I do not blame him. It is a peculiarity of his sex, I think, and he did not make his sex. Of course, I would not have told on him. I would have perished first; but that is a peculiarity of my sex, and I do not take credit for it, for I did not make my sex. Then why is it that I love him? He is strong and handsome, but I could love him without those qualities. If he were plain, I should love him; and I would work for him, slave over him, pray for him, and watch by his bedside until I died. I think I love him merely because he is *mine.* There is no other reason, I suppose. It just *comes* — and cannot explain itself. And it doesn't need to.

ADAM: *Ten Years Later.* After all these years, I see that I was mistaken about Eve in the beginning. It is better to live outside the Garden with her than inside it without her. At first, I thought she talked too much; but now I should be sorry to have that voice fall silent and pass out of my life. Blessed be the one that brought us together and taught me to know the goodness of her heart and the sweetness of her spirit.

133

EVE: *Forty Years Later.* It is my longing, it is my prayer, that we may pass from this life together — a longing which shall never perish from the earth, but shall have a place in the heart of every wife that loves, until the end of time; and it shall be called by my name. But if one of us must go first, it is my prayer that it shall be I; for life without him would not be life. How could I endure it? This prayer is also immortal, and will not cease from being offered up while my race continues. I am the first wife, and in the last wife I shall be repeated.

ADAM: *At Eve's Grave.* Wheresoever she was, *there* was Eden.

# from "Wandering" by Lanford Wilson

Lanford Wilson's almost cartoon-like description of a young man's life as he moves from adolescence to maturity provides ample classroom staging approaches for three performers. As the title of the text suggests, the young man is aimless as he wanders from one event to another; and the performers are encouraged to rotate a single bench, box, or chair to localize the rapid change of scene indicated in the script. The performers should retire to the "Attention" position when not speaking and face the audience in a presentational style of delivery as appropriate.

## Characters

He

She

Him

---

He, She, and Him are all about twenty-five. The stage, which can be very small, should have a bench to be used as chair, bed, couch, bench, whatever. He and She are standing at attention, side by side. Him enters and sits. Actions and props should be pantomimed and the play should be done very rapidly, without pause except toward the end as indicated. The play runs through Him's life, recapping several times at the end. Actions and characterizations should be very simple.

SHE: Where have you been?

HIM: Wandering around.

SHE: Wandering around. I don't know why you can't be a man; you just wait till the Army gets ahold of you, young man.

HE: They'll make a man of you —

SHE: Straighten you out.

HE: A little regimentation.

SHE: Regulation.

HE: Specification.

SHE: Indoctrination.

HE: Boredom.

SHE: You'll get up and go to bed.

HE: Drill; march.

SHE: Take orders.

HE: Fight.

SHE: Do what they tell you.

HE: Keep in step.

SHE: Do your part.

HE: Kill a man.

SHE: You'll be a better person to live with, believe me. As a matter of fact, your father and I are getting damned tired of having you around.

HE: Looking after you.

SHE: Making your bed.

HE: Keeping you out of trouble.

SHE: How old are you, anyway?

HIM: Sixteen.

HE:  Sixteen — well, my God.

SHE:  Shouldn't you be drafted before long?

HIM:  Two years.

SHE:  You just better toe the mark.

HE:  How long at your present address?

HIM:  Six months.

HE:  Any previous experience as an apprentice?

HIM:  No, sir.

HE:  Where did you live before that?

HIM:  I was just wandering around.

HE:  Not good. Draft status?

HIM:  Well, I haven't been called, but—

HE:  We like fighters on our team, fellow.

HIM:  Well, actually, I'm a conscientious—

SHE:  Sit down. Roll up your sleeve. Take off your shirt. Stick out your tongue. Bend over, open your mouth, make a fist, read the top line. Cough. *(HIM coughs.)* Very good.

HIM:  Thank you.

SHE:  Perfect specimen.

HIM:  I do a considerable amount of walking.

HE:  I don't follow you.

HIM:  I don't believe in war.

HE:  There's no danger of war. Our country is never an aggressor.

HIM:  But armies, see—I don't believe in it.

HE:  Do you love your country?

HIM:  No more than any other, the ones I've seen.

HE:  That's treason.

HIM:  I'm sorry.

HE:  Quite all right, we'll take you.

HIM:  I won't go.

HE:  Service is compulsory.

HIM:  It's my right.

HE:  You'll learn.

HIM:  I don't believe in killing people.

HE:  For freedom?

HIM:  No.

HE: For love?

HIM: No.

HE: For money?

HIM: No.

HE: We'll teach you.

HIM: I know, but I won't.

HE: You'll learn.

HIM: I can't.

HE: You're going.

HIM: I'm not.

HE: You'll see.

HIM: I'm sure.

HE: You'll see.

HIM: I'm flat-footed.

HE: You'll do.

HIM: I'm queer.

HE: Get lost.

SHE: I'm lost.

HIM: I'm sorry.

SHE: Aren't you lost?

HIM: I wasn't going anyplace in particular.

SHE: That's unnatural.

HIM: I was just wandering.

SHE: What will become of you?

HIM: I hadn't thought of it.

SHE: You don't believe in anything.

HIM: But you see, I do.

HE: I see.

HIM: It's just that no one else seems to believe—not really.

HE: I see.

HIM: Like this pride in country.

HE: I see.

HIM: And this pride in blood.

HE: I see.

HIM: It just seems that pride is such a pointless thing. I can't believe in killing someone for it.

137

SHE: Oh, my God, honey, it isn't killing. It's merely nudging out of the way.

HIM: But we don't need it.

SHE: Think of our position, think of me, think of the children.

HIM: I am.

SHE: You're shiftless is what it is.

HIM: I'm really quite happy. I don't know why.

SHE: Well, how do you think I feel?

HIM: Not too well, really.

SHE: Where does it hurt?

HE: Nothing to worry about.

SHE: Yes, sir.

HIM: Thank you.

SHE: And that's all for the morning. Mr. Trader is on line six. Thank you. Send Wheeler in.

HE: How are you, old boy?

HIM: Not well, I'm afraid.

SHE: Don't be. It isn't serious.

HE: Just been working too hard.

SHE: Why don't you lie down?

HE: Best thing for you.

SHE: I know, but he was quite handsome—a gentle man.

HE: Bit of a radical though—not good for the family.

SHE: I know.

HE: You're better off.

SHE: I have a life of my own.

HE: You have a life of your own.

SHE: He was such a lost lamb.

HE: Never agreed with anyone.

SHE: Arguments everywhere we went.

HE: What kind of disposition is that?

SHE: I don't know what I ever saw in him.

HE: You need someone who knows his way around.

SHE: I do.

HE: I do.

*Pause*

SHE:  I don't know why you can't be a man.
HE:  Keep in step.
SHE:  Toe the mark.
HE:  Draft status?
SHE:  Stick out your tongue.
HE:  You'll learn.
SHE:  What'll become of you?
HE:  I see.
SHE:  Think of the children.
HE:  Best thing for you.
SHE:  I do.

*Pause*

HE:  I see.
HIM:  I mean that can't be the way people want to spend their lives.
SHE:  Trader on line six.
HIM:  Thank you.
HE:  Just been working too hard.
SHE:  I do.

*Pause*

SHE:  Where?
HIM:  Wandering.
HE:  I see.
HIM:  They'll believe anything anyone tells them.
HE:  I see.
HIM:  I mean that can't be the way people want to spend their lives.
SHE:  That's all for the morning.
HIM:  Quite happy.
HE:  Best thing for you.
SHE:  I do.
HE:  I do.

*Pause*

SHE:  Where have you been?

*Pause*

HIM:  Can it?

# from "Please Hear What I'm Not Saying"
# —Author Unknown

Here is a sample of non-dramatic literature to plant the initial seeds of adapting or compiling a script for classroom performance. The anonymous literary text needs an introduction and appropriate transitions, but is suitable for an ensemble of six or eight performers if additional excerpts from short poems, essays, letters, or song lyrics are integrated to feature a specific program theme. Performers are encouraged to explore numerous staging techniques that identify a specific setting or for each character's intention or motivation.

Don't be fooled by me.
Don't be fooled by the face I wear.
For I wear a mask; I wear a thousand masks,
    masks that I'm afraid to take off,
    and none of them are me.
Pretending is an art that's second nature with me,
    but don't be fooled; for God's sake don't be fooled.
I give the impression that I'm secure,
    that all is sunny and unruffled with me,
    within as well as without;
    that confidence is my name and coolness is my game;
    that the water's calm and I'm in command,
    and that I need no one.

But don't believe me.
Please.
My surface may seem smooth, but my surface is my mask,
    my ever-varying and ever-concealing mask.
Beneath lies no smugness, no complacence.
Beneath dwells the real me in confusion, in loneliness.
But I hide this.
I don't want anybody to know it.

I panic at the thought of my weakness, and fear being
    exposed.
That's why I frantically create a mask to hide behind,
    a nonchalant, sophisticated facade to help me pretend;
    to shield me from the glance that knows.

But such a glance is precisely my salvation.
My only true salvation,
    and I know it.
That is if it's followed by acceptance;
    if it's followed by love.
It's the only thing that can liberate me from myself,
    from the barriers that I so painstakingly erect.
It's the only thing that will assure me of what I can't assure myself;
    that I'm really worth something.
But I don't tell you this.
I don't dare.
I'm afraid to.
I'm afraid your glance will not be followed by acceptance and love.
I'm afraid you'll think less of me, that you'll laugh;
    and your laugh would kill me.

I'm afraid that deep-down I'm nothing, that I'm just no good;
    and that you will see this and reject me.
So I play my game, my desperate pretending game;
    with a façade of assurance without, and a trembling child within.
And so begins the parade of masks,
    the glittering but empty parade of masks.
And my life becomes a front.
I idly chatter to you in the suave tones of surface talk.
I tell you everything that's really nothing,
    and nothing of what's everything;
    of what's crying within me.
So when I'm going through my routine do not be fooled
    by what I'm saying.

Please listen carefully and try to hear what I'm not saying;
    what I'd like to say, what for survival I need to say,
    but what I can't say.
I dislike hiding, honestly.
I dislike the superficial game I'm playing;
    the superficial, phony game.
I'd like to be genuine and spontaneous, and me;
    but you've got to help me.
You've got to hold out your hand,
    even when that's the last thing I seem to want or need.
Only you can wipe away from my eyes the blank stare
    of the breathing dead.
Only you can call me into aliveness.
Each time you're kind and gentle and encouraging,
    each time you try to understand because you really care,
    my heart begins to grow wings; very small wings,
    very feeble wings, but wings.

With your sensitivity and sympathy, your power of understanding,
    you can breathe life into me.
I want you to know that.
I want you to know how important you are to me,
    how you can be a creator of the person that is me;
    if you choose to.
Please choose to.
You alone can break down the wall behind which I tremble.
You alone can remove my mask.
You alone can release me from my shadow-world of panic;
    my lonely prison.
So do not pass me by.
Please do not pass me by.
It will not be easy for you.
A long conviction of worthlessness builds strong walls.
The nearer you approach me, I blinder I may strike back.
It's irrational, but despite what the books say about man,
    I am irrational.

I fight against the very thing that I cry out for;
    but I am told that love is stronger than strong walls.
And in this lies my hope—my only hope.
Please try to beat down those walls with firm hands,
    but with gentle hands—
    for a child is very sensitive.

Who am I, you may wonder?
I am someone you know very well.
For I am every man you meet, and I am every woman you meet.

# from "Frankie and Johnny"

A familiar folk ballad like "Frankie and Johnny" easily lends itself to adaptation and classroom performance. The characteristic ingredients of direct dialog, narration, simple story line, and immediate build to a climax all contribute to the folk ballad's popularity in Readers Theatre scripting. Here, for example, are opportunities for six performers to explore a complex, emotional character relationship simply and vividly. This sample script also features an individual narrator for each of the title characters, and the staging is suitable for either On-stage or Off-stage focus.

MALE NARRATOR: Frankie and Johnny were lovers.

FEMALE NARRATOR: O, how that couple could love.

MALE NARRATOR: Swore to be true to each other.

FEMALE NARRATOR: True as the stars above.

MALE NARRATOR: He was her man.

FEMALE NARRATOR: But he done her wrong.

MALE NARRATOR: Frankie she was his woman, everybody knows. She spent one hundred dollars for a suit of Johnny's clothes. He was her man.

FEMALE NARRATOR: But he done her wrong.

MALE NARRATOR: Frankie went down to Memphis.

FEMALE NARRATOR: She went on the evening train.

MALE NARRATOR: She paid one hundred dollars for Johnny a watch and chain. He was her man.

FEMALE NARRATOR: But he done her wrong.

MALE NARRATOR: Frankie went down to the corner to buy her a bucket of beer. She says to the fat bartender—

FRANKIE: Has my lovingest man been here? He is my man, but he's doing me wrong.

BARTENDER: Ain't going to tell you no story. Ain't going to tell you no lie. I seen your man 'bout an hour ago with a girl named Alice Fry. If he's your man, he's doing you wrong.

FEMALE NARRATOR: Frankie went back to the hotel.

MALE NARRATOR: She didn't go there for fun.

144

FEMALE NARRATOR: Under her long red kimono she toted a forty-four gun. He was her man.

MALE NARRATOR: But he done her wrong.

FEMALE NARRATOR: Frankie went down to the hotel, looked in the window so high.

MALE NARRATOR: There she saw her loving Johnny a-loving up Alice Fry

FEMALE NARRATOR: He was her man.

MALE NARRATOR: But he done her wrong.

FEMALE NARRATOR: Frankie threw back her kimono. She took out her old forty-four.

MALE NARRATOR: Root-a-toot-toot!

FEMALE NARRATOR: Three times she shot right through that hotel door.

MALE NARRATOR: She shot her man, 'cause he done her wrong.

FEMALE NARRATOR: Johnny grabbed off his Stetson.

JOHNNY: O good Lord, Frankie, don't shoot!

MALE NARRATOR: But Frankie put her finger on the trigger, and the gun went—

FEMALE NARRATOR: Toot-a-toot-toot!

MALE NARRATOR: He was her man.

FEMALE NARRATOR: But she shot him down.

JOHNNY: Roll me over easy, roll me over slow. Roll me over easy, boys, 'cause my wounds are hurting me so. I was her man, but I done her wrong.

MALE NARRATOR: First time she shot him he staggered.

FEMALE NARRATOR: Second time she shot him he fell.

MALE NARRATOR: Third time she shot him—

JOHNNY: O Lordy!

FEMALE NARRATOR: There was a new man's face in hell.

MALE NARRATOR: He was her man.

FEMALE NARRATOR: But he done her wrong.

FRANKIE: Oh, bring on your rubber-tired hearses, bring on your rubber-tired hacks. They're taking my Johnny to the burying ground, but they'll never bring him back. He was my man, but he done me wrong.

MALE NARRATOR: The judge said to the jury—

JUDGE: It's plain as plain can be. This woman shot her man; it's murder in the second degree. He was her man, but he done her wrong.

FEMALE NARRATOR: Now, it was not murder in the second degree.

MALE NARRATOR: It was not murder in the third.

FEMALE NARRATOR: The woman simply dropped her man.

MALE NARRATOR: Like a hunter drops a bird.

FEMALE NARRATOR: He was her man.

MALE NARRATOR: And he done her wrong.

FRANKIE: Oh, put me in that dungeon. Oh, put me in that cell. Put me where the northeast wind blows from the northeast corner of hell. I shot my man 'cause he done me wrong.

FEMALE NARRATOR: Frankie walked up to the scaffold, as calm as a girl could be.

MALE NARRATOR: And turning her eyes to heaven she said—

FRANKIE: Good Lord, I'm coming to Thee. He was my man, and I done him wrong.

# from "Marriage: The Moon and Sixpence"

Here is a brief sample of an "in-progress," compiled workshop script that focuses attention on the theme of marriage. It may serve as a working model for later classroom performance assignments that celebrate occasions like Valentine's Day or commemorate special events like Earth Day. The sample script currently provides roles for a narrator figure and two performers, but is easily adapted to feature additional transitions, music, and excerpts of literature that explore the stated theme.

### "On Taking a Wife" (Thomas Moore)

PERFORMER 1:   Come, come. At your time of life, there's no longer excuses for thus playing the rake. It's time you should think, boy, of taking a wife. Why, so it is, father. Whose wife shall I take?

### "A Prayer to Saint Catherine" (Anonymous)

PERFORMER 2:  Saint Catherine, Saint Catherine—
Lend me thine aid, and grant that
I may never die an old maid.
A husband, Saint Catherine,
A *good* one, Saint Catherine.
Sweet Saint Catherine,
A husband, Saint Catherine.
Handsome, Saint Catherine,
Rich, Saint Catherine,
*Soon,* Saint Catherine!

### "A Bachelor's Complaint" (Charles Lamb)

NARRATOR:  As a single man, I have spent a good deal of my time in noting down the infirmities of married people, and to console myself for those superior pleasures which they tell me I have lost by remaining as I am. I cannot say that the quarrels of men and their wives ever made any great impression upon me. What oftenest offends me is an error of quite a different description: it is that they are too loving.

### "Sonnet XVIII" (William Shakespeare)

PERFORMER 1:  Shall I compare thee to a summer's day?
Thou art more lovely and more temperate:
Rough winds do shake the darling buds of May,
And summer's lease hath all too short a date:
Sometime too hot the eye of heaven shines,
And often is his gold complexion dimm'd;
And every fair from fair sometime declines,

147

By chance, or nature's changing course untrimm'd;
But thy eternal summer shall not fade,
Nor lose possession of that fair thou ow'st,
Nor shall death brag thou wander'st in his shade,
When in eternal lines to time thou grow'st;
>So long as man can breathe, or eyes can see,
>So long lives this, and this gives life to thee.

### "A Bachelor's Complaint" (Charles Lamb)

NARRATOR:  They carry their preference so undisguisedly, they perk it up in the faces of us single people so shamelessly; you cannot be in their company a moment without being made to feel that you are not the object of this preference. It is enough that I know I am not: I do not want this perpetual reminding.

### "Sonnet XLIII" (Elizabeth Barrett Browning)

PERFORMER 2:  How do I love thee? Let me count the ways.
I love thee to the depth and breadth and height
My soul can reach, when feeling out of sight
For the ends of Being and ideal Grace;
I love thee to the level of every day's
Most quiet need, by sun and candlelight.
I love thee freely, as men strive for Right;
I love thee purely, as they turn from Praise.
I love thee with the passion put to use
In my old griefs, and with my childhood's faith.
I love thee with a love I seemed to lose
With my lost saints—I love thee with the breath,
Smiles, tears, of all my life! And if God choose,
I shall but love thee better after death.

### "A Bachelor's Complaint" (Charles Lamb)

NARRATOR:  Nothing is to me more distasteful than that entire complacency and satisfaction which beams in the countenance of a new-married couple—in that of the lady particularly. It tells you that her lot is disposed of in this world; that you can have no hopes of her. It is true, I have none; nor wishes either, perhaps. But this is one of those truths which ought to be taken for granted, not expressed.

*The School for Scandal* (**Richard Brinsley Sheridan**)

PERFORMER 1: Lady Teazle, I'll not bear it!

PERFORMER 2: Sir Peter, you may bear it or not, as you please; but I ought to have my own way in everything, and what's more, I will, too.

PERFORMER 1: Very well, very well. So a husband is to have no influence, no authority.

PERFORMER 2: Authority! No, to be sure! If you wanted authority over me, you should have adopted me, and not married me! I am sure you were old enough.

PERFORMER 1: Old enough! Ay, there it is. Well, Lady Teazle, though my life may be made unhappy by your temper, I'll not be ruined by your extravagance. You shall throw away no more sums on such unmeaning luxury. 'Slife! To spend as much to furnish your dressing-room with flowers in winter as would suffice to turn the Pantheon into a greenhouse!

PERFORMER 2: Am I to blame because flowers are dear in cold weather? You should find fault with the climate, and not with me. For my part, I'm sure, I wish it was spring all the year round, and that roses grew under our feet!

PERFORMER 1: If you had been born to this, I shouldn't wonder at your talking thus; but you forget what your situation was when I married you.

PERFORMER 2: No, no, I don't. 'Twas a very disagreeable one, or I should never have married you!

PERFORMER 1: I am glad you have so good a memory. That, madam, was your situation; and what have I done for you? I have made you a woman of fashion, of fortune, of rank. In short, madam, I have made you my wife.

PERFORMER 2: Well, then. There is but one thing more you can make me add to the obligation, and that is—

PERFORMER 1: My widow, I suppose?

PERFORMER 2: For my part, Sir Peter, I should think you would like to have your wife thought a woman of taste.

PERFORMER 1: 'Zounds, Madam! You had no taste when you married me!

PERFORMER 2: That's very true, indeed; and after having married you, I should never pretend to taste again, I allow. But now, Sir Peter, since we have finished our daily jangle I presume I may go to my engagement at Lady Sneerwell's? Good-bye to you.

PERFORMER 1: So—I have gained much by my intended expostulation Yet, with what a charming air she contradicts everything I say; and how pleasingly she shows her contempt for my authority. Well, though I can't make her love me, there is great satisfaction in quarreling with her. And I think she never appears to such advantage, as when she is doing everything in her power to plague me!

### "A Bachelor's Complaint" (Charles Lamb)

NARRATOR: And this is not the worst: if the husband be a man with whom you have lived on a friendly footing before his marriage—look about you—your tenure is precarious. Innumerable are the ways which wives take to insult and worm you out of their husband's confidence. Laughing at all you say with a kind of wonder, as if you were a strange kind of fellow that said some good things, but an oddity.

### "To Women" (D. H. Lawrence)

PERFORMER 2: The feelings I don't have I don't have.

The feelings I don't have, I won't say I have.

The feelings you say you have, you don't have.

The feelings you would like us both to have, we neither of us have.

So if you want either of us to feel anything at all,

You'd better abandon all idea of feelings altogether.

### "The Time I've Lost in Wooing" (Thomas Moore)

PERFORMER 1:  The time I've lost in wooing,
In watching and pursuing
The light that lies
In woman's eyes,
Has been my heart's undoing.
Tho' wisdom oft has sought me,
I scorn'd the lore she brought me,
My only books
Were woman's looks,
And folly's all they taught me.

### "I Am As I Am" (Jacques Prevert)

PERFORMER 2:  I am as I am.
I'm made that way.
PERFORMER 1:  I am as I am.
I'm made that way.
PERFORMER 2:  I am as I am.
PERFORMER 1:  I'm made that way.
PERFORMER 1:  What do you expect of me?
PERFORMER 2:  What do you expect of me?

### "A Description of Love" (Sir Walter Raleigh)

NARRATOR:  Now what is Love, I pray thee, tell?
PERFORMER 1:  It is that fountain
PERFORMER 2:  And that well
PERFORMER 1:  Where pleasure
PERFORMER 2:  And repentance dwell.
NARRATOR:  It is perhaps the sauncing bell
PERFORMER 1:  That tolls all into heaven
PERFORMER 2:  Or hell:
NARRATOR:  And this is love, as I hear tell.
Yet what is love, I pray thee say?
PERFORMER 1:  It is a work on holy day.
PERFORMER 2:  It is December matched with May.
PERFORMER 1:  It is a tooth-ache, or like pain;

PERFORMER 2:  It is sunshine mixed with rain.

NARRATOR:  It is a game where none doth gain.

PERFORMER 1:  Then take the vantage, while you may:

PERFORMER 2:  It is a thing will soon away.

### "A Bachelor's Complaint" (Charles Lamb)

NARRATOR:  But what I have spoken of hitherto is nothing to the airs which these creatures give themselves when they come, as they generally do, to have children. When I consider how little of a rarity children are, I cannot for my life tell what cause for pride there can possibly be in having them.

---

This sample "in-progress" workshop script may now be easily extended to include additional literature that features the Narrator suggestion "how little of a rarity children are." Performers may, for example, begin to explore the stated theme with a classroom performance assignment that includes a review of children's literature, song lyrics, short stories, essays and letters appropriate to further development of the theme; or performers may review additional literature written by the authors already included in the sample script to discover complementary excerpts that also explore the stated theme.

Some interesting selections to review might include Anne Sexton's "Transformations," A.A. Milne's "The King's Breakfast," Joel Chandler Harris's "Uncle Remus Songs and Sayings," Carl Sandburg's "Child of the Romans," and Muriel Rukeyser's "M-Day's Child is Fair of Face." There are also a number of children's short stories or novels that lend themselves to classroom adaptation, like Rudyard Kipling's "Just So Stories," Dr. Seuss's "Yertle the Turtle and Other Stories," Judy Blume's *Tales of a Fourth Grade Nothing,* and Thomas Rockwell's *How to Eat Fried Worms.*

# from "The Wishing Stone" —Folk Tale

This delightful adaptation of a Chinese folk tale is suitable for children, young adults, or puppets! There are a number of fanciful intrigues and fantastical role-playing opportunities that should offer rich, imaginative performance blueprints for young participants. Classroom props, staging, and scenery are suggestive, and each production may create its own songs to complement the action or dialog. Performers are encouraged to explore personal traits like comic flair, mannerisms, and vocal quality to give uniqueness to each character portrait.

## Cast of Characters

Narrator/Dragon Prince

Papa

Mama

Birch

Oak

Rose

Willow

Tilt

Dragon King

Head Carpenter/Dragon Fairy

Second Carpenter/Dragon Fairy

---

*The Wishing Stone.* Based on a Chinese fairy tale told by Wolfram Eberhard. Adapted by Alex Barret and Julie Rae Patterson-Pratt. Reprinted by permission of Rainer Eberhard. Adaptation copyright © 1999 by Julie Rae Patterson-Pratt. All reproduction and performance privileges are prohibited without prior permission. For more information please contact Julie Rae Patterson-Pratt, Box 122, Hancock, MN 56244.

## Production Note

The script may be performed with all live actors, live actors with puppets playing the fantastical roles, or with all puppets. Scenery should suggest a rural locale. Levels would add variety of movement. The songs do not have copyright music and each production may create its own tunes. While exits are indicated, they are not necessary. All actors can stay On-stage. Actions are pantomimed as described in narration. An * indicates when named character(s) enters.

## Casting Note

Casting for this adaptation is very flexible and may include minor changes in dialog to feature girls in the roles of Birch or Oak. There are additional opportunities to enlarge the size of the ensemble to include individual performers in the speaking roles of the Narrator and Dragon Prince, the Head Carpenter and Dragon Fairy, or the Second Carpenter and Dragon Fairy. The Fairies of the Dragon King may include any number of performers who also serve to change the scene or provide appropriate vocal sound effects to enrich the action of the primary characters.

NARRATOR: *(Enters.)* There once was an old couple* with three children*, but the children had never learned anything and sat around all day doing nothing.

MAMA: *(To PAPA)* Shall we introduce them? We should.

PAPA: No, we should not. We cannot let ourselves trip over our own toes by getting ahead of ourselves now. First we need to set up the story, establish a mood and setting, then we —

MAMA: *(To audience)* This is our son, Birch. *(Aside)* The name was *his* idea.

PAPA: My father's name was Birch. It's a very dignified name.

MAMA: Your father cleaned up horse manure in the neighborhood stable, didn't he?

154

PAPA:  Yes, he was a stable-keeper—an *honorable* profession.

MAMA:  He is our oldest child ...

PAPA:  And our laziest. It's important to tell the story correctly. *(To audience)* Birch wants to be a politician when he grows up so that he can get *paid* for doing nothing.

MAMA:  This is Oak, our middle child. Oak is ... spunky.

PAPA:  He's a pit bull, dear.

MAMA:  Papa!

PAPA:  Oak could make the most vicious warrior cry like a baby.

MAMA:  Well, perhaps on a bad day ...

PAPA:  Finally, this is Rose, our youngest.

MAMA:  *(To audience)* The name was my idea.

PAPA:  Rose likes to dream. In fact, she never stops. The last I remember, she wanted to *be* a flute. *(Aside)* I do think she has a few too many holes in her head.

NARRATOR:  One day, Mama and Papa gathered their children for a serious discussion. *(The children gather around.)*

PAPA:  *(To children)* Year by year, I —

MAMA:  We.

PAPA:  *We* grow older. You are all more than twelve years old, but you never went to school or learned a trade. How will you support me —

MAMA:  Us.

PAPA:  *Us* in our old age? So *we've* decided —

MAMA:  You've decided.

PAPA:  ... to send you out into the world to learn about life, get a job, and develop a trade.

BIRCH:  But Papa!

OAK:  Papa, that's a stupid idea.

PAPA:  Whether it's an intelligent decision doesn't matter anymore.

BIRCH:  You're *making* us leave?

PAPA:  You three will go out, find jobs, and earn money. In three years' time, you shall return with what you've earned in a sack. Your mother and I have decided to divide our land and give each of you a third. The one with the biggest sack of money will get first choice.

155

OAK: The first pick is mine. You might as well give it to me now. Birch is too dumb and too lazy. Rose doesn't even know what day it is.

ROSE: Yes I do. It's today.

OAK: You're so clever.

BIRCH: I am not lazy. When I get first pick, I'm taking the land down by the creek.

OAK: No, that's where *I'm* going to live.

BIRCH: No, you're not!

MAMA: Stop this fighting.

PAPA: We'll give you three years and then we'll decide. You can all leave tomorrow morning. Agreed? Good. What's for dinner?

NARRATOR: So their mama cooked a great bowl of rice, which they all ate together. They said their good-byes and went to sleep. At midnight, Oak got up, rubbed his eyes, went to the bowl, ate some mouthfuls of rice, and set off along the broad highway. When Birch woke up and saw that his brother had already left, he quickly jumped up, ran to the fire, gobbled the rest of the rice, and followed Oak along the road.

BIRCH: Can I come with you?

OAK: No, you can't.

BIRCH: Good. *(He continues to follow OAK.)*

NARRATOR: The sun was already shining through the roof when Rose woke up.

ROSE: The others have gone. I better be off.

NARRATOR: She hurried to get some food. Not fancying the rice water left in the pot, she did not eat. Instead, she ran out of the back door and went along the byway.

PAPA: *(To MAMA)* I feared she would be a failure.

MAMA: Shush yourself.

PAPA: *What!*

MAMA: I guess I should apologize to you.

PAPA: Yes, you should.

MAMA: Yes, I suppose I should. *(Stares at PAPA coldly.)*

NARRATOR: After three days of walking, Oak and Birch happened upon a house still under construction. The head carpenter* sat perched atop the house, throwing long pieces of wood to another worker* on the ground.

HEAD CARPENTER:  Here's another.

SECOND CARPENTER:  Got it.

HEAD CARPENTER:  Another.

SECOND CARPENTER:  Ready.

OAK:  Look at that!

HEAD CARPENTER:  And another.

SECOND CARPENTER:  *(Looks at OAK and misses the wood, which hits him on the head. He falls down.)* Oof.

HEAD CARPENTER:  Oh, no!

BIRCH:  Oh, my.

OAK:  *(To BIRCH)* Look what you've done. Do something.

BIRCH:  What?

HEAD CARPENTER:  Perhaps getting some *help* might help.

BIRCH:  *(Aside to OAK)* I don't know. The next town is a long way from here.

OAK:  What if *we* do something? We can wrap his head in a white cloth.

BIRCH:  What will that do?

OAK:  Nothing. That is what they do in hospitals. Maybe he'll think we're doctors.

BIRCH:  Maybe.

OAK:  Here, this will help. *(Wraps cloth around SECOND CARPENTER's head.)*

NARRATOR:  Now Oak's bandage did not help the injured worker at all. But it did look good. He looked like a patient under a doctor's care and that pleased the carpenter. He hired them both as assistant wood catchers. A less than honorable job, but a good start.

MAMA:  *(To PAPA)* That was lucky for them, having that worker get hit on the head.

PAPA:  Yes, dear, it was.

NARRATOR:  Meanwhile, Rose searched for adventure. She couldn't find it, at least not right away. On the third day, she awoke to the sound of bickering.

PAPA: *(To MAMA)* Just like home. *(MAMA swipes at PAPA and connects.)*

NARRATOR: Rose went to investigate the voices she heard. Soon she found two odd characters* yelling loudly at each other.

WILLOW: You *must* have done something with my glasses.

TILT: No, I swear on the grave of my parakeet.

WILLOW: Things don't just disappear—and you hated that bird!

TILT: I swear I don't know where they are.

WILLOW: Liar! Your teeth grow yellow from your lies.

TILT: No, they don't. *(Tries to check anyway. ROSE joins them.)*

WILLOW: Hello! *(To TILT)* A customer.

ROSE: Excuse me, can I help you?

MAMA: *(To audience)* Isn't our Rose sweet?

WILLOW: The show must go on—glasses or no.

ROSE: My name is Rose.

WILLOW: Well, Rose, you're in for a show. Willow Tit-Willow here. Actor, shadow puppeteer, and owner of Willow and Tilt Productions. This is Tilt Wit-Tillow, my partner. Rose, you are in for the performance of a lifetime. *(They begin to set up a screen, lay out puppets, etc.)*

ROSE: I don't have any money to pay for ...

WILLOW: Nonsense. People always have something valuable. Especially when it comes to entertainment. *(They retreat behind the puppet screen. WILLOW's head pops out. He clears his throat.)* The story of Jade, butterfly charmer and Princess of Malalabopindicia. *(Pronounced Mal-lal-uh-bop-in-deesh-ee-uh)* *(WILLOW goes behind screen. A shadow puppet play in Chinese tradition follows. WILLOW plays the KING and the DRAGON. TILT plays JADE.)*

KING: Jade, all you do is sit and play butterfly games.

JADE: I'm a butterfly *charmer.*

KING: Whatever you are, you do no good for our kingdom. For three years we have suffered a great drought and my kingdom blames me. but I know who's at fault for this deterioration.

JADE: Who?

KING: The Dragon.

JADE: Our dragon?

KING: Yes. Our kingdom's dragon is upset. His anger destroys our land. You must slay the dragon.

JADE: *No!*

KING: You must! Here is my sword and shield. Take them and kill the dragon.

JADE: But—

KING: You must do it! I'd do it but … I've got this lame arm. Our kingdom really needs this. As Princess of Malalabopindicia, it is your obligation. Go.

WILLOW: *(Pops head up.)* Exciting, isn't it? It gets even better. *(He goes back down.)*

JADE: I don't know why I'm doing this. I can't even poke an olive with a toothpick.

DRAGON: *(Roars.)* Who are you? What do you want?

JADE: I … I …

DRAGON: Get out of my lair! *(A flash of fire shoots at JADE.)*

JADE: My, you *are* angry.

DRAGON: I'm *not* angry.

JADE: Then why do you ruin our land?

DRAGON: Because I choose to. Not much to do around here. The life of a dragon isn't all magic and games, you know. What do you want?

JADE: I'm the Princess of Malalabopindicia, the land you are destroying. My father, the King, sent me here to … slay you.

DRAGON: You? You couldn't even slay an olive. Leave my lair before I turn you into a barbecue princess.

JADE: You can't keep destroying our land. What if I make a deal with you?

DRAGON: Compromise is a sign of weakness.

JADE: I'm not asking you to sacrifice your honor. Have you ever seen a butterfly charmer?

DRAGON: No.

JADE: It's a wonderful profession. And it doesn't hurt anyone.

DRAGON: I doubt that.

WILLOW: So Jade sings a butterfly song, soothes the dragon, and all is well again in the land of Malalabopindicia. *(He pops up.)* What did you think?

ROSE: It was ... nice.

WILLOW: *(To TILT)* She didn't like it! Tilt, this is your fault.

TILT: What did I do?

WILLOW: What did you *do?* *(To ROSE)* What did she do?

ROSE: It wasn't her fault.

WILLOW: Well, it certainly wasn't my fault.

ROSE: No ...

WILLOW: What then?

ROSE: It's just that the play ... seemed ... incomplete.

WILLOW: *(Flabbergasted)* Incom—

TILT: *(Very smug)* Incomplete. Maybe we should have done the song.

WILLOW: Not that again.

ROSE: There is a song?

TILT: A final grand song that charms a few butterflies, impresses the dragon, and makes everyone happy.

ROSE: Can you sing it?

WILLOW: *(Together)* No.        TILT: *(Together)* Yes.

WILLOW: We have no musicians.

ROSE: Give me your flute. I want to hear the song.

WILLOW: You certainly are the persistent one, aren't you?

MAMA: She certainly is.

PAPA: Don't interrupt.

WILLOW: All right. I suppose I could sing it alone. Tilt, give me a B.

TILT: A bee?

WILLOW: Yes, a B.

TILT: But I'm allergic. If I'm stung, I swell up like an elephant.

WILLOW: Then give me something else.

TILT: Here's a slice of watermelon.

WILLOW: This is fruitless!

TILT: It can't be ... It has seeds.

WILLOW: Aarrggh ... *(To audience)* Do you see how an artist must suffer?

ROSE: Sing the butterfly song. *(WILLOW and TILT retreat behind the screen and sing to a fast-paced, happy tune. WILLOW sings and*

*ROSE plays the flute.)*

WILLOW: The butterflies have disappeared
The wildflowers have turned all gray
In the event that we all feared:
The start of night, the end of day.

Bring back the sun.
Bring back the bright skies.
Bring back the sun.
Bring back the butterflies.

WILLOW, ROSE, and TILT:
So part the clouds, reveal the sun.
Lower the moon beneath the sky.
I will not sleep until it's done.
The return of the butterfly.

TILT: And everyone lived happily ever after.

WILLOW: It *was* magnificent! *(They all bow to each other.)* You are the final perfect ingredient. A natural! Tilt, you saw how beautifully she played the flute. And that golden voice! Come with us and entertain mile-long crowds of eager audiences. Rose, would you like to join our traveling show?

ROSE: *Would I?* In a heartbeat. *(Everyone shakes hands repeatedly.)*

NARRATOR: And so Rose's career as a traveling musician begins.

PAPA: Oh, no! How does she expect to get rich as a musician?

MAMA: Is *that* what she really expected?

PAPA: What?

MAMA: Oh, nothing.

NARRATOR: Time passes quickly for Rose. It goes a bit slower for Oak and Birch. Oak was promoted to head carpenter eventually. Birch had a ... more difficult time advancing.

BIRCH: There. My first shed. How does it look? I made it myself! *(The shed creaks loudly and collapses.)*

MAMA: *(To audience)* Carpentry wasn't poor Birch's trade.

PAPA: *So?* He certainly could have traded in whatever trade he had before this one.

161

MAMA:  Neither of them enjoyed their work very much, did they?

PAPA:  *So? (MAMA swipes PAPA but doesn't connect.)*

NARRATOR:  Rose, on the other hand, loved her job. She hardly had enough money to buy food but she hardly cared. She traveled across the countryside entertaining thousands of delighted audiences. She got lost in her love of singing. When the time came, three years later, to meet Birch and Oak, Rose forgot.

ROSE:  Oh, no!

WILLOW:  *(Together)* What is it?    TILT:  *(Together)* What's wrong?

ROSE:  What day is it?

WILLOW:  It's today, of course. *(ROSE shoots a dirty look.)* You taught me that trick, young lady.

ROSE:  I'm late for a three-year meeting.

WILLOW:  That's a long meeting.

TILT:  Are you three years late?

ROSE:  I have got to go. I need to get back to my family. I promised.

WILLOW:  Rose, your life is that of a traveling musician. You don't need your family anymore. We're your family. Besides, you don't have any money.

ROSE:  Willow, Tilt, you have to understand. I need to meet with my family and claim a share of land.

WILLOW:  Aha! There's money involved.

ROSE:  Please help me get home.

NARRATOR:  So Willow and Tilt took Rose as far as they could— to the shoreline of a large sea.

WILLOW and TILT:  Sorry, we don't swim.

ROSE:  Neither do I.

NARRATOR:  Rose knew she must find a way. She said good-bye to Willow and Tilt and they reluctantly left her. Though she tried, she could find no way to cross the sea. Not knowing what else to do, she expressed her longing in song.

ROSE:  *(A slow, melancholy tune)*
One tiny teardrop
Falls in the water
Salt in salt forgotten.

But I remember the
Smile of my father.
His old shirt missing a button.
*(She breaks down sobbing.)*
*(The NARRATOR becomes the DRAGON PRINCE who parts the sea and walks to ROSE's side.)*
PRINCE: Beautiful.
ROSE: *(Without looking)* Thank you.
PRINCE: No, thank you. You sing with such sadness. My Father, the Dragon King, is enchanted by your song. He begs you to come down to his kingdom and sing something for him. *(Bows.)*
ROSE: I must get home to my family.
PRINCE: Sing once for the king and the journey home shall be your fee. *(Joyfully, ROSE agrees. The PRINCE parts the sea and they enter the water.)*
PAPA: Ahh, Oak and Birch have returned home.
MAMA: Thank goodness. *(She hugs them too much.)*
OAK: I found us jobs as carpenter's helpers our first day out. I was promoted ... right away ... to head carpenter. The money was very good.
PAPA: How much is good?
MAMA: Shhh! *(OAK pulls out a medium-sized money sack.)*
PAPA: Would you look at that sack of money!
BIRCH: I have a sack too. *(He pulls out a small coin purse.)*
OAK: Look at it—no larger than a mouse's burp.
MAMA: *(While counting)* I count only two of our three children.
BIRCH: She's always late.
OAK: She won't have a thing.
PAPA: Nonetheless, it was part of our agreement. We shall wait.
OAK and BIRCH: So we waited.
NARRATOR: And they waited. Rose arrived at the Dragon King's lair near the same time Oak and Birch arrived home. *(NARRATOR becomes PRINCE again as he and ROSE move into the lair.)*
ROSE: Oh, my ...
PRINCE: Welcome to the lair, Rose. You must be hungry. Eat. *(She does.)* You are our most honored guest.

DRAGON KING: *(Enters with his FAIRIES.)* Welcome, young one. I heard you play the flute and sing. Would you mind entertaining an old dragon like me?

ROSE: *(Bows.)* I'd love to.

DRAGON KING: Sing me the song I heard you sing on the beach.

ROSE: One tiny teardrop
> Falls in the water
> Salt in salt and it's forgotten.

> But I remember the
> Laugh of my mother,
> The green blouse she never tucked in.

> So take me back into the water,
> Calm my fears; it's that or nothing.
> It's that or nothing.

DRAGON KING: That was wonderful. But so sad. You seem as if you would be such a happy one.

ROSE: Usually I am. I miss my family very much and wish to go home.

DRAGON KING: Can you sing anything more to your nature?

ROSE: I must be going.

DRAGON KING: Young Rose, time is insignificant. Stay as long as you like. Stay until you finish a new song and I'll see that you get home.

ROSE: I would be honored to sing for you again.

DRAGON KING: Excellent. *(To FAIRIES)* Show Rose to her lodging. *(They escort ROSE to her own space.)* A delightful girl. Still, she has much to learn about happiness.

PRINCE: She does seem to love singing.

DRAGON KING: Yes, I'm afraid she has forgotten that.

MAMA: See how hard Rose worked on the Dragon King's song?

PAPA: Yes, but it *still* took her three days. *(MAMA swings and connects.)*

PRINCE: Have you finished?

ROSE: Yes, I have. I really must go home soon.

PRINCE: Since you have been so gracious to my father, I wish to give you something. The Dragon King is a generous one, and when you complete your song, he will offer you a gift to take home. Ask for this stone that fits around my neck.

ROSE: A stone?

PRINCE: It is a magic wishing stone. Accept nothing else.

ROSE: Thank you.

PRINCE: Now, follow me to the lair where you shall entertain the king.

DRAGON KING: Ahh, our Lady is here to sing. Hello, Rose.

ROSE: *(Bows.)* Sir Dragon King.

DRAGON KING: Don't fret, young Rose. We'll get you home immediately after your song. *(PRINCE and FAIRIES gather around.)*

ROSE: *(Singing a lively tune)*

> The sun woke him up
> Early in the day.
> "What a fine breeze,"
> I heard him say.

> He put on his shirt
> He buttoned up his pants
> Went out the door
> And hopped over the fence.

> The first thing he saw
> Was a hopping purple toad
> Whose every purple plop
> Echoed in the road.
> "Why purple?" he asked
> In an off color voice.
> "Why, my young lad,
> Purple was my choice."

> It was a garden frolic sort of day
> And he jumped, skipped, ran, and played

Through the magic garden
Where everything was happy
Whether day or night
Because they chose to be that way.


*(ROSE lowers her head to ponder.)*

DRAGON KING: That was wonderfully true to your nature. Rose, what's wrong?

ROSE: I chose my color like the toad in the song, but I don't think my Papa will approve.

DRAGON KING: Because you chose to be a musician?

ROSE: Yes.

DRAGON KING: I think you have chosen wisely and honorably. *(ROSE thanks him with a bow. The DRAGON KING returns the bow.)* Before you leave for home, you may choose one thing from this lair to bring with you. Take anything. Gold. Silver. Jewels.

ROSE: I would like to have the stone the Dragon Prince wears around his neck.

DRAGON KING: *(Pause)* My young Rose, with the wishing stone comes much responsibility. Are you prepared to accept that?

ROSE: I am.

DRAGON KING: Very well. You have proven yourself honorable. Take the stone. *(DRAGON KING gets the stone and places it around ROSE's neck.)* Remember: greed or evil can destroy this stone's magic, like it can with any good thing.

ROSE: I'll remember.

DRAGON KING: Fairies, escort Rose home. Good luck to you! *(The FAIRIES escort ROSE by the elbows.)*

NARRATOR: *(Removing PRINCE garb)* The Dragon King's fairies escorted Rose right to her doorstep, where the rest of the family waited.

ROSE: I'm home! Oh, Mama, Papa, Birch, Oak!

PAPA, OAK, BIRCH: It's about time.

MAMA: Shhh! Oh, Rose. *(Rushes over to hug and kiss her.)*

OAK: *(To BIRCH)* I bet she doesn't have a coin on her.

PAPA: You've all returned now. Three years have passed and it's time to decide your fates. Rose, what have you done in the past three years?

ROSE:   Well, I met two actors named Willow and Tilt and ... I became a musician.

PAPA:   *This* is what you've done with yourself?

ROSE:   Would you like to hear a song I wrote?

PAPA:   *(Together)* Certainly not.      MAMA:   *(Together)* Oh, yes.

PAPA:   So, what did you bring home with you?

ROSE:   I have this flute.

OAK:   Worth hardly two coins.

ROSE:   The Dragon King gave me this stone for singing him a song.

PAPA:   A *stone?!* From the Dragon King? Has our currency system been replaced with a stone system? Ridiculous! Rose, I'm ashamed of you. *(PAPA retreats.)*

MAMA:   I'm sorry, Rose. I'll speak with him. *(MAMA follows PAPA. OAK and BIRCH stick out their tongues and hide.)*

ROSE:   Now I have nothing. *(Takes off stone, holds it in both hands.)* Oh great wishing stone, please give me back the respect of my father. *(The DRAGON KING's FAIRIES appear.)*

FAIRIES:   Poor fool, your wish is granted.

ROSE:   Thank you!

NARRATOR:   With that, Rose fell asleep on the cold stone floor, clutching her flute in one hand and her wishing stone in the other. *(OAK and BIRCH come out of hiding.)*

OAK:   Did you see that?

BIRCH:   What?

OAK:   The wishing stone—it really works!

BIRCH:   So?

OAK:   *(Giving BIRCH a dirty look)* I have an idea. You grab this feather and tickle her nose. I'll snatch the stone.

BIRCH:   I have a better idea. *You* take the feather.

OAK:   Don't argue with me or I'll get the stone myself and wish you a nose made out of bamboo stalk.

BIRCH:   I'll take the feather. *(BIRCH tickles ROSE's nose. ROSE swats and OAK grabs her flute. They display their disgust and try again—this time getting the stone.)*

167

OAK: Aha!

BIRCH: Give it to me.

OAK: Wait your turn. I wish that Birch and I each had brand-new expensive warrior's clothes. *(The FAIRIES appear.)*

FAIRIES: Poor fools, your wish is granted. *(OAK and BIRCH are garbed in warrior's clothing.)*

BIRCH: It works!

OAK: Poor fool? I'm no fool.

BIRCH: We need to hide it so Rose doesn't suspect us.

OAK: If we hide it, she'll still know it's gone. We need to replace it. Find one like this, put it on a rope, and set it next to Rose.

NARRATOR: That is just what Birch did while Oak admired the precious wishing stone, dreaming of all the riches he could have. The next day, Rose woke early. She began to hum a sweet little tune. Her papa heard her lovely voice and was moved to speak with her.

PAPA: Rose, you have the voice of a canary. It's beautiful. *(Pauses.)* I want to apologize; you've proven me wrong. I forgot part of the promise. Your brothers may have earned more money, but they didn't learn like you. That's the important part, Rose, you are the richest of my children! I want to give you first choice of the land.

ROSE: Papa!

BIRCH and OAK: *(Who have been eavesdropping)* Papa, you can't!

OAK: You can't give Rose first pick. She didn't do anything. Look at my new clothes.

BIRCH: And mine too!

PAPA: Where did you get those clothes?

OAK: *(Without a beat)* We bought them.

PAPA: With what? You gave me your money.

OAK: I ... had a little saved.

PAPA: Birch?

BIRCH: I made a wish.

ROSE: What?

OAK: *(Quickly)* He said, "I ... missed." I had a little coin saved up for him, too.

PAPA: Is that right?

BIRCH: Almost. I ... I found a stone outside just like Rose's.

OAK: Give me that!

ROSE: The wishing stone! *(BIRCH and OAK tussle.)*

BIRCH: No, I found it. It's mine.

OAK: It's mine. Give it back.

ROSE: Birch, stop it! Oak, don't!

MAMA: *(Commanding)* Children, quit this at once. *(They do.)* Now, let us talk things over.

OAK: *(Under his breath)* You lazy dog.

BIRCH: You mean pit bull. *(They resume the fight.)*

OAK: Give me that stone.

BIRCH: I'll wish your nose into a celery stalk. *(At the climax of the struggle, the stone flies into the air, crashes to the ground, and splits in two. ROSE cries out in anguish. The DRAGON KING's FAIRIES appear.)*

FAIRIES: Poor fools! The power went to your heads. The greed in your hearts destroyed the stone. You don't deserve even its pieces. *(The two halves of the stone disappear.)*

BIRCH: *(Together)* No, no!     OAK: *(Together)* No, wait!

BIRCH: It's not fair.

OAK: This is your fault. *(They begin to fight yet again.)*

BIRCH: What?

OAK: You did this!

BIRCH: No, you did it!

PAPA: *(Stopping the fight)* Children, stop this at once! This has gone too far.

MAMA: It went too far too long ago.

PAPA: How do you expect to gain my—

MAMA: Our.

PAPA: ... *our* respect by being so bad?

BIRCH and OAK: *Bad?*

MAMA and PAPA: *Yes, bad!*

PAPA: Rose, take our hands. Now, you two, look at your sister. Does she look rich?

BIRCH and OAK: No.

MAMA: But she is.

OAK: I knew it. She's been lying the whole time.

MAMA: No. She's rich because she is happy.

PAPA: That's right. Rose, we offer you first choice of our land.

OAK: *(Together) No!*   BIRCH: *(Together) Never!*

ROSE: Thank you, Papa. Thank you, Mama. *(They embrace.)* But I can't live here. *(BIRCH and OAK perk up.)*

MAMA: But why?

ROSE: I'm a traveling musician now—the road is my choice and my path.

OAK: So that means I get first pick.

BIRCH: What about me?

PAPA: No. You two still have much to learn. I can't trust you with one rock, and you want a field of them? No, it's back to carpentry for you two.

MAMA: Rose, if you ever need a home again, you may have the land by the creek.

ROSE: I'm grateful. Thank you both.

NARRATOR: That's a happy ending. Well, at least, happy for Rose. Oak and Birch left home and tried to earn enough money to persuade Papa and Mama to give them the choicest land.

MAMA: Poor Birch spends as much as he makes. *(BIRCH exits.)*

PAPA: Oak lost his job as head carpenter because of his hot head. *(OAK exits.)* Now he works as a stable-keeper, cleaning up horse manure.

MAMA: Well, it's an honorable profession. *(MAMA and PAPA both laugh.)*

NARRATOR: And so, in the end ... *(WILLOW and TILT rush in.)*

WILLOW: We're not too late, are we?

PAPA: Too late for what?

WILLOW: For Rose. We've been looking all over for her.

ROSE: Willow? Tilt? *(They all embrace.)*

WILLOW: We've been looking far and wide for you. It didn't help that my glasses were stolen.

TILT: They must be broken. I told you.

MAMA: You mean these? *(Points to the glasses on WILLOW's head.)*

WILLOW: What? Why, I can't ... I knew they were there all the time.

I was just testing you.

ROSE: Oh, really? *(They all laugh except WILLOW—who reluctantly joins in.)* Mama, Papa, this is Willow and Tilt.

WILLOW: Willow Tit-Willow here. Actor, shadow puppeteer, and owner of Willow and Tilt Productions. This is Tilt Wit-Tillow, my partner.

TILT: Pleased to meet you.

NARRATOR: So Rose said good-bye to her Papa and Mama and went on her way. She promised to return home often and tell them of her adventures. And they all lived happily ...

WILLOW: Wait! You can't properly end a show without a good song. Your daughter taught me that.

PAPA: I'm sorry, but this is my story.

MAMA: *Our* story.

PAPA: Our story. *(To audience)* Thank you so much for coming. Now we've come to the end of our tale of the wishing stone. And they all lived happily ...

WILLOW: This won't do at all. Rose, how about an excellent song?

PAPA: I won't stand for this.

MAMA: Then sit down! *(Pulls him down.)*

ROSE: *(Starts the happy song.)*

Some people thought the end was near.
They carried thick signs and spread the fear
That butterflies are gone and would never return.
They were all wrong, but I hope they have learned

*(All characters, except OAK, BIRCH, and PAPA join in and sing.)*

That the end wasn't near.
The beginning is all that is here.

*(PAPA joins in)*

The clouds are gone.
The skies are clear.

The dragon rests,
And butterflies appear.

NARRATOR: And they all ... *(Indicating OAK and BIRCH)* well, almost all of them, lived happily ... *(Looks to see if any interruption is coming)* ever after. *(He sighs. All the characters dance off.)*

WILLOW: *(Popping his head out)* Now, *that's* an ending!

# from "A Primer of the Daily Round" by Howard Nemerov

Here is a brief companion piece of literature by poet Howard Nemerov that provides an interesting contrast to "A Was An Archer," included in the Chapter Five exercise titled "Carry Your Character With You!" The poem lends itself to a classroom performance that features a single narrator figure and an ensemble that relies on pantomime or physical activity to visualize the dramatic action described. This brief poem may also serve as a warm-up for the rehearsal period and as a movement exercise for performers to explore basic principles of space and staging.

A peels an apple, while B kneels to God,
C telephones to D, who has a hand
On E's knee, F coughs, G turns up the sod
For H's grave, I do not understand
But J is bringing one clay pigeon down
While K brings down a nightstick on L's head,
And M takes mustard, N drives into town,
O goes to bed with P, and Q drops dead,
R lies to S, but happens to be heard
By T, who tells U not to fire V
For having to give W the word
That X is now deceiving Y with Z,
  Who happens just now to remember A
  Peeling an apple somewhere far away.

"A Primer of the Daily Round" by Howard Nemerov. © Copyright 1975, University of Chicago Press. Reprinted by permission of Margaret Nemerov.

# from *A Midsummer Night's Dream* by William Shakespeare

William Shakespeare's early comedy (1595-1596) is also one of his most imaginative, introducing us to the world of sprites and spirits. The comic scene of "Pyramus and Thisby" (Act V, Scene i) is a hilarious parody of naive and inexperienced performers in artless role-playing. These "rude mechanicals" offer a number of inventive characterizations for classroom performance, and encourage the use of hand-props, costumes, and small scenic units to capture the comic spirit of the selected scene. There are also opportunities here to pursue arena, thrust, or found space staging.

### Prologue

QUINCE: If we offend, it is with our good will.
    That you should think, we come not to offend,
    But with good will. To show our simple skill,
    That is the true beginning of our end.
    Consider, then, we come but in despite.
    We do not come, as minding to content you,
    Our true intent is. All for your delight
    We are not here. That you should here repent you,
    The actors are at hand; and, by their show,
    You shall know all that you are like to know.
    *(Enter PYRAMUS, THISBY, WALL, MOONSHINE, and LION.)*
    Gentles, perchance you wonder at this show;
    But wonder on, till truth make all things plain.
    This man is Pyramus, if you would know;
    This beauteous lady Thisby is certain.
    This man, with lime and rough-cast, doth present
    Wall, that vile Wall which did these lovers sunder;
    And through Wall's chink, poor souls, they are content
    To whisper. At the which let no man wonder.
    This man, with lantern, dog, and bush of thorn,
    Presenteth Moonshine; for, if you will know,

By moonshine did these lovers think no scorn
To meet at Ninus' tomb, there, there to woo.
This grisly beast, which Lion hight by name,
The trusty Thisby, coming first by night,
Did scare away, or rather did affright;
And, as she fled, her mantle she did fall,
Which Lion vile with bloody mouth did stain.
Anon comes Pyramus, sweet youth and tall,
And finds his trusty Thisby's mantle slain;
Whereat, with blade, with bloody blameful blade,
He bravely broach'd his boiling bloody breast.
And Thisby, tarrying in mulberry shade,
His dagger drew, and died. For all the rest,
Let Lion, Moonshine, Wall, and lovers twain
At large discourse, while here they do remain.
*(Exit LION, THISBY, and MOONSHINE.)*
WALL: In this same interlude it doth befall
That I, one Snout by name, present a wall;
And such a wall, as I would have you think,
That had in it a crannied hole or chink,
Through which the lovers, Pyramus and Thisby,
Did whisper often very secretly.
This loam, this rough-cast, and this stone doth show
That I am that same wall; the truth is so.
And this the cranny is, right and sinister,
Through which the fearful lovers are to whisper.
*(PYRAMUS comes forward.)*
PYRAMUS: O grim-look'd night! O night with hue so black!
O night, which ever art when day is not!
O night, O night! Alack, alack, alack,
I fear my Thisby's promise is forgot.
And thou, O wall, O sweet, O lovely wall,
That stand'st between her father's ground and mine,
Thou wall, O wall, O sweet and lovely wall,
Show me thy chink, to blink through with mine eyne!
*(WALL holds up his fingers.)*

175

Thanks, courteous wall. Jove shield thee well for this!
But what see I? No Thisby do I see.
O wicked wall, through whom I see no bliss!
Curs'd be thy stones for thus deceiving me!
*(Enter THISBY.)*

THISBY: O wall, full often hast thou heard my moans,
For parting my fair Pyramus and me.
My cherry lips have often kiss'd thy stones,
Thy stones with lime and hair knit up in thee.

PYRAMUS: I see a voice. Now will I to the chink,
To spy an I can hear my Thisby's face.
Thisby!

THISBY: My love! Thou art my love, I think.

PYRAMUS: Think what thou wilt, I am thy lover's grace,
And, like Limander, am I trusty still.

THISBY: And I like Helen, till the Fates me kill.

PYRAMUS: Not Shafalus to Procus was so true.

THISBY: As Shafalus to Procus, I to you.

PYRAMUS: O, kiss me through the hole of this vile wall!

THISBY: I kiss the wall's hole, not your lips at all.

PYRAMUS: Wilt thou at Ninny's tomb meet me straightway?

THISBY: 'Tide life, 'tide death, I come without delay.
*(Exit PYRAMUS and THISBY.)*

WALL: Thus have I, Wall, my part discharged so;
And, being done, thus Wall away doth go. *(Exit.)*
*(Enter LION and MOONSHINE.)*

LION: You, ladies, you, whose gentle hearts do fear
The smallest monstrous mouse that creeps on floor,
May now perchance both quake and tremble here,
When lion rough in wildest rage doth roar.
Then know that I, as Snug the joiner, am
A lion fell, nor else no lion's dam;
For, if I should as lion come in strife
Into this place, 'twere pity on my life.

MOON: This lanthorn doth the horned moon present;
Myself the man I' th' moon do seem to be.

All that I have to say is to tell you that the
Lanthorn is the moon, I, the man in the moon,
This thorn-bush my thorn-bush,
And this dog my dog.
*(Enter THISBY.)*
THISBY:  This is old Ninny's tomb. Where is my love?
LION:  *(Roaring)* Oh—
*(THISBY runs off left as PYRAMUS enters right.)*
PYRAMUS:  Sweet Moon, I thank thee for thy sunny beams;
I thank thee, Moon, for shining now so bright;
For, by thy gracious, golden, glittering gleams,
I trust to take of truest Thisby sight.
　　But stay, O spite!
　　But mark, poor knight.
What dreadful dole is here?
　　Eyes, do you see?
　　How can it be?
O dainty duck! O dear!
　　Thy mantle good,
　　What, stain'd with blood!
Approach, ye Furies fell!
　　O Fates, come, come,
　　Cut thread and thrum;
Quail, crush, conclude, and quell!
O wherefore, Nature, didst thou lions frame?
Since lion vile hath here deflow'r'd my dear,
Which is—no, no—which was the fairest dame
That liv'd, that lov'd, that lik'd, that look'd with cheer.
　　Come, tears, confound,
　　Out, sword, and wound
The pap of Pyramus;
　　Ay, that left pap,
　　Where heart doth hop. *(Stabs himself.)*
Thus die I, thus, thus, thus.
　　Now am I dead,
　　Now am I fled;

177

My soul is in the sky.
    Tongue, lose thy light;
    Moon, take thy flight. *(MOONSHINE exits.)*
Now die, die, die, die, die. *(PYRAMUS dies.)*
*(Enter THISBY.)*
THISBY:  Asleep, my love?
    What, dead my dove?
O Pyramus, arise!
    Speak, speak. Quite dumb?
    Dead, dead?
A tomb must cover thy sweet eyes.
    These lily lips,
    This cherry nose,
These yellow cowslip cheeks,
    Are gone, are gone!
    Lovers, make moan.
His eyes were green as leeks.
    O Sisters Three,
    Come, come to me,
With hands as pale as milk;
    Lay them in gore,
    Since you have shore
With shears his thread of silk.
    Tongue, not a word.
    Come, trusty sword,
Come, blade, my breast imbrue! *(Stabs herself.)*
    And farewell, friends.
Thus Thisby ends.
    Adieu, adieu, adieu. *(THISBY dies.)*
*(PYRAMUS leaps up.)*
PYRAMUS:  I assure you, the wall is now
Down that parted their fathers.
WIll it please you to see the Epilogue,
Or to hear a Bergomask dance
Between two of our company?

# from "The Love Song of J. Alfred Prufrock" by T. S. Eliot

T. S. Eliot's "The Love Song of J. Alfred Prufrock" lends itself to an imaginative classroom exploration of staging to suggest a specific place and time. The opening line, for example, indicates character action that may have occurred before the poem begins; and there is meaningful non-verbal action throughout the text that will need to be defined in performance. Depicting a vivid locale and considering the movement of time within the poem are essential ingredients in an interpretation of the literature. The poem may also be adapted to feature multiple narrator figures and a chorus of occasional voices.

S'io credesse che mia reposta fosse
A persona che mai tornasse al mondo,
Questa fiamma staria senza piu scosse.
Ma perciocche giammai di questo fondo
Non torno vivo alcum, s'l'odo il vero,
Senza tema d'infamia ti rispondo.[1]

Let us go then, you and I,
When the evening is spread out against the sky
Like a patient etherised upon a table;
Let us go, through certain half-deserted streets,
The muttering retreats
Of restless nights in one-night cheap hotels
And sawdust restaurants with oyster-shells:
Streets that follow like a tedious argument
Of insidious intent
To lead you to an overwhelming question ...

---

1. "If I thought my answer were to one who could ever return to the world, this flame should shake no more; but since, if what I hear is true, no one ever returned alive from this depth, I answer you without fear of shame." —A statement made by a spirit in hell in Dante's twenty-seventh canto of the *Inferno*.

Oh, do not ask, 'What is it?'
Let us go and make our visit.

In the room the women come and go
Talking of Michelangelo.

The yellow fog that rubs its back upon the window-panes,
The yellow smoke that rubs its muzzle on the window-panes
Licked its tongue into the corners of the evening,
Lingered upon the pools that stand in drains,
Let fall upon its back the soot that falls from chimneys,
Slipped by the terrace, made a sudden leap,
And seeing that it was a soft October night,
Curled once about the house, and fell asleep.

And indeed there will be time
For the yellow smoke that slides along the street,
Rubbing its back upon the window-panes;
There will be time, there will be time
To prepare a face to meet the faces that you meet;
There will be time to murder and create,
And time for all the works and days of hands
That lift and drop a question on your plate;
Time for you and time for me,
And time yet for a hundred indecisions,
And for a hundred visions and revisions,
Before the taking of a toast and tea.

In the room the women come and go
Talking of Michelangelo.

And indeed there will be time
To wonder, 'Do I dare?' and, 'Do I dare?'
Time to turn back and descend the stair,
With a bald spot in the middle of my hair—
[They will say: 'How his hair is growing thin!']

My morning coat, my collar mounting firmly to the chin,
My necktie rich and modest, but asserted by a simple pin—
[They will say: 'But how his arms and legs are thin!']
Do I dare
Disturb the universe?
In a minute there is time
For decisions and revisions which a minute will reverse.

    For I have known them all already, known them all:—
Have known the evenings, mornings, afternoons,
I have measured out my life with coffee spoons;
I know the voices dying with a dying fall
Beneath the music from a farther room.
    So how should I presume?

    And I have known the eyes already, known them all—
The eyes that fix you in a formulated phrase,
And when I am formulated, sprawling on a pin,
When I am pinned and wriggling on the wall,
Then how should I begin
To spit out all the butt-ends of my days and ways?
    And how should I presume?

    And I have known the arms already, known them all—
Arms that are braceleted and white and bare
[But in the lamplight, downed with light brown hair!]
Is it perfume from a dress
That makes me so digress?
Arms that lie along a table, or wrap about a shawl.
    And should I then presume?
    And how should I begin?

          .   .   .   .

Shall I say, I have gone at dusk through narrow streets
And watched the smoke that rises from the pipes
Of lonely men in shirt-sleeves, leaning out of windows?

181

I should have been a pair of ragged claws
Scuttling across the floors of silent seas.

           .    .    .    .

And the afternoon, the evening, sleeps so peacefully!
Smoothed by long fingers,
Asleep ... tired ... or it malingers,
Stretched on the floor, here beside you and me.
Should I, after tea and cakes and ices,
Have the strength to force the moment to its crisis?
But though I have wept and fasted, wept and prayed,
Though I have seen my head [grown slightly bald] brought in
    upon a platter,
I am no prophet—and here's no great matter;
I have seen the moment of my greatest flicker,
And I have seen the eternal Footman hold my coat, and snicker,
And in short, I was afraid.

And would it have been worth it, after all,
After the cups, the marmalade, the tea,
Among the porcelain, among some talk of you and me,
Would it have been worth while,
To have bitten off the matter with a smile,
To have squeezed the universe into a ball
To roll it toward some overwhelming question,
To say: 'I am Lazarus, come from the dead,
Come back to tell you all, I shall tell you all'—
If one, settling a pillow by her head,
    Should say: 'That is not what I meant at all.
    That is not it, at all.'

And would it have been worth it, after all,
Would it have been worth while,
After the sunsets and the dooryards and the sprinkled streets,
After the novels, after the teacups, after the skirts that trail along
    The floor—
And this, and so much more?

182

It is impossible to say just what I mean!
But as if a magic lantern threw the nerves in patterns on a screen:
Would it have been worth while
If one, settling a pillow or throwing off a shawl,
And turning toward the window, should say:
    'That is not it at all.
    That is not what I meant, at all.'

              .    .    .    .

No! I am not Prince Hamlet, nor was meant to be;
Am an attendant lord, one that will do
To swell a progress, start a scene or two,
Advise the prince; no doubt, an easy tool,
Deferential, glad to be of use,
Politic, cautious, and meticulous;
Full of high sentence, but a bit obtuse;
At times, indeed, almost ridiculous—
Almost, at times, the Fool.
    I grow old ... I grow old ...
I shall wear the bottoms of my trousers rolled.

    Shall I part my hair behind? Do I dare to eat a peach?
I shall wear white flannel trousers, and walk upon the beach.
I have heard the mermaids singing, each to each.
    I do not think that they will sing to me.

    I have seen them riding seaward on the waves
Combing the white hair of the waves blown back
When the wind blows the water white and black.

    We have lingered in the chambers of the sea
By sea-girls wreathed with seaweed red and brown
Till human voices wake us, and we drown.

# from *Act Without Words* by Samuel Beckett

Desert. Dazzling light. Delusion. Samuel Beckett's simple arrangement of the dramatic events in this pantomime scenario is a nice extension of "The Body Beautiful!" exercise in Chapter Five. The precisely choreographed movement and focus on gesture should encourage performers to actively explore physical reactions and responses in rehearsal. The brief scenario also provides imaginative opportunities to explore a compiled script of thematic literature that provides spoken transitions between each unit of dramatic action suggested in the pantomime.

The man is flung backwards on stage from right wing.
He falls, gets up immediately, dusts himself, turns
aside, reflects.
Whistle from right wing.
He reflects, goes out right.
Immediately flung back on stage he falls, gets up
immediately, dusts himself, turns aside, reflects.
Whistle from left wing.
He reflects, goes out left.

Immediately flung back on stage he falls, gets up
immediately, dusts himself, turns aside, reflects.
Whistle from left wing.
He reflects, goes toward left wing, hesitates, thinks
better of it, halts, turns aside, reflects.
A little tree descends from flies, lands. It has a single
bough some three yards from ground and at its
summit a meager tuft of palms casting at its foot a
circle of shadow.

---

He continues to reflect.

Whistle from above.

He turns, sees tree, reflects, goes to it, sits down in its
    shadow, looks at his hands.

A pair of tailor's scissors descends from flies, comes to
    rest before tree, a yard from ground.

He continues to look at his hands.

Whistle from above.


He looks up, sees scissors, takes them and starts to trim
    his nails.

The palms close like a parasol, the shadow disappears.

He drops scissors, reflects.

A tiny carafe, to which is attached a huge label inscribed
    WATER, descends from flies, comes to rest some
    three yards from ground.

He continues to reflect.

Whistle from above.


He turns, sees cube, takes it up, carries it over and sits
    it down under carafe, tests its stability, gets up on it,
    tries in vain to reach carafe, renounces, gets down,
    carries cube back to its place, turns aside, reflects.

A second smaller cube descends from flies, lands.

He continues to reflect.

Whistle from above.


He turns, sees second cube, looks at it, at carafe, goes to
    second cube, takes it up, carries it over and sets it
    down under carafe, tests its stability, gets up on it,
    tries in vain to reach carafe, renounces, gets down,
    takes up second cube to carry back to its place,
    hesitates, thinks better of it, sets it down, goes to
    big cube, takes it up, carries it over and puts it on
    small one, tests their stability, gets up on them, the
    cubes collapse, he falls, gets up immediately, brushes
    himself, reflects.

185

He takes up small cube, puts it on big one, tests their
stability, gets up on them, and is about to reach
carafe when it is pulled up a little way and comes
to rest beyond his reach.
He gets down, reflects, carries cubes back to their
place, one by one, turns aside, reflects.
A third still smaller cube descends from flies, lands.
He continues to reflect.
Whistle from above.

He turns, sees third cube, looks at it, reflects, turns
aside, reflects.
This third cube is pulled up and disappears in flies.
Beside carafe a rope descends from flies, with knots to
facilitate ascent.
He continues to reflect.
Whistle from above.

He turns, sees rope, reflects, goes to it, climbs up it and
is about to reach carafe when rope is let out and
deposits him back on ground.
He reflects, looks around for scissors, sees them, goes
and picks them up, returns to rope and starts to cut
it with scissors.
The rope is pulled up, lifts him off ground, he hangs on,
succeeds in cutting rope, falls back on ground, drops
scissors, falls, gets up again immediately, brushes
himself, reflects.

The rope is pulled up quickly, and disappears in flies.
With length of rope in his possession he makes a lasso
with which he tries to lasso carafe.
The carafe is pulled up quickly and disappears in flies.
He turns aside, reflects.

He goes with lasso in his hand to tree, looks at bough,
    turns and looks at cubes, looks again at bough,
    drops lasso, goes to cubes, takes up small one,
    carries it over and sets it down under bough, goes
    back for big one, takes it up and carries it over under
    bough, makes to put it on small one, hesitates, thinks
    better of it, sets it down, takes up small one and puts
    it on big one, tests their stability, turns aside and
    stops to pick up lasso.

The bough folds down against trunk.
He straightens up with lasso in his hand, turns and
    sees what has happened.
He drops lasso, turns aside, reflects.
He carries back cubes to their places, one by one, goes
    back for lasso, carries it over to cubes and lays it in
    a neat coil on small one.
He turns aside, reflects.
Whistle from right wing.

He reflects, goes out right.
Immediately flung back on stage he falls, gets up
    immediately, brushes himself, turns aside, reflects.
Whistle from left wing.

He does not move.
He looks at his hands, looks around for scissors, sees
    them, goes and picks them up, starts to trim his
    nails, stops, reflects, runs his finger along blade of
    scissors, goes and lays them on small cube, turns
    aside, opens his collar, frees his neck and fingers it.
The small cube is pulled up and disappears in flies,
    carrying away rope and scissors.
He turns to take scissors, sees what has happened.

187

He turns aside, reflects.

He goes and sits down on big cube.

The big cube is pulled from under him. He falls. The big
cube is pulled up and disappears in flies.

He remains lying on his side, his face towards
auditorium, staring before him.

The carafe descends from flies and comes to rest a few
feet from his body.

He does not move.

Whistle from above.

He does not move.

The carafe descends further, dangles and plays about
his face.

He does not move.

The carafe is pulled up and disappears in flies,

The bough returns to horizontal, the palms open, the
shadow returns.

Whistle from above.

He does not move.

The tree is pulled up and disappears in flies.

He looks at his hands.

(End)

# from *The Velveteen Rabbit* by Margery Williams
# adapted by William Prenevost

This charming adaptation of Margery Williams' classic children's story is especially suitable for a young audience. There are multiple role-playing opportunities here for four performers, and the production may be easily accommodated in a classroom. Theatrical ingredients that appeal to a young child's imagination, like improvisation, music, and sound effects, should also enrich the classroom production.

Performers are encouraged to sketch broadly-drawn portraits that reveal imaginative character action or movement, and to anticipate empathic, vocal responses from the audience!

## Characters

Player One: Lead Narrator, Skin Horse, Doctor
Player Two: Narrator, Velveteen Rabbit
Player Three: Narrator, Child, Wild Rabbit
Player Four: Narrator, Nana, Fairy, Wild Rabbit

## Production Note

Music for "Love Song," written by Lesley Duncan may be heard on Elton John's album *Tumbleweed Connection,* (Uni Records 93096/BlueSeas Music). The lyrics are indicated on the album cover and the song is accompanied by two guitar chords.

Another tune may be substituted for "Love Song" in both the introduction and conclusion of the script. Instrumental music may also be introduced to separate each episode or to provide theme music.

## Scene

The scene opens with Players 2, 3, and 4 at Center-stage. Player 2 in-between and slightly in front of Players 3 and 4. Player 1 stands Up-stage Left singing "Love Song" with guitar accompaniment. He moves towards the other players as they harmonize with him the chorus of the song. When the song is completed, a chord is struck on the guitar and Players 2, 3, and 4 turn their backs to the audience. Player 1 steps forward.

189

PLAYER 1: Imagine, if you will, a rabbit. Now, not a real rabbit like you see hopping around outside, underneath the bushes. But a rabbit make of velveteen, all soft, shiny, and new.

PLAYER 2: *(Facing audience)* A rabbit fat and bunchy, as a rabbit should be.

PLAYER 3: *(Facing audience)* A rabbit with brown and white spots on his coat.

PLAYER 4: *(Facing audience)* A rabbit with real thread whiskers and ears lined with pink sateen.

PLAYER 1: On Christmas morning ... *(He indicates "one moment" to the audience, turns around to face the other PLAYERS, raises his right hand as if to conduct a chorus, then sings them the pitch with "La." He leads them into " 'Tis the Season" sung in "La." As he continues his speech, he moves Up-stage Left.)* ... the rabbit sat wedged in the top of the child's stocking with a sprig of holly between his paws ... *(PLAYER 2 sits in a position to suggest the rabbit. PLAYERS 3 and 4 reach a natural pause and rest in the song for the next line.)* ... the effect was charming. *(PLAYER 1 looks at PLAYER 2, then conducts PLAYERS 3 and 4 to resume the song.)* There were other things in the stocking; nuts and oranges, a toy engine, chocolate covered almonds, and a clockwork mouse, but the Rabbit was quite the best of all. *(PLAYERS 3 and 4 have completed the song. PLAYER 2, as the Rabbit, smiles.)* For at least two hours, the Child loved him, and then ... *(PLAYER 1 conducts PLAYERS 3 and 4 into the song once again. This time it is sung with "Ta" and with a harshness as they walk around PLAYER 2 waving their arms to create a sense of chaos.)* Aunts and Uncles and friends came, and there was a great rustling of tissue paper and unwrapping of gifts. *(PLAYER 1 moves backside of PLAYER 2; and PLAYERS 3 and 4 are frozen, arms extended, in front of PLAYER 2. The singing stopped when they froze on "gifts.")* ... and in the excitement of looking at all the new presents, the Velveteen Rabbit was quite forgotten. *(Slight pause as the PLAYERS form a tableaux. Two snap fingers as if to say "darn it." Then the PLAYERS break to make a new formation. PLAYERS 4 and 1 stand on either side of PLAYER 2 who*

190

*stands Center-stage. PLAYER 3 moves to Up-stage Left as he starts the next speech.)*

PLAYER 3:  For a long time, he lived in the toy box or on the nursery floor, and no one thought very much about him. He was naturally shy, and being only made of velveteen, some of the more expensive toys quite snubbed him. *(PLAYERS 1 and 4 turn profile, arms folded, and snub PLAYER 2 with a "Hm!" Returning to the original backs-to-audience position, PLAYERS 1 and 3 begin mechanical sounds and gesticulations.)* The mechanical toys were very superior, and looked down upon everyone else; they were full of modern ideas, and pretended they were real. *(Mechanical noise and gesture stops, PLAYER 4 starts whistling "Columbia, Gem of the Ocean" and PLAYER 1, suggesting the boat, slowly turns around to audience.)* The model boat, who had lived through two seasons and lost most of his paint, caught the tone from them and never missed an opportunity of referring to his rigging in technical terms.

PLAYER 1:  Aye matey! Take the o'whatchamacallit. And put it on the o' ... *(Trying to remember)* ... poopdeck! *(PLAYER 1 returns to neutral back position.)*

PLAYER 3:  The Rabbit could not claim to be a model of anything, for he didn't know that real rabbits existed; he thought they were all stuffed with sawdust like himself, and he understood that sawdust was quite out-of-date and should never be mentioned in modern circles. Even Timothy, the jointed wooden lion, who was made by the disabled soldiers, and should have had broader views, put on airs and pretended he was connected with the government.

PLAYER 4:  *(Having been imitating the lion as if wearing a trench coat, opens one side of the coat and says ...)* C.I.A.!

PLAYER 3:  Among them all, the poor little Rabbit was made to feel himself very insignificant and commonplace, and the only person who was kind to him at all was the Skin Horse. *(PLAYER 1 turns around and puts his hand on the shoulder of PLAYER 2. During the next speech, PLAYERS 1 and 2 will move Stage Left and freeze in the Rabbit and Skin Horse personae. PLAYER 4 moves Stage Right.)*

PLAYER 4: The Skin Horse had lived longer in the nursery than any of the others. He was so old that his brown coat was bald in patches and showed the seams underneath, and most of the hairs in his tail had been pulled out to string bead necklaces. He was wise, for he had seen a long succession of mechanical toys arrive to boast and swagger, and by-and-by break their mainsprings and pass away, and he knew that they were only toys, and would never turn into anything else. *(Slight pause)* For nursery magic is very strange and wonderful, and only those playthings that are old and wise and experienced, like the Skin Horse, understand all about it. *(Moving toward Center-stage)* One day, when they were laying side by side near the nursery fender, before Nana came to tidy the room, the little Rabbit asked ...

PLAYER 2: What is Real? Does it mean having things that buzz inside you and a stick-out handle?

PLAYER 1: Real isn't how you're made, it's a thing that happens to you. When a child loves you for a long, long time, not just to play with, but *really* loves you, then you become Real.

PLAYER 2: Does it hurt?

PLAYER 1: Sometimes.

PLAYER 4: *(Aside)* The Skin Horse was always truthful.

PLAYER 1: But when you're Real, you don't mind being hurt.

PLAYER 2: Does it happen all at once, like being wound up, or bit by bit?

PLAYER 1: No, it doesn't happen all at once. You become! And it takes a long time. That's why it doesn't often happen to people who break easily, or who have sharp edges, and have to be carefully kept. Generally, by the time you are Real, most of your hair has been loved off, and your eyes drop out and you get loose in the joints and very shabby. But these things don't matter at all, because once you are *Real* you can't be ugly, except to people who don't understand.

PLAYER 2: I suppose *you* are Real?

PLAYER 4: *(Aside)* Said the Rabbit. And then he wished he had not said it, for he thought the Skin Horse might be sensitive. But the Skin Horse only smiled.

PLAYER 1:  The Child's Uncle made me Real. And that was a great many years ago. But once you are Real you can't become unreal again. It lasts for always.

PLAYER 4:  The Rabbit sighed. He thought it would be a long time before this magic called Real happened to him.

PLAYER 2:  *(Stepping forward into narrative persona)* He longed to become Real, to know what it felt like; and yet the idea of growing shabby and losing his eyes and whiskers was rather sad. He wished that he could become it without these uncomfortable things happening to him. *(PLAYER 2 freezes and there is a slight pause. On the next speech, PLAYER 3 moves to Center-stage, while PLAYER 4 assuming NANA mimes tidying up.)*

PLAYER 3:  There was a person called Nana who ruled the nursery. Sometimes she took no notice of the playthings lying about, and sometimes, for no reason whatever, she went swooping about like a great wind and hustled them away in the Child's toy box. She called this …

PLAYER 4:  Tidying up!

PLAYER 3:  And all the playthings hated it, especially the tin ones. The Rabbit didn't mind it so much, for wherever he was thrown, he came down soft. *(PLAYERS 2 and 4 suggest this action.)*

PLAYER 1:  *(Moving from frozen position to Up-stage Right)* One evening, when the Child was going to bed, he couldn't find the plastic dog that always slept with him.

PLAYER 3:  Where's my doggy?

PLAYER 1:  Well, Nana was in a hurry, and it was too much trouble to go hunting for plastic dogs at bedtime, so she simply looked about her and, noticing the opened toy box, she made a swoop.

PLAYER 4:  Here, take your old Bunny! He'll do to sleep with you!

PLAYER 1:  And she dragged the Rabbit out by one ear, and put him into the Child's arms. *(PLAYER 4 pulls PLAYER 2's ear, but PLAYER 2 stays in place as PLAYER 4 carries an imagined toy over to PLAYER 3 who takes it in his arms. Two steps forward.)*

PLAYER 2:  That night, and for many nights after, the Velveteen Rabbit slept in the Child's bed. At first he found it rather uncomfortable, for the Child liked to hug him very tight, and

193

sometimes he pushed him so far under the pillow that the Rabbit could scarcely breathe. And he missed, too, those long moonlight hours in the nursery, when all the house was silent, and his talks with the Skin Horse. But very soon he grew to like it, for the Child used to talk to him, and make nice tunnels for him under the covers that he said were like the burrows real rabbits lived in. And they had splendid games together, in whispers, when Nana had gone to her supper and left the light on. *(PLAYER 2 starts moving backward and finally sits just below PLAYER 3. PLAYER 2 continues softly.)* And when the Child dropped off to sleep, the Rabbit would snuggle down close under his little warm chin and dream, with the Child's hands clasped close round him all night long. *(Pause)*

PLAYER 4: And so time went on, and the little Rabbit was very happy. So happy that he never noticed how his beautiful velveteen fur was getting shabbier and shabbier, and his tail coming unsewn, and all the pink rubbed off his nose where the Child had kissed him.

PLAYER 1: Spring came, and they had long days in the garden, for wherever the Child went, the Rabbit went too.

PLAYER 2: He had rides in the wheelbarrow, and picnics on the grass, and lovely fairy huts built for him under the raspberry canes behind the flower border.

PLAYER 3: And once, when the Child was called away suddenly to take his nap, the Rabbit was left out on the lawn until long after dark.

PLAYER 4: And Nana had to come and look for him with a flashlight because the Child couldn't go to sleep unless he was there.

PLAYER 2: He was wet through with the dew and quite earthy from diving into the burrows the Child had made for him in the flower bed.

PLAYER 1: And Nana grumbled as she rubbed him off with the corner of her apron.

PLAYER 4: You must have your old Bunny! Fancy all that fuss for a toy!

PLAYER 3: Give me my Bunny! *(PLAYERS 4 and 3 exchange the imagined bunny "presentationally" facing out.)* You mustn't say that. He isn't a toy. He's *real!*

PLAYER 1: When the little Rabbit heard that, he was happy, for he knew that what the Skin Horse had said was true at last. The nursery magic had happened to him, and he was a toy no longer. *(PLAYERS 3 and 4 are walking to the back of the house or audience for the next scene.)*

PLAYER 2: *(With tender sincerity)* I am Real. The Child said it himself! *(Stepping forward into narrator persona)* That night he was almost too happy to sleep, and so much love stirred in his little sawdust heart that it almost burst. And into his boot-button eyes, that had long ago lost their polish, there came a look of wisdom and beauty. *(Pause)*

PLAYER 1: That was a wonderful spring for the Velveteen Rabbit! *(On that line, PLAYER 1 has taken PLAYER 2's Up Center-stage position and PLAYER 2 has returned to the Center-stage spot where the Rabbit repeatedly sits.)* Near the house where they lived, there was a woods, and in the long June evenings, the Child liked to go there to play. And he'd take o' Bunny with him of course. But the Child liked to go off and pick flowers or play Robin Hood in the trees, so he always made the Rabbit a little nest somewhere where he would be quite cozy. You see, he was a kind-hearted little Child and he wanted Bunny to be comfortable. Well, one afternoon, while the Velveteen Rabbit was lying there alone, watching the ants that ran to and fro between his velvet paws in the grass, he saw two strange beings creep out of the tall grass near him. *(PLAYERS 3 and 4 start making their way down the aisle toward the stage.)* They were rabbits like himself, but quite furry and brand-new. They must have been very well made, for their seams didn't show at all, and they changed shape in a strange way when they moved; one minute they were long and thin and the next minute fat and bunchy. Their feet padded softly on the ground, and they crept quite close to him. And the Velveteen Rabbit stared hard to see which side the clockwork stuck out, for he knew that people who jump generally have something to wind them up. But he couldn't see it. They were evidently a new kind of rabbit altogether. He stared at them and they stared back. And all the time their noses twitched.

PLAYER 4: Why don't you get up and play with us?

PLAYER 2: I don't feel like it.

PLAYER 4: Well, it's as easy as anything. All you do is jump, like this. *(PLAYER 4 jumps.)*

PLAYER 3: I don't believe you can!

PLAYER 2: I can! I can jump higher than anything!

PLAYER 1: *(Aside)* He meant when the Child threw him, but he didn't want to say that.

PLAYER 3: Can you hop on your hind legs? *(PLAYER 3 jumps backwards.)*

PLAYER 1: *(Aside)* Now that was a dreadful question, for the Velveteen Rabbit had no hind legs at all. The back of him was made all in one piece. So he sat still in the tall grass and hoped they wouldn't notice.

PLAYER 2: I don't feel like it.

PLAYER 1: But wild rabbits have very sharp eyes. And they stretched out their necks and looked.

PLAYER 4: He hasn't got any hind legs! Fancy a rabbit without any hind legs! *(PLAYERS 3 and 4 laugh.)*

PLAYER 2: I have! I have too got hind legs! I'm sitting on them.

PLAYER 3: Then stretch them out and show us, like this! *(PLAYERS 3 and 4 do a short dance.)*

PLAYER 1: And they began to dance and whirl around, and the little Rabbit just sat there, watching.

PLAYER 2: I ... I don't like dancing. It makes me dizzy. I'd rather sit still.

PLAYER 1: But all the while he was longing to dance for a funny new feeling ran through him, and he felt he would give anything in the world to be able to jump about like these rabbits did. Then they came close, so close to the Velveteen Rabbit that their long whiskers brushed against him. Then suddenly they wrinkled their noses, flattened their ears and jumped backwards.

PLAYER 3: He doesn't smell right!

PLAYER 4:  He isn't a rabbit at all!

PLAYERS 3 and 4:  *(Pointing at PLAYER 2)* He isn't real!

PLAYER 2:  I *am* Real! I *am* Real! The Child said so!

PLAYER 1:  And he nearly began to cry. Just then, there was a sound of footsteps, the little Child was fast approaching. And with a stamp of feet, and a flash of white tails, the two strange rabbits disappeared. *(PLAYERS 3 and 4 jump and turn on "then," "steps," "stamp," and "flash" until they are completely back facing the audience; yet frozen in their rabbit positions. After "disappeared" PLAYER 1 snaps his fingers and they relax into neutral positions.)*

PLAYER 2:  Come back and play with me! Oh, do come back! I *know* I am Real!

PLAYER 1:  For a long time he lay very still, watching the tall grass and hoping they would come back. But they never returned, and presently the sun sank lower and the little white moths fluttered out, and the Child came and carried him home. *(Pause)*

PLAYER 4:  Weeks passed, and the little Rabbit grew very old and shabby, but the Child loved him just as much.

PLAYER 3:  He loved him so hard that he loved all his whiskers off, and the pink lining to his ears turned grey, and his brown spots faded.

PLAYER 1:  He even began to lose his shape, and he scarcely looked like a rabbit anymore, except to the Child.

PLAYER 2:  To him he was always beautiful, and that was all that the little Rabbit cared about. He didn't mind how he looked to other people, because the nursery magic had made him Real, and when you are Real, shabbiness doesn't matter.

PLAYER 4:  And then, one day, the Child became very ill.

PLAYER 1:  His face grew very flushed. *(PLAYERS 1 and 4 circle PLAYER 3 during this exchange.)*

PLAYER 4:  And he talked in his sleep.

PLAYER 1:  And his little body was so hot …

PLAYER 4:  That it burned the Rabbit when he held him close.

PLAYER 1:  Strange people came and went in the nursery.

PLAYER 4:  And a light burned all night. *(PLAYERS 1 and 4 help*

*PLAYER 3 sit down, then stand by his side.)*

PLAYER 2:  And through it all, the little Velveteen Rabbit lay there, hidden from sight under the bedclothes, and he never stirred, for he was afraid that if they found him, someone might take him away, and he knew the Child needed him.

PLAYER 1:  It was a long, weary time, for the Child was too ill to play, and the little Rabbit found it rather dull with nothing to do all day long. But he snuggled down patiently, and looked forward to the time when the Child should be well again.

PLAYER 4:  All sorts of delightful things he planned, and while the Child lay half asleep, he crept up close to the pillow and whispered them in his ear. And then one day, the fever turned and ...

PLAYERS 1, 2, 3, and 4:  The Child got better!

PLAYER 3:  It was a bright, sunny morning and the windows stood wide open. They had carried the Child out onto the porch where he could breathe the fresh air.

PLAYER 2:  While the little Rabbit lay tangled up among the bedclothes, thinking.

PLAYER 3:  The Child was going to go with his parents to the lake tomorrow. Everything was arranged.

PLAYER 2:  They had talked about it all while the Rabbit lay half under the covers with just his head peeping out.

PLAYER 1:  It only remained now for them to carry out the doctor's orders.

PLAYER 4:  The room was to be disinfected, and all the books and toys that the Child had played with in the room must be burnt.

PLAYER 2:  Hurrah! Tomorrow we are going out to the lake!

PLAYER 3:  The Child had often talked about the lake, and he wanted very much to see all the clear blue water and the sandy shore.

PLAYER 4:  *(Assuming Nana)* How about this old Bunny?

PLAYER 1:  *(Assuming Doctor)* That?

PLAYER 3:  Said the doctor.

PLAYER 1:  Why, it's a mass of scarlet fever germs! Burn it at once.

PLAYER 4:  But it is the Child's favorite.

PLAYER 1:  What? Nonsense! Get him a new one. He mustn't have that one anymore.

PLAYER 2:  And so the little Rabbit was put into a sack with the old coloring books and a lot of rubbish, and carried out to the end of the garden by the back alley.

PLAYER 1:  That was a fine place to make a bonfire, only the Child's father was too busy just then to attend to it.

PLAYER 3:  That night the Child slept in a different bedroom, and he had a new bunny to sleep with him. It was a splendid bunny, all white plush with real glass eyes, but the Child was too excited to care very much about it. For tomorrow he was going out to the lake and that in itself was such a wonderful thing that he could think of nothing else.

PLAYER 1:  And while the Child was asleep, dreaming of the lake, the little Rabbit lay among the old coloring books in the back by the alley. And he felt very lonely.

PLAYER 2:  The sack had been left untied, and so by wriggling a bit he was able to get his head through the opening and look out.

PLAYER 4:  He was shivering a little, for he had always been used to sleeping in a proper bed, and by this time his coat had worn so thin and threadbare from hugging that it was no longer any protection to him.

PLAYER 3:  Nearby he could see the thicket of raspberry canes, growing tall and close like tropical jungle, in whose shadow he had played with the Child on bygone mornings.

PLAYER 2:  He thought of those long sunlit hours in the garden— how happy they were—and a great sadness came over him.

PLAYER 4:  He seemed to see them all pass before him, each more beautiful than the other, the fairy huts in the flower bed.

PLAYER 1:  The quiet evenings in the wood when he lay in his nest and watched the little ants run over his paws.

PLAYER 3:  The wonderful day when he first knew he was Real.

PLAYER 1:  He thought of the Skin Horse, so wise and gentle, and all that he had told him.

PLAYER 2:  *(As the Rabbit)* What use is it to be loved, and lose one's beauty and become Real if it all ends like this?

PLAYER 4:  And a tear, a real tear, trickled down his little shabby velvet nose and fell to the ground.

PLAYER 3: And then a strange thing happened. For where the tear had fallen, a flower grew out of the ground, a mysterious flower. It had slender green leaves the color of emeralds, and in the center of the leaves a blossom like a golden cup. *(PLAYER 4 enacts the flower coming out of the ground.)*

PLAYER 2: It was so beautiful that the little Rabbit forgot to cry, and just lay there watching it.

PLAYER 1: And presently the blossom opened, and out of it there stepped a fairy.

PLAYER 3: She was quite the loveliest fairy. Her dress was of pearl and dewdrops, and there were flowers round her neck and in her hair, and her face was like the most perfect flower of all. And she came close to the little Rabbit and said.

PLAYER 4: Little Rabbit, don't you know who I am? I'm the nursery magic fairy. I take care of all the playthings that the children have loved. When they are old and worn out and the children don't need them anymore, then I come and take them away with me and turn them into Real.

PLAYER 2: But wasn't I Real before?

PLAYER 4: You were Real to the Child because he loved you. Now you shall be Real to everyone.

PLAYER 1: It was light now, for the moon had risen. All the forest was beautiful. The dew on the tall grass sparkled like silver dust. In the open glade between the tree trunks, the wild rabbits danced with their shadows on the velvet grass, but when they saw the Fairy, they all stopped and stood around in a ring to stare at her.

PLAYER 4: I've brought you a new playfellow. You must be very kind to him and teach him all he needs to know in Rabbitland, for he is going to live with you forever and ever!

PLAYER 3: And she kissed the little Rabbit and put him down on the grass.

PLAYER 4: Run and play, little Rabbit! *(Pause. PLAYER 4 walks away from PLAYER 2, who sits in usual Center-stage spot.)*

PLAYER 2: *(As to himself)* Run and play? I can't run and play. I haven't any hind legs.

PLAYER 3: He did not know that when the Fairy kissed him, she had changed him altogether. And he might have sat there a long time, too shy to move, if just then something hadn't tickled his nose.

PLAYER 2: *(PLAYER 2 moves hand to scratch nose and discovers whiskers, then feels out his ears, then feels his fur down to legs. PLAYER 2 carefully stands and acknowledges the realization of his physical self.)* I am real. I'm *really* Real!!! *(PLAYER 2 jumps and dances down the aisle.)*

PLAYER 1: And he gave one joyous leap. And the thrill of using those hind legs was so great that he went springing about on the turf, jumping, dancing, and whirling round as the others did.

PLAYER 4: *(As Narrator)* And he grew so excited that when at last he did stop to thank the Fairy, she had gone. *(Pause)*

PLAYER 2: He was a Real Rabbit at last, at home with the other rabbits. *(Slight pause)*

PLAYER 1: Autumn passed and winter, and in the spring when the days grew warm and sunny once again, the Child returned to the wood to play.

PLAYER 4: And while he was playing, a rabbit crept out from the tall grass and peeped at him. He had strange markings under his fur, as though long ago he had been spotted.

PLAYER 2: And about his little soft nose and his round black eyes there was something familiar, so that the Child thought to himself,

PLAYER 3: Why, he looks just like my old Bunny that was lost when I had scarlet fever.

PLAYER 1: And he never knew that it really was his old Bunny, come back to look at the Child who had first helped him to become Real.

*(Close with song.)*

# from "Jabberwocky" by Lewis Carroll

This familiar nonsense poem by Lewis Carroll encourages performers to explore the value of sound combinations and vocal sound effect techniques in classroom performance. It is important in this selection to pay attention to the sense of tempo suggested, and to voice the obscure words with excellent diction and vocal variety that gives fresh insight to the meaning of the poem. This selection is also a good vocal warm-up exercise to pursue in the rehearsal period. Please note opportunities here to integrate a narrator figure and multiple characters in the preliminary classroom performance blueprint.

> 'Twas brillig and the slithy toves
>     Did gyre and gimble in the wabe;
> All mimsy were the borogoves,
>     And the mome raths outgrabe.
>
> "Beware the Jabberwock, my son!
>     The jaws that bite, the claws that catch!
> Beware the Jubjub bird, and shun
>     The frumious Bandersnatch!"
>
> He took his vorpal sword in hand;
>     Long time the manxome foe he sought—
> Then rested he by the Tumtum tree,
>     And stood awhile in thought.
>
> And, as in uffish thought he stood,
>     The Jabberwock, with eyes of flame,
> Came whiffling through the tulgey wood,
>     And burbled as it came!
>
> One, two! One, two! And through and through
>     The vorpal blade went snicker-snack!
> He left it dead, and with its head
>     He went galumphing back.

"And hast thou slain the Jabberwock?
    Come to my arms, my beamish boy!
O frabjous day! Callooh, Callay!"
    He chortled in his joy.

'Twas brillig, and the slithy toves
    Did gyre and gimble in the wabe;
All mimsy were the borogoves,
    And the mome raths outgrabe.

# from *The Importance of Being Earnest*
# by Oscar Wilde

Oscar Wilde's "trivial play for serious people," *The Importance of Being Earnest,* is an amusing British comedy of manners text that depicts the artificial attitudes and customs of polite society. The characters are not realistic, and the imagined obstacles they face are not without moments of amusing invention and intrigue. In the first of the "Wild(e) Card" scenes, Jack—rascal and spendthrift—is being interrogated by Lady Bracknell, who is suspicious of his intentions regarding her daughter, Gwendolyn. Every movement or stance should be elegant; and every exchange of dialog should be crisp.

BRACKNELL: I feel bound to tell you that you are not down on my list of eligible young men, although I have the same list as the dear Duchess of Bolton has. We work together, in fact. However, I am quite ready to enter your name, should your answers be what a really affectionate mother requires. Do you smoke?

JACK: Well, yes, I must admit I smoke.

BRACKNELL: I am glad to hear it. A man should always have an occupation of some kind. There are far too many idle men in London as it is. How old are you?

JACK: Twenty-nine.

BRACKNELL: A very good age to be married at. I have always been of the opinion that a man who desires to get married should know either everything or nothing. Which do you know?

JACK: I know nothing, Lady Bracknell.

BRACKNELL: I am pleased to hear it. I do not approve of anything that tampers with natural ignorance. Ignorance is like a delicate, exotic fruit; touch it and the bloom is gone. The whole theory of modern education is radically unsound. Fortunately in England, at any rate, education produces no effect whatsoever. If it did, it would prove a serious danger to the upper classes, and probably lead to acts of violence in Grosvenor Square. What is your income?

JACK: Between seven and eight thousand a year.

BRACKNELL: In land, or in investments?

JACK: In investments, chiefly.

BRACKNELL: That is satisfactory. What between the duties expected of one during one's lifetime, and the duties exacted from one after one's death, death has ceased to be either a profit or a pleasure. It gives one position, and prevents one from keeping it up. That's all that can be said about land.

JACK: I have a country house with some land, of course, attached to it, about fifteen hundred acres, I believe; but I don't depend on that for my real income. In fact, as far as I can make out, the poachers are the only people who make anything out of it.

BRACKNELL: A country house! How many bedrooms? Well, that point can be cleared up afterwards. You have a town house, I hope? A girl with a simple, unspoiled nature, like Gwendolyn, could hardly be expected to reside in the country.

JACK: Well, I own a house in Belgrave Square, but it is let by the year to Lady Bloxham. Of course, I can get it back whenever I like, at six months' notice.

BRACKNELL: Lady Bloxham? I don't know her.

JACK: Oh, she goes about very little. She is a lady considerably advanced in years.

BRACKNELL: Ah, nowadays, that is no guarantee of respectability of character. What number in Belgrave Square?

JACK: 149.

BRACKNELL: The unfashionable side. I thought there was something.

However, that could be easily altered.

JACK: Do you mean the fashion, or the side?

BRACKNELL: Both, if necessary, I presume. What are your politics?

JACK: Well, I am afraid I really have none. I am a Liberal Unionist.

BRACKNELL: Oh, they count as Tories. They dine with us. Or come in the evening, at any rate. Now to minor matters. Are your parents living?

JACK: I have lost both my parents.

BRACKNELL: To lose one parent, Mr. Worthing, may be regarded as a misfortune; to lose both looks like carelessness. Who was your father? He was evidently a man of some wealth. Was he born in what the radical papers call the purple of commerce, or did he rise from the ranks of the aristocracy?

JACK: I am afraid I really don't know. The fact is, Lady Bracknell, I said I had lost my parents. It would be nearer to the truth to say that my parents seem to have lost me. I don't actually know who I am by birth. I was ... well, I was found.

BRACKNELL: Found!

JACK: The late Mr. Thomas Cardew, an old gentleman of a very charitable and kindly disposition, found me, and gave me the name of Worthing, because he happened to have a first-class ticket to Worthing in his pocket at the time. Worthing is a place in Sussex. It is a seaside resort.

BRACKNELL: Where did the charitable gentleman who had a first-class ticket for this seaside resort find you?

JACK: In a hand-bag.

BRACKNELL: A hand-bag!

JACK: Yes, Lady Bracknell. I was in a hand-bag—a somewhat large, black leather hand-bag, with handles to it—an ordinary hand-bag in fact.

BRACKNELL: In what locality did this Mr. Thomas Cardew come upon this ordinary hand-bag?

JACK: In the cloakroom at Victoria Station. It was given to him in mistake for his own.

BRACKNELL: The cloakroom at Victoria Station?

JACK: Yes. The Brighton line.

BRACKNELL: The line is immaterial, Mr. Worthing. I confess I feel somewhat bewildered by what you have just told me. To be born, or at any rate, bred, in a hand-bag, whether it had handles or not, seems to me to display a contempt for the ordinary decencies of family life that reminds one of the worst excesses of the French Revolution. And I presume you know what that unfortunate movement led to? As for the particular locality in which the hand-bag was found, a cloakroom at a railway station might serve to conceal a social indiscretion—has probably, indeed, been used for that purpose before now—but it could hardly be regarded as an assured basis for a recognized position in good society.

JACK: May I ask you then what you would advise me to do? I need hardly say I would do anything in the world to ensure Gwendolyn's happiness.

BRACKNELL: I would strongly advise you, Mr. Worthing, to acquire some relations as soon as possible, and to make a definite effort to produce at any rate one parent, of either sex, before the season is quite over.

JACK: Well, I don't see how I could possibly manage to do that. I can produce the hand-bag at any moment. It is in my dressing-room at home. I really think that should satisfy you, Lady Bracknell.

BRACKNELL: Me, sir! What has it to do with me? You can hardly imagine that I and Lord Bracknell would dream of allowing our only daughter—a girl brought up with the utmost care—to marry into a cloakroom, and form an alliance with a hand-bag! Good morning, Mr. Worthing!

The second "Wild(e) Card" scene features Gwendolyn, the young lady from the city, and Cecily, an innocent young girl who has always resided in the country, in their first meeting. Each is now engaged to be married to a gentleman who calls himself Ernest Worthing, the name assumed by both Jack and his friend Algernon to appeal to the young ladies' romantic imagination. Hand-held scripts to indicate the frequent reference to diaries and Off-stage focus to locate the garden meeting place are good performance choices.

CECILY: Pray let me introduce myself to you. My name is Cecily Cardew.

GWENDOLYN: Cecily Cardew? What a very sweet name! Something tells me that we are going to be great friends. I like you already more than I can say. My first impressions of people are never wrong.

CECILY: How nice of you to like me so much after we have known each other such a comparatively short time. Pray sit down.

GWENDOLYN: With pleasure!

CECILY: And you will always call me Cecily, won't you?

GWENDOLYN: If you wish.

CECILY: Then that is all quite settled, is it not?

GWENDOLYN: I hope so. Perhaps this might be a favourable opportunity for my mentioning who I am. My father is Lord Bracknell. You have heard of Papa, I suppose?

CECILY: I don't think so.

GWENDOLYN: Outside the family circle, Papa, I am glad to say, is entirely unknown. I think that is quite as it should be. The home seems to me to be the proper sphere for the man. And certainly once a man begins to neglect his domestic duties he becomes painfully effeminate, does he not? And I don't like that. It makes men so very unattractive. Cecily, my Mamma, whose views on education are remarkably strict, has brought me up to be extremely shortsighted; it is part of her system; so do you mind my looking at you through my glasses?

CECILY: Oh, not at all, Gwendolyn! I am very fond of being looked at.

GWENDOLYN: You are here on a short visit, I suppose?

CECILY: Oh, no! I live here.

GWENDOLYN: Really? Your mother, no doubt, or some female relative of advanced years, resides here also?

CECILY: Oh, no. I have no mother, nor, in fact, any relations.

GWENDOLYN: Indeed?

CECILY: My dear guardian, with the assistance of my tutor, Miss Prism, has the arduous task of looking after me.

GWENDOLYN: Your guardian?

CECILY: Yes, I am Mr. Worthing's ward.

GWENDOLYN: Oh! It is strange he never mentioned to me that he had a ward. How very secretive of him! He grows more interesting hourly. I am not sure, however, that the news inspires me with feelings of unmixed delight. I am very fond of you, Cecily; I have liked you ever since I met you! But I am bound to state that now I know that you are Mr. Worthing's ward, I cannot help expressing a wish that you were—well, just a little older than you seem to be—and not quite so very alluring in appearance. In fact, if I may speak candidly—

CECILY: Pray do! I think that whenever one has anything unpleasant to say, one should always be quite candid.

GWENDOLYN: Well, to speak with perfect candour, Cecily, I wish that you were fully forty-two, and more than usually plain for your age. Ernest has a strong, upright nature. He is the very soul of truth and honour. Disloyalty would be as impossible to him as deception. But even men of the noblest possible moral character are extremely susceptible to the influence of the physical charms of others. Modern, no less than ancient history, supplies us with many most painful examples of what I refer to. If it were not so, indeed, history would be quite unreadable.

CECILY: I beg your pardon, Gwendolyn, did you say Ernest?

GWENDOLYN: Yes.

CECILY: Oh, but it is not Mr. Ernest Worthing who is my guardian. It is his brother—his elder brother.

GWENDOLYN: Ernest never mentioned that he had a brother.

CECILY: I am sorry to say that they have not been on good terms for a long time.

GWENDOLYN: Ah! That accounts for it. And now that I think of it, I have never heard any man mention his brother. The subject seems distasteful to most men. Cecily, you have lifted a load from my mind. I was growing almost anxious. It would have been terrible if any cloud had come across a friendship like ours, would it not? Of course you are quite sure it is not Mr. Ernest Worthing who is your guardian?

CECILY: Quite sure. In fact, I am going to be his.

GWENDOLYN: I beg your pardon?

CECILY: Dearest Gwendolyn, there is no reason why I should make a secret of it to you. Our little country newspaper is sure to chronicle the fact next week. Mr. Ernest Worthing and I are engaged to be married!

GWENDOLYN: My darling Cecily, I think there must be some slight error. Mr. Ernest Worthing is engaged to me. The announcement will appear in the Morning Post on Saturday at the latest.

CECILY: I am afraid you must be under some misconception. Ernest proposed to me exactly ten minutes ago.

GWENDOLYN: It is very curious, for he asked me to be his wife yesterday afternoon at 5:30. If you wish to verify the incident, pray do so. I never travel without my diary. One should always have something sensational to read on the train. I am so sorry, dear Cecily, if it is any disappointment to you, but I am afraid I have the prior claim.

CECILY: It would distress me more than I can tell you, dear Gwendolyn, if it caused you any mental or physical anguish, but I feel bound to point out that since Ernest proposed to you he clearly has changed his mind.

GWENDOLYN: If the poor fellow has been entrapped into any foolish promise I shall consider it my duty to rescue him at once, and with a firm hand.

CECILY: Whatever unfortunate entanglement my dear boy may have got into, I will never reproach him with it after we are married.

GWENDOLYN: Do you allude to me, Miss Cardew, as an entanglement? You are presumptuous. On an occasion of this kind it becomes more than a moral duty to speak one's mind. It becomes a pleasure.

CECILY: Do you suggest, Miss Fairfax, that I entrapped Ernest into an engagement? How dare you! This is no time for wearing the shallow mask of manners. When I see a spade I call it a spade.

GWENDOLYN: I am glad to say that I have never seen a spade. It is obvious that our social spheres have been widely different. *(Looks around the garden.)* Are there many interesting walks in the vicinity, Miss Cardew?

CECILY: Oh, yes! A great many. From the top of one of the hills quite close one can see five counties.

GWENDOLYN: Five counties! I don't think I should like that. I hate crowds.

CECILY: I suppose that is why you live in town.

GWENDOLYN: Quite a well-kept garden this is, Miss Cardew.

CECILY: So glad you like it, Miss Fairfax.

GWENDOLYN: I had no idea there were so many flowers in the country.

CECILY: Oh, flowers are as common here, Miss Fairfax, as people are in London.

GWENDOLYN: Personally, I cannot understand how anybody manages to exist in the country, if anybody who is anybody does. The country always bores me to death.

CECILY: Ah! This is what the newspapers call agricultural depression, is it not? I believe the aristocracy are suffering very much from it just at present. It is almost an epidemic amongst them, I have been told. May I offer you some tea, Miss Fairfax?

GWENDOLYN: Thank you. *(Aside)* Detestable girl! But I require tea!

CECILY: Sugar?

GWENDOLYN: No, thank you. Sugar is not fashionable anymore.

CECILY: Cake or bread and butter?

GWENDOLYN: Bread and butter, please. Cake is rarely seen at the best houses nowadays. *(Drinks tea.)* You have filled my tea with lumps of sugar, and though I asked most distinctly for bread and butter, you have given me cake. I am known for the gentleness of my disposition, and the extraordinary sweetness of my nature, but I warn you, Miss Cardew, you may go too far.

CECILY: To save my poor, innocent, trusting boy from the machinations of any other girl there are no lengths to which I would not go.

GWENDOLYN: From the moment I saw you I distrusted you. I felt that you were false and deceitful. I am never deceived in such matters. My first impressions of people are invariably right.

CECILY: It seems to me, Miss Fairfax, that I am trespassing on your valuable time. No doubt you have many other calls of a similar character to make in the neighborhood.

# from *The Canterbury Tales* by Geoffrey Chaucer adapted by Arnold Wengrow

Geoffrey Chaucer's medieval, metrical tale is a relatively long poem that tells a number of individual stories in verse. This adaptation by Arnold Wengrow is a more contemporary text that features a small ensemble, minimal staging, and suggestive change of locale. The adaptation also encourages a highly physical, almost dance-like approach to movement, use of pantomime to indicate scenery, and selective costume pieces like hat, shawl, or cape to suggest change of character.

## Characters

Three Actresses

Four Actors

## Setting

There is a burst of cheerful music as the house lights fade down. Simultaneously, the stage lights cross-fade up, and all the actors and actresses make lively entrances from all directions. Some come bounding on like dancers, with jetés and pirouettes. Others enter like circus acrobats, with handsprings, cartwheels, and somersaults. They ad-lib enthusiastic greetings among themselves (and perhaps to the audience), shake hands, slap backs, exchange hugs, improvise a few dance steps to the music. The men and women are in festive, flirtatious moods.

Quickly, they gather at Center into a group with as many different postures and positions of arms, legs, and bodies as they can imagine. Two of the actors hoist the first actress to their shoulders. Then, extending arms and hands to the audience as if inviting them to join in the merriment, they speak the Prologue with gusto, like a circus ringmaster.

As each actor or actress speaks, he or she takes an expansive pose to capture the audience's attention, and then takes a new pose as he or she finishes speaking and returns to the group. There should be no break between the lines, however, until indicated, so the effect is of an animated, constantly shifting tableau.

## Production Note

This excerpt from the original adaptation of Geoffrey Chaucer's The Canterbury Tales includes only "The Prologue" and "The Wife of Bath's Tale." There are, however, several other well-known theatrical stories in the original text suitable for classroom performance. "The Pardoner's Tale," "The Reeve's Tale," "The Nun Priest Tale," and "The Merchant's Tale" may also be adapted in a more contemporary performance style by students as part of an extended study of the medieval period.

## PROLOGUE

FIRST ACTRESS: When April with his showers sweet ...

SECOND ACTRESS: The drought of March has pierced into the root ...

THIRD ACTRESS: And bathed each vein with liquor that has such power to generate therein and sire the flower;

FIRST ACTOR: When Zephyr also has with his sweet breath quickened again in every grove and heath ...

SECOND and THIRD ACTORS: *(With masculine bravado)* The tender shoots and buds,

FOURTH ACTOR: *(Jogs like a runner.)* And the young sun one-half his course in the sign of the Ram has run,

ACTRESSES: *(In falsetto voices with flirtatious walks, head away from the men.)*
And many little birds make melody that sleep away the night with open eye,

ACTORS: *(Sneaking up behind the women and giving them a quick pinch or squeeze)* So Nature pricks them and their hearts engage!

*(The ACTRESSES squeal and wiggle their fingers in reproach. The Company makes a new, expansive group tableau and immediately belts out the next line. Some of the men pick up two or three of the women as they do so, one hoisting an actress over his shoulders, caveman fashion. Another lifts an actress like a ballerina and a third like a groom carrying his bride over the threshold.)*

COMPANY: Then folks do long to go on pilgrimages!

*(The Company holds the tableau as the music, which has been continuous under the dialog, builds. Then they break the tableau with laughter and exclamations and dance singly or in twos to the edge of the stage. The FIRST ACTOR and FIRST ACTRESS dance together at Center.)*

FIRST ACTOR and FIRST ACTRESS: *(Calling the Company together over the music)* And specially from shire's end of England down to Canterbury they wend.

*(The Company dances back to Center, then forms a line and dances, as if they were riding horses around the stage. The SECOND ACTOR leaps to Center.)*

SECOND ACTOR: It happened, in that season, on a day in Southwark, at the Tabard Inn, as I lay ready to start upon my pilgrimage to Canterbury, full of devout homage, there came at nightfall some nine and twenty in a company.

*(The Company has been dancing behind or around the SECOND ACTOR, and they now hoist him to their shoulders.)*

And pilgrims were they all that toward Canterbury town would ride!

COMPANY: *(Forming a group tableau again and belting out the line)* And pilgrims were they all that toward Canterbury town would ride!

*(Cheers from the Company as the music builds. Then, with cartwheels, somersaults, handsprings, jetés, pirouettes, leaps and bounds, the ACTORS and ACTRESSES take sitting and lounging*

*positions around the stage. The music fades out.*

*During the next sequence, each ACTOR and ACTRESS stands to introduce a variety of characters. The Company responds warmly with applause, ad-libs, laughter to each introduction, and the ACTOR or ACTRESS goes to a new position after each introduction.)*

THIRD ACTOR:   A knight there was, a most distinguished man, who, from the moment that he first began to ride about the world, loved chivalry, truth, honor, generosity, and courtesy.

FOURTH ACTOR:  With him there was his son, a fine young squire, a lover and a lusty bachelor, a lad of fire, wonderfully agile and very strong. *(He picks up one of the women to demonstrate his strength, but also to flirt.)* He was always singing. *(He sings an operatic "Do Re Me Fa So La Ti Do" as he returns the woman to her place.)* Or fluting the whole day long!

FIRST ACTOR:  A friar there was, a very jolly man. In all the orders four was none that can equal his gossip and his well-turned speech.

SECOND ACTOR:   A clerk from Oxford was with us also, who turned to getting knowledge of long ago.he had but little gold within his coffer, but all that he might borrow from a friend. *(He has approached one of the Company and has his hand out for a hand-out; the other ACTOR is reluctant, but the others urge him to be generous.)* On books and learning he would only spend.of study he took the utmost care and heed, and he never spoke one word more than was his need.and an air of moral virtue filled his speech, and gladly would he learn and gladly teach.

*(The women applaud the clerk enthusiastically, but the men, especially the one who lent the clerk the money, are more dubious. Now all the Company rise, and there is a rapid round of introductions, with handshakes and bows.)*

THIRD ACTOR:  A yeoman there was,

FOURTH ACTRESS:  A prioress,

FIFTH ACTRESS:  A nun,

SECOND, THIRD, and FOURTH ACTORS:  Three priests,

THIRD ACTRESS:  A monk,

214

FIRST ACTOR:  A merchant,

FIRST ACTRESS:  A lawyer,

SECOND ACTRESS:  A weaver,

SECOND ACTOR:  A dyer,

FOURTH ACTRESS:  A cook,

THIRD ACTOR:  A sailor,

FIRST ACTOR:  A plowman,

SIXTH ACTRESS:  A doctor,

> *(The Company has formed another tableau.)*

COMPANY:  And pilgrims are we all that toward Canterbury town would ride!

HOST:  *(Indicating for the Company to take their sitting positions again)* Great cheer the Host gave to everyone, saying thus: "Now masters, verily, you are all welcome here, and heartily. For by my truth, and telling you no lie, I have not seen this year a company here in this inn, fitter for a sport than now. I would make you happy, if I knew how. And of a game have I this moment thought to give you joy and cost you naught. You're off to Canterbury — well, God speed! Blessed St. Thomas answer your need! And I don't doubt, before the journey's done you mean to while the time in tales and fun.

So let me propose then for your enjoyment, just as I said, a suitable employment, each of you, to beguile the long day, shall tell two stories as you wend your way to Canterbury; and each of you on coming home, shall tell another two. And he who tells his tale the best shall have a supper at the others' cost. I'll ride along with you myself to Canterbury. Now if you'll agree to what you've heard, tell me at once without another word."

SECOND ACTOR:  *(Rising)* Of course we all agreed ...

> *(All the pilgrims now rise, and talking animatedly among themselves begin to mount their imaginary horses. The music fades in under.)*

FIRST ACTRESS:  And begged him, too, that he should be the judge of our tales ...

SECOND ACTRESS:  And all that he proposed we do.

215

THIRD ACTOR:  So forth we rode ...
THIRD ACTRESS:  With right good cheer!
FOURTH ACTOR:  And began our tales ...
COMPANY:  As you shall hear!
> *(The pilgrims are now cantering in a line as the music builds and the lights fade. End of Prologue)*

## THE WIFE OF BATH'S TALE

### Characters

Wife of Bath
Two Actors
Six Actresses
Knight
Queen
King Arthur
Old Woman
Three Ladies

### Setting

Before the lights fade completely, they come back up. It is midday, and the pilgrims have stopped for their lunch. Pantomime of a picnic. The WIFE OF BATH is flirting with two of the younger men. The women are gossiping about her behind her back.

*(The Director may choose to minimize the connecting scenes between the tales. In this case, when the lights come back up, the pilgrims are grouped in tableau in sitting positions, and the WIFE OF BATH is already at Center and speaks immediately.)*

One of the young men has made a rude suggestion to her and she playfully reprimands him. The young men laugh as she moves to Center. She is a jolly, bawdy soul, full of spirit, quick to take offense, but equally quick to laugh at herself.

WIFE OF BATH: *(Deaf she may be but she knows when she's being talked about, and she approaches the women to scold.)*
    In all the parish there was no good wife
    Should make offering at church before her,
       on my life!
    And if one did, indeed so wrath was she
    It put her out of all her charity.
    *(Returning to flirt with the men)*
    On Sunday, she wore the finest kerchiefs on her
      head.
    Her hose were of the choicest scarlet red.
    *(She lifts her skirt to show her red stockings, which makes the men laugh and whistle and the women cluck.)*
    And likewise, her shoes were soft and new.
FIRST ACTOR: *(Going to her and putting an arm around her waist)*
    Bold was her face, handsome, and red of hue.
    *(Steals a big kiss on her cheek.)*
WIFE OF BATH: *(Pushing him away in mock offense, but, of course, pleased)*
    A respectable woman all her life! What's more
    She'd brought five husbands in all to the church
      door.
SECOND ACTOR: *(He has joined in the fun and steals a kiss.)*
    Not counting other company in youth!
WIFE OF BATH: *(Giving both ACTORS playful slaps)*
    But of that there's no need to speak, in truth.
    *(The Company laughs. FIRST and SECOND ACTOR now pick her up by the arms, so that her feet appear to walk without touching the ground.)*
    Three times she journeyed to Jerusalem;
    Seen many strange rivers and passed over them.
    At Rome she'd been, and she'd been in Bologne.
    In Spain at Santiago, and at Cologne.
    She could tell much of her travels, by the way.
    *(The ACTORS, who have been carrying her about, set her down with a jolt.)*

FIRST ACTOR:  She was gap-toothed besides ...
SECOND ACTOR:  It is no lie to say.
>   *(She shows her teeth proudly and backs the young men to a sitting position.)*
WIFE OF BATH:  But she knew the remedies for love's mischances,
>   For in that art she'd learned all the old, old
>   >   dances!
>   *(She takes Center stage and speaks expansively to the group.)*
>   "Experience is the best teacher,
>   And that's good enough for me,
>   And all my experience just goes to show
>   That marriage, good friends, is a misery and a
>   >   woe.
>   Now thanks be to God the Father evermore
>   Five husbands have I had at the church door.
>   Yes, it's a fact I've had so many,
>   And all worthy men, as good as any.
>   But someone told me not so long ago,
>   That since Our Lord himself would never go
>   To a wedding, save that at Cana in Galilee,
>   Thus, by this same example, showed He me
>   That I never should have married more than
>   >   once.
>   Lo and behold! What sharp words, for the
>   >   nonce,
>   But well I know and say, and do not lie,
>   God bade us all increase and multiply;
>   That worthy text can I well understand.
>   And well I know my husbands were under God's
>   >   command
>   To leave father and mother, and cleave to me;
>   But there was no specific mention of what the
>   >   number was to be.
>   So why not take two or even eight?
>   And why speak ill of the married state?
>   Now, there's the case of old King Solomon;

I understand he had many more wives than one;
A thousand, I've heard; would God it were
    permitted me
To be refreshed one-half as oft as he!
God knows, this king, one must admit,
On each first night had a merry fit
With each of them, so much was he alive!
So praise be to God that I have wedded five!
And I'll welcome the sixth wherever he appears.
I can't keep continent for years and years.
Wedding's no sin as far as I can learn;
Better to marry than to burn.
Show me a text where God disparages
Or sets a prohibition on marriages!
Men may to woman virginity advise,
But that's advice, no commandment, in my eyes.
And certainly, if there were no seed sown,
Where then should new virginity be grown?
God summons folk unto him in many ways;
And if in chastity some are called to live their
    days,
Why, He speaks to those who would live perfectly.
But by your leave, my friends, that's not for me.
I will bestow the flower of life, and the honey,
Upon the acts and fruit of matrimony.
Now, friends, as I hope to drink good ale,
I'll go on and tell my tale.
*(As the lights fade, there is a musical bridge while the actors
exit. If the stage is large enough, it is also effective to have the
actors clear to the sides of the stage and sit in view until time for
their entrances as characters in the tale. When the lights come
back up, the KNIGHT is on stage, riding an imaginary horse.
Music under and out during his speech.)*
KNIGHT:  Long, long ago, in the days of King Arthur,
    A knight at his court, a lusty bachelor,
    One spring day, came riding by a river.

219

*(MAIDEN enters and walks slowly ahead of the KNIGHT. She looks back several times with come-hither glances.)*

He saw a maiden walking all forlorn,

Ahead of him, alone as she was born.

*(Looking around to make sure no one is watching, he catches her by the waist from behind. She squeals but offers little resistance. He locks her in a dramatic "movie" embrace, or she can take the initiative and lock him in the embrace.)*

And in spite of all she did and said,

Straightaway by force he took her maidenhead.

*(After the kiss, the MAIDEN squeals at length in a high-pitched voice, ad libs "You naughty man," slaps the KNIGHT and runs off. At the same time, two of the King's OFFICERS enter quickly from one side, while KING ARTHUR, the QUEEN, and three LADIES enter from the other. The OFFICERS lift the KNIGHT by his arms and carry him to the KING, where they deposit him on his knees. The OFFICERS exit.)*

QUEEN: *(The LADIES chatter and twitter as she speaks.)*

This act of violence made such a stir

And caused such appealing unto King Arthur ...

KING ARTHUR: *(All the nagging is getting on his nerves and he raises his hand threateningly as much to silence the women as to condemn the KNIGHT.)*

That the king condemned this knight to lose his head.

According to the law, he was as good as dead.

*(The QUEEN and the LADIES have begun to find the KNIGHT very attractive, and he might have given them an appealing look or two, or a wink, or even blown them a few pretend kisses.)*

LADIES: But then the ladies ...

QUEEN: And the Queen

Prayed to the King so long to show him grace ...

*(She strokes the KING's arm entreatingly.)*

KING ARTHUR: *(Sighing with irritation)*

That he relented at last and gave the case

To the Queen, to hear and decide, as she

    should choose,

To show him mercy — or refuse.

QUEEN: The Queen thanked the King with all her might,

*(She gives him a big smack on the cheek, and he exits in vexation. She crooks her finger at the KNIGHT coyly. He rises and approaches her. The LADIES giggle behind the QUEEN's back.)*

And afterwards she summoned the knight.

"I'll grant your life, if you answer as I require.

What is the thing in all the world that women
     most desire?

*(More giggles from the LADIES. The QUEEN suddenly becomes imperious.)*

You have twelve months and a day, to search
     and learn

Sufficient answer in this grave concern.

*(The KNIGHT is very perplexed and starts to leave. She calls him back.)*

And remember, you're on your honor to return."

KNIGHT: The knight was sad, and sorrowfully he sighed.

But there! All other choices were denied.

And in the end he chose to go away

And to return after a year and a day

With such an answer as God might convey.

*(He bows. The QUEEN and LADIES exit, gossiping and giggling.)*

So he took his leave and went his way.

*(The KNIGHT begins to circle the stage. During the next sequence he encounters several women who are crossing the stage briskly in various directions, pausing only long enough to give him their answers.)*

He knocked at every house, searched every place

Wherein he hoped to find he had the grace

To learn what women love the most.

He never touched a country, town, or coast

Where he could find what seemed to be ...

*(FIRST and SECOND ACTRESSES are entering from opposite directions and pass each other and the KNIGHT at the same time.)*

FIRST ACTRESS: Two persons ...

SECOND ACTRESS:  Who were willing to agree.

> *(FIRST and SECOND ACTRESSES glare at each other and continue their opposite ways. The other ACTRESSES are entering and passing the KNIGHT.)*

THIRD ACTRESS:  Some said that women wanted wealth and treasure.

FOURTH ACTRESS:  Honor, some said.

FIFTH ACTRESS:  *(Giggling)* Fun and pleasure.

SIXTH ACTRESS:  Gorgeous clothes, said some ...

FIRST ACTRESS:  *(Seductively)* And others, fun in bed.

SECOND ACTRESS:  Often to be widowed and often to be re-wed.

> *(The ACTRESSES exit.)*

KNIGHT:  The knight this tale is told about

> Perceived at last he never would find out
> What it is that women love the best.

> *(He begins crossing in the opposite direction.)*

> Most saddened was the spirit in his breast
> As home he went; he dared delay no longer.

> *(All the ACTRESSES enter together from one side, holding hands, and they swirl and snake their way across the stage. They twirl around the KNIGHT as he approaches them.)*

> As he rode in a dejected mood,
> Suddenly he saw at the edge of a wood
> Four and twenty ladies, maybe more, dancing.
> Eagerly he approached
> That from them some wisdom he might learn.
> But before he came to where they were,
> Dancers and dance all vanished into air.

> *(The ACTRESSES, except for one, have exited.)*

> There wasn't a living creature to be seen.

> *(One ACTRESS has broken off from the chain as it swirled around the KNIGHT and waits huddled to one side behind the KNIGHT, who is watching where the other women exited.)*

OLD WOMAN:  *(ACTRESS contorts her face and body and speaks with an old crone's voice.)*

> Save one old woman crouched upon the green.

KNIGHT:  *(Going over to her in curiosity but recoiling as she rises*

*with her twisted body and distorted face.)*
A fouler-looking creature I suppose
Could scarce be imagined.

OLD WOMAN: *(She leers lasciviously at the young KNIGHT and walks around him, pawing and patting him; he finds her repulsive.)*
Sir Knight, there's no road on from here.
Tell me what you're looking for, my dear.
Perchance you'll find it best for you.
We old women know a thing or two.
*(OLD WOMAN laughs her crone's laugh and tries to give him a kiss, but he backs away.)*

KNIGHT: Dear mother, I am a dead man unless I can tell
What women most desire.
Tell me that and I'll pay you well.

OLD WOMAN: *(Grabbing his hand in a vise-like grip, she strokes his hand greedily.)*
Give me your hand, and pledge to do
Whatever I may require of you,
If what I ask lies within your might.
And I'll give you your answer before the night.

KNIGHT: *(Dubious, but desperate)*
Upon my honor, I agree.

OLD WOMAN: *(Gleeful with her prize)*
Then I guarantee your life is safe.
*(She roughly pulls the KNIGHT's head close to her face and appears to be trying to kiss him.)*
She whispered a sentence in his ear,
And bade him be glad and have no fear.
*(The OLD WOMAN laughs and, still holding tightly on the KNIGHT's hand, leads him eagerly, making little kissing gestures, to one side of the stage, where the QUEEN and the LADIES have entered.)*

KNIGHT: *(Shaking her off with relief)*
When they were come into the court, this knight
Said he had kept his promise, as was right,
And ready was his answer, as he said.

LADY 1:  Many a noble wife ...

LADY 2:  And many a maid ...

LADY 3:  And many a widow, since they are so wise ...

QUEEN:  And the Queen herself sitting as high justice,
  Were assembled to hear his answer there.
  *(She beckons the KNIGHT to approach.)*
  And then the knight was bidden to appear.
  Command was given for silence in the hall,
  And then that the knight should tell
     them all
  What thing all worldly women love the best.

KNIGHT:  "My liege and lady," said he,
  "A woman desires that same sovereignty
  Over her husband as over her lover.
  She wants mastery, he must not be above her.
  This is your greatest wish. *(He kneels.)* Whether
     you kill
  Me or spare me, I await your will."
  *(The LADIES and the QUEEN are pleased with the answer and
  use the next lines to confer among themselves.)*

LADY 1:  In all the court there was no wife ...

LADY 2:  Or maid ...

LADY 3:  Or widow that denied the thing he said.

LADIES:  *(In unison)* All agreed!

QUEEN:  *(Goes to the KNIGHT, indicates for him to rise, embraces
  him, perhaps a bit too warmly.)*
  He was worthy to have his life.

OLD WOMAN:  *(Coming forward; the KNIGHT and the LADIES recoil.)*
  Mercy, my sovereign lady Queen!
  Before the court's dismissed, give me my right.
  'Twas I who taught this answer to this knight;
  For which he swore and pledged his honor to it,
  That the first thing I asked of him he'd do it,
  So far as it should lie within his might.
  Before this court, now, I ask you, Sir Knight,
  To keep your word and take me for your wife.

*(Gasps from the QUEEN and LADIES as the OLD WOMAN clutches at the KNIGHT.)*
Well you know that I have saved your life.
If this be false, deny it upon your sword.
KNIGHT: Alas, old lady, by Our Lord,
    That I so promised I will not protest.
    But for God's love pray make a new request.
    Take all my wealth and let my body go.
    *(He tries to dislodge himself from her grip, but she holds on all the tighter.)*
OLD WOMAN: Nay then, curse me if I do!
    For though I may be foul and old and poor,
    I will not, for all the gold and precious ore
    That from the earth is dug or lies above,
    Be aught except your wife and your true love.
    *(She is trying to give him kisses again and is running her fingers over his arms.)*
KNIGHT: *(Pulls free.)* My love! Nay, rather my damnation!
    *(To the QUEEN, seeking her damnation)*
    Alas! That any of my place and station
    Should ever make so foul a misalliance.
    *(The QUEEN shakes her head "No" sternly and exits with all except LADY 2, who watches sympathetically.)*
    But in the end his pleading and defiance ...
OLD WOMAN: *(Gleefully goes to the KNIGHT and giving him a hammerlock, drags him to another part of the stage.)*
    Went for nothing! He was forced to wed,
    And take his ancient wife and go to bed.
    *(She gives a girlish giggle in her crone's voice and paws the KNIGHT hungrily.)*
LADY 2: Now, some may well suspect
    A lack of care, since we neglect
    To tell you of the joy and all the array    .
    That at the wedding feast were seen that day.
    Make a brief answer to this charge I shall;
    I say, there was no joy or feast at all. *(Exits.)*

KNIGHT:  Nothing but heaviness and grievous sorrow,
For privately he wedded her on the morrow.
*(The OLD WOMAN gives him a big kiss and a smothering bear hug; he breaks free, wipes his mouth ostentatiously, and crosses away from her.)*
And all day long he stayed hidden like an owl.
*(Each time he turns back to look at her, she blows him coy little kisses and primps her hair and twisted face.)*
So sad was he, his wife looked so foul!
*(Seeing that he is not going to take the initiative, the OLD WOMAN lurches over to the KNIGHT and drags him to the "bed.")*
Great was the anguish churning in his head
When at last she brought him to their bed.
*(The "bed" can be accomplished in a variety of ways. One method is to have six actors/actresses enter quickly and form the bed with their bodies: A person for each of the four posters, and one each for the headboard and footboard. The KNIGHT and the OLD WOMAN would then stand in the middle of the group. If this method is used, it is effective if the "bed" people are not just neutral, but, keeping their bodies frozen, react with horror and titillation on their faces to the events taking place. A second method is to have two actors bring on a large cardboard cartoon of a bed to be held in a vertical position. The OLD WOMAN and the KNIGHT would then stand behind it, with only their heads and shoulders showing.)*
He rolled about and turned to and fro.
OLD WOMAN:  *(Coy and girlish; looks over at him and bats her eyes. He keeps moving farther and farther away; she keeps edging closer and closer.)*
His old wife lay there, always smiling so,
Until she finally said, "Bless us, husband,
     my dear,
Is this how knights and wives get on together
     here.
Is this the custom in King Arthur's house?
Are all his knights so fastidious?

226

I am your own true love, and, more, your wife;
And I am she who saved your very life.
And truly, since I've never done you wrong,
Why do you treat me so, this first night long?
You're carrying on as a man half-witted!
Say, for God's love, what sin have I committed?
I shall amend it, if you tell me how."
KNIGHT:  Amend it? Alas, never, now!
Nothing can ever be right again.
You are so old and so abominably plain
And so poor and of family so low born,
*(Each of his accusations causes her to pout or sniff or screw up her face even more.)*
It's little wonder that I toss and turn.
Would God my heart would break within my breast!
OLD WOMAN:  Is that the cause of your unrest?
KNIGHT:  Yes, truly, and do you wonder?
OLD WOMAN:  Now, sir, I could amend what you suppose a blunder,
If I cared to, and that within days three,
If you would but bear yourself courteously towards me.
But since you speak of gentle birth
Such as descends from old wealth,
And claim for that you are a gentleman,
I say such arrogance is not worth a hen.
Find him who is most virtuous,
Alone or publicly, and who most tries
To do whatever noble deeds he can,
And take him for the greatest gentleman.
He is not gentle, be he duke or earl,
If acting churlish makes a man a churl.
And therefore, husband dear, I thus conclude:
Although my ancestors perhaps are rude,
Yet may the High Lord God, and so hope I,
Grant me the grace to live right virtuously.

227

Now since you say that I am foul and old,
Then fear you not to be made a cuckold;
For dirt and age, I'm sure you'll agree,
Are mighty wardens over chastity.
Nevertheless, since I know your delight,
I'll satisfy your worldly appetite.
You have two choices; which one will you try?
To have me foul and old until I die
And be to you a true and humble wife,
And never anger you in all my life;
Or else to have me young and very fair
And take your chance with those who will repair
Unto your house, and all because of me,
Or in some other place, as well may be.
Now choose which you like better and reply.

KNIGHT: The knight considered, and did sorely sigh,
But at the last replied as you shall hear:
"My lady and my love, and wife so dear,
I put myself in your wise care.
Do you choose which may be the best
To bring us both most honor and most rest.
What pleases you suffices me."

OLD WOMAN: Then have I got of you the mastery,
Since I may choose and rule as I see fit?

KNIGHT: Yes, truly, wife, that's it.

OLD WOMAN: *(The KNIGHT is turned away from the OLD WOMAN.*
*As she speaks, her voice and body gradually become unknotted,*
*and she becomes a beautiful young woman. The transformation*
*can also be assisted if her hair as the OLD WOMAN was in loose*
*twists, which she now undoes to let her long hair fall free.)*
Kiss me, no quarrels, by my oath
And word of honor, you'll find me both.
That is, both fair and faithful as a wife;
May I go howling mad, and take my life
If I be not to you as good, as true
As ever wife was since the world was new.

228

And now, at dawn, if I'm not as fairly seen
As any lady, empress, or great queen
Between the distant east and west,
Do with my life and death as you like best.
Now turn you round, husband, and look at me.
KNIGHT: *(Turning to face her)*
And when indeed the knight had looked to see ...
OLD WOMAN: Lo, she was fair and young and rich in charms.
KNIGHT: In joy he clasped her in his arms;
    *(They embrace.)*
His heart went bathing in bath of blisses
And he gave his wife a thousand kisses.
OLD WOMAN: And she obeyed in fullest measure
With all that would delight and give him
    pleasure.
*(The WIFE OF BATH has entered and is watching this happy resolution. The "bed," too, if composed of people, is smiling. Musical tag comes in under.)*
WIFE OF BATH: And they lived happily ever after until the
    end.
Now I pray for husbands young and fresh.
And the good luck to outlive them all!
*(The lights fade, the music builds, then music fades under and out.)*

# from "The Little Girl and the Wolf" by James Thurber

This James Thurber fable presents a humorous view of the classic children's story with a modern, upbeat moral that is sure to provoke thoughtful laughter. There are inventive performance opportunities here for a narrator figure and the two title characters. The text lends itself to open-space staging and pantomime. Traditional theatrical ingredients like an oversized script for the Narrator, suggestive costumes for the characters, hand-props, and contemporary music should provide additional dimensions of light-hearted satire to a classroom adaptation or staged reading.

One afternoon a big wolf waited in a dark forest for a little girl to come along carrying a basket of food to her grandmother. Finally a little girl did come along and she was carrying a basket of food. "Are you carrying that basket to your grandmother?" asked the wolf. The little girl said yes, she was. So the wolf asked her where her grandmother lived and the little girl told him and he disappeared into the wood.

When the little girl opened the door of her grandmother's house she saw that there was somebody in bed with a nightcap and nightgown on. She had approached no nearer than twenty-five feet from the bed when she saw that it was not her grandmother but the wolf, for even in a nightcap a wolf does not look any more like your grandmother than the Metro-Goldwyn lion looks like Calvin Coolidge. So the little girl took an automatic out of her basket and shot the wolf dead.

Moral: It is not so easy to fool little girls nowadays as it used to be.

---

# from *The Gap* by Eugene Ionesco

Theatre of the absurd texts like Eugene Isonesco's *The Gap* provide a flood of images, signs, and symbols that provoke an audience to reason and to think. The juxtaposition of the familiar with the strange in a series of apparently disconnected events is a typical theatre of the absurd scripting principle, and encourages classroom performances that focus on character actions rather than dialog. In the text that follows, performers should pay careful attention to gestures, facial expressions, and movement to suggest the interior feelings and thoughts of the characters. The text may also be performed using Off-stage focus.

WIFE: Dear friend, tell me all.

FRIEND: I don't know what to say.

WIFE: I know.

FRIEND: I heard the news last night. I did not want to call you. At the same time I couldn't wait any longer. Please forgive me for coming so early with such terrible news.

WIFE: He didn't make it! How terrible! We were still hoping ...

FRIEND: It's hard, I know. He still had a chance. Not much of one. We had to expect it.

WIFE: I didn't expect it. He was always so successful. He could always manage somehow, at the last moment.

FRIEND: In that state of exhaustion. You shouldn't have let him!

WIFE: What can we do, what can we do? How awful!

FRIEND: Come on, dear friend, be brave. That's life.

WIFE: I feel faint. I'm going to faint.

FRIEND: I shouldn't have blurted it out like that. I'm sorry.

WIFE: No, you were right to do so. I had to find out somehow or other.

FRIEND: I should have prepared you, carefully.

WIFE: I've got to be strong. I can't help thinking of him, the wretched man. I hope they won't put it in the papers. Can we count on the journalists' discretion?

FRIEND: Close your door. Don't answer the telephone. It will get around. You could go to the country. In a couple of months, when you are better, you'll come back, you'll go on with your life. People forget such things.

WIFE: People won't forget so fast. That's what they're all waiting for. Some friends will feel sorry, but the others, the others ...

*(The ACADEMICIAN enters, fully dressed in uniform with decorations and his sword on his side.)*

ACADEMICIAN: Up so early, my dear? *(To the FRIEND)* You've come early, too. What's happening? Do you have the final results?

WIFE: What a disgrace!

FRIEND: You mustn't crush him like this, dear friend. *(To the ACADEMICIAN)* You have failed.

ACADEMICIAN: Are you quite sure?

FRIEND: You should never have tried to pass the baccalaureate examination.

ACADEMICIAN: They failed me. The rats! How dare they do this to me!

FRIEND: The marks were posted late in the evening.

ACADEMICIAN: Perhaps it was difficult to make them out in the dark. How could you read them?

FRIEND: They had set up spotlights.

ACADEMICIAN: They're doing everything to ruin me.

FRIEND: I passed by in the morning; the marks were still up.

ACADEMICIAN: You could have bribed the concierge into pulling them down.

FRIEND: That's exactly what I did. Unfortunately the police were there. Your name heads the list of those who failed. Everyone's standing in line to get a look. There's an awful crush.

ACADEMICIAN: Who's there? The parents of the candidates?

FRIEND: Not only they.

WIFE: All your rivals, all your colleagues must be there. All those you attacked in the press for ignorance; your undergraduates;

your graduate students; all those you failed when you were chairman of the board of examiners.

ACADEMICIAN: I am discredited! But I won't let them. There must be some mistake.

FRIEND: I saw the examiners. I spoke with them. They gave me your marks. Zero in mathematics.

ACADEMICIAN: I had no scientific training.

FRIEND: Zero in Greek, zero in Latin.

WIFE: You, a humanist, the spokesman for humanism, the author of that famous treatise "The Defense of Poesy and Humanism."

ACADEMICIAN: I beg your pardon, but my book concerns itself with twentieth-century humanism *(To the FRIEND)* What about composition? What grade did I get in composition?

FRIEND: Nine hundred. You have nine hundred points.

ACADEMICIAN: That's perfect. My average must be all the way up.

FRIEND: Unfortunately not. They're marking on the basis of two thousand. The passing grade is one thousand.

ACADEMICIAN: They must have changed the regulations.

WIFE: They didn't change them just for you. You have a frightful persecution complex.

ACADEMICIAN: I tell you they changed them.

FRIEND: They went back to the old ones, back to the time of Napoleon.

ACADEMICIAN: Utterly outmoded. Besides, when did they make those changes? It isn't legal. I'm chairman of the Baccalaureate Commission of the Ministry of Public Education. They didn't consult me, and they cannot make any changes without my approval. I'm going to expose them. I'm going to bring government charges against them.

WIFE: Darling, you don't know what you're doing. You're in your dotage. Don't you recall handing in your resignation just before taking the examination so that no one could doubt the complete objectivity of the board of examiners?

ACADEMICIAN: I'll take it back.

WIFE: You should never have taken that test! I warned you. After all, it's not as if you needed it. But you have to collect all the honors, don't you? You're never satisfied. What did you need this diploma for? Now all is lost. You have your Doctorate, and your Master's, your high school diploma, your elementary school certificate, and even the first part of the baccalaureate.

ACADEMICIAN: There was a gap.

WIFE: No one suspected it.

ACADEMICIAN: But *I* knew it. Others might have found out. I went to the office of the Registrar and asked for a transcript of my record. They said to me: "Certainly Professor, Mr. President, Your Excellency." Then they looked up my file, and the Chief Registrar came back looking embarrassed indeed. He said: "There's something very peculiar, very peculiar. You have your Master's, certainly, but it's no longer valid." I asked him why, of course. He answered: "There's a gap behind your Master's. I don't know how it happened. You must have registered and been accepted at the university without having passed the second part of the baccalaureate examination."

FRIEND: And then?

WIFE: Your Master's degree is no longer valid?

ACADEMICIAN: No, not quite. It's suspended. "The duplicate you are asking for will be delivered to you upon completion of the baccalaureate. Of course you will pass the examination with no trouble." That's what I was told, so you see now that I had to take it.

FRIEND: Your husband, dear friend, wanted to fill the gap. He's a conscientious person.

WIFE: It's clear you don't know him as I do. That's not it at all. He wants fame, honors. He never has enough. What does one diploma more or less matter? No one notices them anyway, but he sneaks in at night, on tip-toe, into the living room, just to look at them, and count them.

ACADEMICIAN: What else can I do when I have insomnia?

FRIEND: The questions asked at the baccalaureate are usually known in advance. You were admirably situated to get this particular information. You could also have sent in a replacement to take the test for you. One of your students, perhaps. Or if you wanted to take the test without people realizing that you already knew the questions, you could have sent your maid to the black market, where one can buy them.

ACADEMICIAN: I don't understand how I could have failed in my composition. I filled three sheets of paper. I treated the subject fully, taking into account the historical background. I interpreted the situation accurately ... at least plausibly. I didn't deserve a bad grade.

FRIEND: Do you recall the subject?

ACADEMICIAN: Hum ... let's see ...

FRIEND: He doesn't even remember what he discussed.

ACADEMICIAN: I do ... wait ... hum.

FRIEND: The subject to be treated was the following: "Discuss the influence of Renaissance painters on the novelists of the Third Republic." I have here a photostatic copy of your examination paper. Here is what you wrote.

ACADEMICIAN: *(Grabs the photostat and reads.)* "The trial of Benjamin: After Benjamin was tried and acquitted, the assessors holding a different opinion from that of the President murdered him, and condemned Benjamin to the suspensions of his civic rights, imposing on him a fine of nine hundred francs ..."

FRIEND: That's where the nine hundred points came from.

ACADEMICIAN: "Benjamin appealed his case ... Benjamin appealed his case ..." I can't make out the rest. I've always had bad handwriting. I ought to have taken a typewriter along with me.

WIFE: Horrible handwriting, scribbling and crossing out; ink spots didn't help you much.

ACADEMICIAN: *(Continues reading after having retrieved the text his WIFE had pulled from his hand.)* "Benjamin appealed his case. Flanked by policemen dressed in zouave uniforms ... in zouave uniforms ..." It's getting dark. I can't see the rest ... and I don't have my glasses.

WIFE: What you've written has nothing to do with the subject.

FRIEND: Your wife's quite right, friend. It has nothing to do with the subject.

ACADEMICIAN: Yes, it has. Indirectly.

FRIEND: Not even indirectly.

235

ACADEMICIAN: Perhaps I chose the second question.

FRIEND: There was only one.

ACADEMICIAN: Even if there was only that one, I treated another quite adequately. I went to the end of the story. I stressed the important points, explaining the motivation of the characters, highlighting their behavior. I explained the mystery, making it plain and clear. There was even a conclusion at the end. I can't make out the rest. *(To the FRIEND)* Can you read it?

FRIEND: It's illegible. I don't have any glasses either.

WIFE: *(Taking the text)* It's illegible and I have excellent eyes. You pretended to write. Mere scribbling.

ACADEMICIAN: That's not true. I've even provided a conclusion. It's clearly marked here in heavy print: "Conclusion or sanction ... Conclusion or sanction ..." They can't get away with it. I'll have this examination rendered null and void.

WIFE: Since you treated the wrong subject, and treated it badly, setting down only titles, and writing nothing in between, the mark you received is justified. You'd lose your case.

FRIEND: You'd most certainly lose. Drop it. Take a vacation.

ACADEMICIAN: You're always on the side of the Others.

WIFE: After all, these professors know what they're doing. They haven't been granted their rank for nothing. They passed examinations, received serious training. They know the rules of composition.

FRIEND: For mathematics, a movie star. For Greek, one of the Beatles. For Latin, the champion of the automobile race, and many others.

ACADEMICIAN: These people aren't any more qualified than I am. And for composition?

FRIEND: A woman, a secretary in the editorial division of the review *Yesterday, the Day Before Yesterday, and Today.*

ACADEMICIAN: Now I know. This wretch gave me a poor grade out of spite because I never joined the political party. It's an act of vengeance. But I have ways and means of rendering the examination null and void. I'm going to call the President.

WIFE: Don't! You'll make yourself look even more ridiculous. *(To the FRIEND)* Please try to restrain him. He listens to you more than to me. *(The FRIEND shrugs his shoulders, unable to cope with the situation. The WIFE turns to her husband, who has just lifted the receiver off the hook.)* Don't call!

ACADEMICIAN: *(On the telephone)* Hello. Bill? It is I ... What? What did you say? But, listen my dear friend ... but, listen to me. Hello! Hello! *(Puts down the receiver.)*

FRIEND: What did he say?

ACADEMICIAN: He said ... He said ... "I don't want to talk to you. My mummy won't let me make friends with boys at the bottom of the class." Then he hung up on me.

WIFE: You should have expected it. All is lost. How could you do this to me? How could you do this to me?

ACADEMICIAN: Think of it! I lectured at the Sorbonne, at Oxford, at American universities. Ten thousand theses have been written on my work; hundreds of critics have analyzed it. I hold an *honoris causa* doctorate from Amsterdam as well as a secret university Chair with the Duchy of Luxembourg. I received the Nobel Prize three times. The King of Sweden himself was amazed by my erudition. A doctorate *honoris causa, honoris causa* ... and I failed the baccalaureate examination!

WIFE: Everyone will laugh at us! *(The ACADEMICIAN takes off his sword and breaks it on his knee.)*

FRIEND: *(Picking up the pieces)* I wish to preserve these in memory of our ancient glory. *(The ACADEMICIAN is tearing down his diplomas and decorations, throwing them on the floor, and stepping on them.)*

WIFE: *(Trying to salvage the remains)* Don't do this! Don't! That's all we've got left.

**Curtain**

# from "Ringing the Bells" by Anne Sexton

Anne Sexton is often viewed as a "confessional poet" who reveals her most private thoughts in instinctive, almost mechanical imagery. Knowing that the author was frequently institutionalized, and ultimately committed suicide, should provide meaningful performance insight in "Ringing the Bells." The poem lends itself to simple staging, a number of voiceless supporting performers, and sound effects that punctuate the author's point of view. The poem may also serve as an introduction to a later, compiled script that features a number of Anne Sexton's narratives detailing periods of institutional confinement.

And this is the way they ring
the bells in Bedlam
and this is the bell-lady
who comes each Tuesday morning
to give us a music lesson
and because the attendants make you go
like bees caught in the wrong hive,
we are the circle of crazy ladies
who sit in the lounge of the mental house
and smile at the smiling woman
who passes us each a bell,
who points at my hand
that holds my bell, E flat,
and this is the gray dress next to me
who grumbles as if it were special
to be old, to be old,
and this is the small hunched squirrel girl
on the other side of me
who picks at the hairs over her lip,
who picks at the hairs over her lip all day,
and this is how the bells really sound,
as untroubled and clean

as a workable kitchen,
and this is always my bell responding
to my hand that responds to the lady
who points at me, E flat;
and although we are no better for it,
they tell you to go. And you do.

# from "The Elephant's Child" by Rudyard Kipling adapted by Melvin R. White

Rudyard Kipling's vivid stories of talking animals and exotic locales continue to enchant and fascinate readers of all ages. This adaptation of "The Elephant's Child," by Melvin R. White, is suitable for group reading or classroom performance. This adaptation is also an excellent introduction to basic Readers Theatre performance principles for children or adults performing for children, and may be staged with or without theatrical ingredients like costumes, movement, music, and props.

## Cast of Characters

Storyteller — Effective storyteller, warm, friendly, and intimate with the audience

Elephant's Child — Large boy with juvenile, "different" voice, the "shining halo" type; innocent but curious

Aunt Ostrich — A screeching soprano, possibly tall and thin

Uncle Giraffe — A tall man; timid-soul type

Aunt Hippopotamus — Resembles the large woman in the circus; has gruff voice, but is ladylike

Uncle Baboon — An older man, solemn and dignified; has a whiskered voice

Mr. Kolokolo Bird — An obliging and charming man

Mr. Python-Rock-Snake — Literal and precise, with excessive sibilance ("s" sound)

Mr. Crocodile — The villain; deep-voiced, with superb diction

*("Spanking" music may be provided by either a guitarist or violinist if desired.)*

STORYTELLER: In the high and far-off times, there was once an Elephant, a new Elephant, an Elephant's Child, who was full of 'satiable curiosity—that means he asked ever so many questions. He lived in Africa, and he filled all Africa with his 'satiable curiosity. He asked his tall aunt, the Ostrich: *(Music is out by now.)*

ELEPHANT: *(Lumbers over to her.)* Aunt Ostrich, why do your tail-feathers grow just so?

OSTRICH: Naughty Elephant's Child, you ask too many questions. Come here!

STORYTELLER: And his tall aunt, the Ostrich, spanked him *(Spanking music. OSTRICH may pantomime spanking in time to the music, with ELEPHANT reacting to each pantomimed blow physically and vocally.)* with her hard, hard claw. Then he asked his tall uncle, the Giraffe:

ELEPHANT: *(Lumbers over to him.)* Uncle Giraffe, what makes your skin so spotty?

GIRAFFE: Naughty Elephant's Child, you are too inquisitive. Come here!

STORYTELLER: And his tall uncle, the Giraffe, spanked him *(Spanking music)* with his hard, hard hoof. *(Pantomime and reactions as above)* And still he was full of 'satiable curiosity! He inquired of his broad aunt, the Hippopotamus:

ELEPHANT: *(Lumbers over to her.)* Aunt Hippopotamus, why are your eyes so red?

HIPPO: Naughty Elephant's Child, you talk too much. Come here!

STORYTELLER: And his broad aunt, the Hippopotamus, spanked him, too *(Spanking music. Pantomime and reactions as before)* with her broad, broad hoof. Next he asked his hairy uncle, the Baboon:

ELEPHANT: *(Lumbers over to him.)* Uncle Baboon, what makes your hair grow just so?

BABOON: Naughty Elephant's Child, you are never quiet. Come here!

240

STORYTELLER: And naturally, his hairy uncle, the Baboon, spanked him *(Spanking music. Pantomime and reactions as before)* with his hairy, hairy paw. And still he was full of 'satiable curiosity! He asked questions about everything he saw ...

ELEPHANT: *(Lumbers from one character to another on the following sequence of questions.)* How can birds fly?

STORYTELLER: Or heard ...

ELEPHANT: Why do lions roar?

STORYTELLER: Or felt ...

ELEPHANT: What makes the rain feel wet?

STORYTELLER: Or smelled ...

ELEPHANT: Why do bananas smell so good?

STORYTELLER: Or touched ...

ELEPHANT: What's this?

STORYTELLER: And all his uncles and his aunts spanked him. *(Spanking music. Pantomime and reactions as before)* And still he was full of 'satiable curiosity! *(Several climactic chords of music for transition purposes)* One fine morning in the middle of a big parade, this 'satiable Elephant's Child asked a new question that he had never asked before:

ELEPHANT: *(Speaking to all his relatives)* What does the Crocodile have for dinner?

OSTRICH: Hush, Child!

GIRAFFE: Be quiet, inquisitive one!

HIPPO: Shhh, someone might hear, naughty Elephant's Child!

BABOON: What a question to ask, talkative one!

STORYTELLER: Then everybody said:

ALL: Hush!

STORYTELLER: In a loud and dreadful tone, and they spanked him *(Spanking music. Pantomime and reactions as before)* immediately and without stopping, for a long time. *(Repeat spanking music, pantomime, and reactions)* By and by, when that was finished, the Elephant's Child decided to take a walk, and came upon a Kolokolo Bird sitting in the middle of a thornbush, and he said:

ELEPHANT: *(Lumbers over to him.)* My father has spanked me,

*(One chord of spanking music)* and my mother has spanked me, *(Two chords of spanking music)* and all my aunts and uncles have spanked me *(Chords build to finish)* for my 'satiable curiosity, and *still* I want to know what the Crocodile has for dinner! Can you tell me, Mr. Kolokolo Bird?

KOLOKOLO BIRD:  Go to the banks of the great gray-green, greasy Limpopo River, all set about with fever-trees, and find out.

STORYTELLER:  The very next morning, this 'satiable Elephant's Child prepared for this journey:

ELEPHANT:  Let's see ... I'll take a hundred pounds of bananas ...

STORYTELLER:  The little short red kind.

ELEPHANT:  And a hundred pounds of sugarcane ...

STORYTELLER:  The long purple kind.

ELEPHANT:  And seventeen melons ...

STORYTELLER:  The green crackly kind.

ELEPHANT:  *(Speaking to all his relatives)* Good-bye, all my dear families. I am going to the great gray-green, greasy Limpopo River, all set about with fever-trees, to find out what the Crocodile has for dinner.

STORYTELLER:  And they all spanked him once more for luck, *(Spanking music. Pantomime and reactions as before)* though he asked them most politely:

ELEPHANT:  Please stop!

STORYTELLER:  Then he went away, a little warm but not at all astonished. He went from Graham's Town to Kimberley, and from Kimberley to Khama's County, and from Khama's County he went east by north, till at last he came to the banks of the great gray-green, greasy Limpopo River, all set with fever-trees.

ELEPHANT:  *(Looking around)* Why, this is precisely as the Kolokolo Bird told me.

STORYTELLER:  Now you must know and understand that till that very week, and day, and hour, and minute, this 'satiable Elephant's Child had never seen a Crocodile, and didn't know what one was like. It was all his 'satiable curiosity. The first thing that he found was a Bi-Colored-Python-Rock-Snake curled around a rock. Said the Elephant's Child most politely:

ELEPHANT: *(Lumbers over to him)* 'Scuse me, but have you seen such a thing as a Crocodile in these parts?

SNAKE: *(Speaking with excessive sibilance)* Have I seen a Crocodile? What will you ask me next?

ELEPHANT: 'Scuse me, but could you kindly tell me what he has for dinner?

STORYTELLER: Then the Bi-Colored-Python-Rock-Snake uncoiled himself very quickly from the rock, and spanked the Elephant's Child with his scalesome, flailsome tail. *(Spanking music. Pantomime and reactions as before)*

ELEPHANT: This is odd, because my father and my mother, and my uncle and my aunt, not to mention my other aunt, the Hippopotamus, and my other uncle, the Baboon, have all spanked me for my 'satiable curiosity—and I suppose this is the same thing.

STORYTELLER: So he said good-bye very politely to the Bi-Colored-Python-Rock-Snake, and went on, a little warm, but not at all astonished, till he trod on what he thought was a log of wood at the very edge of the great gray-green, greasy Limpopo River, all set about with fever-trees. But it was really the Crocodile, and the Crocodile winked one eye, like this. *(Sound of something heavy closing)*

ELEPHANT: *(Stumbling as he approaches the Crocodile)* 'Scuse me, but do you happen to have seen a Crocodile in these parts?

STORYTELLER: Then the Crocodile winked the other eye. *(Sound of something heavy closing)* And he lifted his tail out of the mud; and the Elephant's Child stepped back most politely, because he did not wish to be spanked again.

CROCODILE: *(Speaking ingratiatingly in his deep bass voice)* Come hither, Little One. Why do you ask such things?

ELEPHANT: 'Scuse me, but my father has spanked me, *(One spanking chord)* and my mother has spanked me, *(Two spanking chords)* not to mention my tall aunt, the Ostrich, and my tall uncle, the Giraffe, who can kick ever so hard, as well as my broad aunt, the Hippopotamus, and my hairy uncle, the Baboon, and the Bi-Colored-Python-Rock-Snake, with the

243

scalesome, flailsome tail, just up the bank, who spanks harder than any of them. *(Spanking chords to climactic finish) So,* if it's all the same to you, I don't want to be spanked any more.

CROCODILE: Come hither, Little One, for I am the Crocodile.

STORYTELLER: And he wept crocodile tears to show it was quite true. Then the Elephant's Child grew all breathless, and panted, and leaned over the bank and said:

ELEPHANT: You're the very person I've been looking for all these long days. Will you please tell me what you have for dinner?

CROCODILE: Come hither, Little One, and I'll whisper.

STORYTELLER: And the Elephant's Child put his head down close to the Crocodile's musky, tusky mouth, and the Crocodile caught him by his little nose, which up to that very week, day, hour, and minute, had been no bigger than a boot, though much more useful. Then the Crocodile said—and he said it between his teeth, like this:

CROCODILE: *(Speaking with his teeth and jaws tightly closed)* I think today I will begin with the Elephant's Child!

STORYTELLER: At this, the Elephant's Child was much annoyed, and he said, speaking through his nose, like this:

ELEPHANT: *(Speaking through his nose, and pantomiming pulling away from the CROCODILE)* Let go! You're hurting me!

STORYTELLER: Then the Bi-Colored-Python-Rock-Snake scuffled down from the bank and said:

SNAKE: *(May scuffle over to the ELEPHANT'S CHILD.)* My young friend, if you do not now, immediately and instantly, pull as hard as ever you can, it is my opinion that your acquaintance in the large-pattern leather ulster ...

STORYTELLER: And by this he meant the Crocodile.

SNAKE: ... will jerk you into yonder limpid stream before you can say Jack Robinson.

STORYTELLER: This is the way Bi-Colored-Python-Rock-Snakes always talk. Then the Elephant's Child sat back on his little haunch, and pulled, *(One sustained chord of pulling music)* and pulled, *(Two chords)* and pulled, *(Three chords, music accompanied by pulling activity by the ELEPHANT'S CHILD)* and his nose began to stretch. *(Short chord)* The Crocodile floundered into the water, making it all creamy with great sweeps of his tail, and *he* pulled, and pulled, and pulled. *(Again, music of pulling and stretching)* And the Elephant's Child's nose kept on stretching; *(Chords)* and the Elephant's Child spread all his little four legs and pulled, *(One chord)* and pulled, *(Two chords)* and pulled, *(Three chords)* and his nose kept on stretching; *(Stretching music)* and the Crocodile thrashed his tail like an oar, and *he* pulled, *(One chord)* and pulled, *(Two chords)* and pulled. *(Three chords)* And at each pull the Elephant's Child's nose grew longer and longer *(Stretching music)* and it hurt him Hijjus! Then the Elephant's Child felt his legs slipping, and he said through his nose, which was now nearly five feet long:

ELEPHANT: *(Speaking through nose)* This is too much for me!

STORYTELLER: Then the Bi-Colored-Python-Rock-Snake knotted himself in a double-clove-hitch round the Elephant's Child's hind legs, and he said:

SNAKE: *(Throughout the following, SNAKE and ELEPHANT'S CHILD pantomime as the narration suggests.)* Rash and inexperienced traveler, we'll now seriously devote ourselves to a little high tension, because if we do not, it is my impression that yonder self-propelling man-of-war with the armor-plated upper deck ...

STORYTELLER: And by this he meant the Crocodile.

SNAKE: ... will permanently vitiate your future career.

STORYTELLER: This is the way all Bi-Colored-Python-Rock-Snakes always talk. So he pulled, *(One chord of pulling music)* and the Elephant's Child pulled, *(Higher chord of pulling music)* and the Bi-Colored-Python-Rock-Snake pulled; *(Another chord higher)* and at last the Crocodile let go of the Elephant's Child's nose with a plop that you could hear all up and down the Limpopo. *(Plop chord)* Then the Elephant's Child sat down most hard and sudden; but first he was careful to say to the Bi-Colored-Python-Rock-Snake:

ELEPHANT: Thank you!

STORYTELLER: And next he was kind to his poor pulled nose, and wrapped it all up in cool banana leaves, and hung it in the great gray-green, greasy Limpopo to cool. The Bi-Colored-Python-Rock-Snake asked:

SNAKE: What are you doing that for?

ELEPHANT: 'Scuse me, but my nose is badly out of shape, and I am waiting for it to shrink.

SNAKE: Then you will have to wait a long time. Some people do not know what is good for them.

STORYTELLER: The Elephant's Child sat there for three days waiting for his nose to shrink. But it never grew any shorter, and besides, it made him squint. For you will see and understand that the Crocodile had pulled it out into a really truly trunk same as all elephants have today. *(Transition chords)* At the end of the third day a fly came and stung him on the shoulder, and before he knew what he was doing he lifted up his trunk and hit that fly dead with the end of it. *(Pantomime hitting the fly)* Cried the Bi-Colored-Python-Rock-Snake:

SNAKE: 'Vantage number one! You couldn't have done that with a mere-smere nose. Try to eat a little now.

STORYTELLER: Before he thought what he was doing the Elephant's Child put out his trunk *(Pantomime throughout)* and plucked a large bundle of grass, dusted it clean against his forelegs, and stuffed it into his own mouth. Exclaimed the Bi-Colored-Python-Rock-Snake:

SNAKE: 'Vantage number two! You couldn't have done that with a mere-smere nose. Don't you think the sun is very hot here?

ELEPHANT: It is.

STORYTELLER: And before he thought what he was doing, he schlooped up a schloop of mud from the banks of the great gray-green greasy Limpopo, and slapped it on his head, where it made a cool schloopy-sloshy mudcap all trickly behind his ears. *(With pantomime, as always)* Said the Bi-Colored-Python-Rock-Snake:

SNAKE: 'Vantage number three! You couldn't have done that with a mere-smere nose. Now how do you feel about being spanked again?

ELEPHANT:  'Scuse me, but I should not like it at all.

SNAKE:  How would you like to spank somebody?

ELEPHANT:  I should like it very much indeed.

SNAKE:  Well, you'll find that new nose of yours very useful with which to spank people.

ELEPHANT:  Thank you. I'll remember that; and now I think I'll go home to all my dear families and try.

STORYTELLER:  *(Throughout the following narration, ELEPHANT'S CHILD pantomimes all business as suggested.)* So the Elephant's Child went home across Africa frisking and whisking his trunk. When he wanted fruit to eat he pulled fruit down from a tree ...

ELEPHANT:  I'm hungry. I'll have some fruit. *(Reaches up in tree and takes it.)*

STORYTELLER:  ... instead of waiting for it to fall as he used to do. When he wanted grass he plucked grass up from the ground, instead of going on his knees as he used to do.

ELEPHANT:  I'm still hungry. I think I'll have some of that grass. *(Fly bites him.)* Ouch, that fly bit me. *(Pantomimes breaking off a branch from a tree and hitting flies from his shoulder with it.)*

STORYTELLER:  When the flies bit him he broke off the branch of a tree and used it as a fly-whisk; and he made himself a new, cool, slushy-squishy mudcap whenever the sun was hot. When he felt lonely walking through Africa he sang to himself down his trunk. *(ELEPHANT sings very loudly.)* The noise of his singing was louder than several brass bands. He went especially out of his way to find a broad Hippopotamus (she was no relative of his), and he spanked her very hard, just to make sure that the Bi-Colored-Python-Rock-Snake had spoken the truth. *(Transition chords)* One dark evening he came back to all his dear families, and he coiled up his trunk and said:

ELEPHANT:  *(Speaking to all his relatives)* How do you do?

STORYTELLER:  They were very glad to see him, and immediately said:

OSTRICH:  Elephant's Child ...

GIRAFFE:  Come here ...

HIPPO:  And be spanked ...

BABOON: For your 'satiable curiosity.

ELEPHANT: Pooh! I don't think you people know anything about spanking; but I do, and I'll show you.

STORYTELLER: Then he uncurled his trunk and knocked two of his dear relations *(Crashing sound)* head over heels. They said, quite amazed:

BABOON: O, bananas! Where did you learn that trick?

OSTRICH: What have you done to your nose?

ELEPHANT: I got a new one from the Crocodile on the banks of the great gray-green, greasy Limpopo River. I asked him what he had for dinner, and he gave me this to keep.

BABOON: It looks very ugly.

ELEPHANT: It does, Uncle Baboon, but it's very useful. Let me show you.

STORYTELLER: He picked up his hairy uncle, the Baboon, by one hairy leg, and threw him into a hornet's nest. *(Pantomime)* Then that bad Elephant's Child spanked all his dear families for a long time, *(Spanking chords)* till they were very warm and greatly astonished. He pulled out his tall Ostrich aunt's tail-feathers. *(Pantomime)*

OSTRICH: *(Reacts to pain of losing feathers, and screams.)* My feathers!

STORYTELLER: And he caught his tall uncle, the Giraffe, by the hind leg, and dragged him through a thorn-bush. *(Pantomime)*

GIRAFFE: Owww! The thorns!

STORYTELLER: And he shouted at his broad aunt, the Hippopotamus, and blew bubbles *(Pantomime)* into her ear when she was sleeping in the water after meals.

HIPPO: Don't blow bubbles!

STORYTELLER: But he never let anyone touch Kolokolo Bird. At last, things grew so exciting that his dear families went off one by one in a hurry to the banks of the great gray-green, greasy Limpopo River, all set about with fever-trees, to borrow new noses from the Crocodile. *(One by one the relatives may leave the playing space, if desired, during the narration.)* When they came back nobody spanked anybody any more. *(If background music was used under the opening narration, it may be employed*

*here also.)* And ever since that day, all elephants you will ever see, besides those that you won't, have trunks precisely like the trunk of the 'satiable Elephant's Child.
*(Music up to climax and out.)*

# from *Nicholas Nickleby* by Charles Dickens

Despite ready-made characters, a wide range of events or incidents, and intriguing setting, adapting the novel for classroom performance presents a number of creative challenges. Descriptive details and narration need to be compressed to meet the confines and available playing space and a limited performance time. The following adaptation of one chapter in Charles Dickens' expansive novel *Nicholas Nickleby* is a good example of cutting and editing a selected episode for classroom performance.

### "Nicholas Nickleby Leaving the Yorkshire School"

NARRATOR: The poor creature, Smike, paid bitterly for the friendship of Nicholas Nickleby; all the spleen and ill humor that could not be vented on Nicholas were bestowed on him. Stripes and blows, stripes and blows, morning, noon, and night, were his penalty for being compassionated by the daring new master. Squeers was jealous of the influence which the said new master soon acquired in the school, and hated him for it; Mrs. Squeers had hated him from the first; and poor Smike paid heavily for all. One night he was poring hard over a book, vainly endeavoring to master some task which a child of nine years could have conquered with ease, but which to the brain of the crushed boy of nineteen was a hopeless mystery. Nicholas laid his hand upon his shoulder.

SMIKE: I can't do it.

NICHOLAS: Do not try. You will do better, poor fellow, when I am gone.

SMIKE: Gone? Are you going?

249

NICHOLAS:  I cannot say. I was speaking more to my own thoughts than to you. I shall be driven to that at last! The world is before me, after all.

SMIKE:  Is the world as bad and dismal as this place?

NICHOLAS:  Heaven forbid. Its hardest, coarsest toil is happiness to this.

SMIKE:  Should I ever meet you there?

NICHOLAS:  *(Willing to soothe him)* Yes.

SMIKE:  No! No! Should I—say I should be sure to find joy.

NICHOLAS:  You would, and I would help and aid you, and not bring fresh sorrow upon you, as I have done here.

NARRATOR:  The boy caught both his hands, and uttered a few broken sounds which were unintelligible. Squeers entered at that moment, and he shrunk back into his old corner. Two days later, the cold feeble dawn of a January morning was stealing in at the windows of the common sleeping-room.

SQUEERS:  Now, then, are you going to sleep all day up there?

NICHOLAS:  We shall be down directly, sir.

SQUEERS:  Down directly! Ah! You had better be down directly, or I'll be down upon some of you in less time than directly. Where's that Smike?

NICHOLAS:  He is not here, sir.

SQUEERS:  Don't tell me a lie. He is.

NARRATOR:  Squeers bounced into the dormitory, and swinging his cane in the air ready for a blow, darted into the corner where Smike usually lay at night. The cane descended harmlessly. There was nobody there.

SQUEERS:  What does this mean? Where have you hid him?

NICHOLAS:  I have seen nothing of him since last night.

SQUEERS:  Come, you won't save him this way. Where is he?

NICHOLAS:  At the bottom of the nearest pond, for anything I know.

NARRATOR:  In a fright, Squeers inquired of the other boys whether any one of them knew anything of their missing school-mate. There was a general hum of denial, in the midst of which one shrill voice was heard to say—as indeed everybody thought—

BOY: Please, sir. I think Smike's run away, sir.

SQUEERS: Ha! Who said that?

NARRATOR: Squeers made a plunge into the crowd, and caught a very little boy.

SQUEERS: You think he has run away, do you?

BOY: Yes. Please, sir.

SQUEERS: And what reason have you to suppose that any boy would run away from this establishment, eh?

NARRATOR: The child raised a dismal cry by way of answer, and Squeers beat him until he rolled out of his hands.

SQUEERS: There! Now if any other boy thinks Smike has run away, I shall be glad to have a talk with him. *(A profound silence follows)* Well, Nickleby, you think he has run away, I suppose?

NICHOLAS: I think it extremely likely.

SQUEERS: Maybe you know he has run away?

NICHOLAS: I know nothing about it.

SQUEERS: He didn't tell you he was going, I suppose?

NICHOLAS: He did not. I am very glad he did not, for then it would have been my duty to tell you.

SQUEERS: Which, no doubt, you would have been very sorry to do?

NICHOLAS: I should, indeed.

NARRATOR: Mrs. Squeers now hastily made her way to the scene of the action.

MRS. SQUEERS: What's all this here to-do? What on earth are you talking to him for, Squeey? The cow-house and stables are locked up, so Smike can't be there; and he's not downstairs anywhere. Now, if you takes the chaise and goes one road, and I borrow Swallow's chaise and goes t'other, one or other of us is moral sure to lay hold of him.

NARRATOR: The lady's plan was put in execution without delay, Nicholas remaining behind in a tumult of feeling. Death, from want and exposure, was the best that could be expected from the prolonged wandering of so helpless a creature. Nicholas lingered on, in restless anxiety, picturing a thousand possibilities, until the evening of the next day, when Squeers returned alone.

SQUEERS:  No news of the scamp!

NARRATOR:  Another day came, and Nicholas was scarcely awake when he heard the wheels of a chaise approaching the house. It stopped, and the voice of Mrs. Squeers was then heard, ordering a glass of spirits for somebody, which was in itself a sufficient sign that something extraordinary had happened. Nicholas hardly dared look out of the window, but he did so, and the first object that met his eyes was the wretched Smike, bedabbled with mud and rain, haggard and worn and wild.

SQUEERS:  Lift him out! Bring him in, bring him in!

MRS. SQUEERS:  Take care! We tied his legs under the apron, and made 'em fast to the chaise, to prevent him giving us the slip again!

NARRATOR:  With hands trembling with delight, Squeers loosened the cord; and Smike more dead than alive, was brought in and locked up in a cellar, until such a time as Squeers should deem it expedient to operate upon him. The news that the fugitive had been caught and brought back ran like wildfire through the hungry community, and expectation was on tiptoe all the morning. In the afternoon, Squeers, having refreshed himself with his dinner and an extra libation or so, made his appearance, accompanied by his amiable partner, with a fearful instrument of flagellation, strong, supple, wax-ended and new.

SQUEERS:  Is every boy here?

NARRATOR:  Every boy was there.

SQUEERS:  Each boy keep his place. Nickleby! Go to your desk.

NARRATOR:  There was a curious expression on Nickleby's face; but he took his seat, without opening his lips in reply. Squeers left the room, and shortly afterward returned, dragging Smike by the collar—or rather by that fragment of his jacket which was nearest the place where his collar ought to have been.

SQUEERS:  Now, what have you got to say for yourself? Stand a little out of the way, Mrs. Squeers. I've hardly got room enough.

SMIKE:  Spare me, sir!

SQUEERS:  Oh, that's all you've got to say, is it? Yes, I'll flog you within an inch of your life, and spare you that!

NARRATOR:   One cruel blow had fallen on him, when Nicholas
　　Nickleby cried out—

NICHOLAS:　Stop!

SQUEERS:　Who cried, "Stop!"?

NICHOLAS:　I did. This must not go on.

MRS. SQUEERS:　Must not go on?

NICHOLAS:　No! Must not! Shall not! I will prevent it! You have
　　disregarded all my quiet interference on this miserable lad's
　　behalf; you have returned no answer to the letter in which I
　　begged forgiveness for him, and offered to be responsible that
　　he would remain quietly here. Don't blame me for this public
　　interference. You have brought it upon yourself, not I.

SQUEERS:　*(To SMIKE)* Sit down, beggar!

NICHOLAS:　Wretch, touch him again at your peril! I will not stand
　　by and see it done. My blood is up, and I have the strength of
　　ten such men as you. By Heaven! I will not spare you, if you
　　drive me on! I have a series of personal insults to avenge, and
　　my indignation is aggravated by the cruelties practiced in this
　　cruel den. Have a care, or the consequences will fall heavily
　　upon your head!

NARRATOR:　Squeers, in a violent outbreak, spat at him, and
　　struck him a blow across the face. Nicholas instantly sprung
　　upon him, wrested his weapon from his hand, and, pinning him
　　by the throat, beat the ruffian till he roared for mercy. He then
　　flung him away with all the force he could muster, and the
　　violence of his fall precipitated Mrs. Squeers over an adjacent
　　form; Squeers, striking his head against the same form in his
　　descent, lay at his full length on the ground, stunned and
　　motionless.

NICHOLAS:　Now, let that be the end of the matter!

NARRATOR:　Having brought affairs to this happy termination, and
　　having ascertained to his satisfaction that Squeers was only
　　stunned, and not dead—upon which point he had some
　　unpleasant doubts at first—Nicholas packed up a few clothes in
　　a small valise, and finding that nobody offered to oppose his
　　progress, marched boldly out by the front door, and struck into

the road. Then such a cheer arose as the walls of Dotheboys Hall had never echoed before, and would never respond to again. When the sound had died away, the school was empty; and of the crowd of boys not one remained. This, indeed, was the solemn occasion of Nicholas Nickleby leaving the Yorkshire school.

# from "The Diamond Necklace"
# by Guy de Maupassant

The short story is one of the most popular texts for Readers Theatre adaptation and classroom performance. Its brevity, singleness of action, and short exchange of crisp lines of dialog promote explicit vocal and physical characterization. The following adaptation of Guy de Maupassant's classic short story "The Diamond Necklace" includes a number of clearly-defined characters, dramatic story line, and unexpected climax that is sure to surprise!

NARRATOR 1: The girl was one of those pretty and charming young creatures who sometimes are born, as if by a mistake of destiny, in a family of clerks. She had no dowry, no expectations, no way of being known, understood, loved, married, by any rich and distinguished man; so she let herself by married to a little clerk at the Ministry of Public Instruction.

NARRATOR 2: She had no gowns, no jewels, and she loved nothing else. She felt made for that alone. She was filled with a desire to please, to be envied, to be bewitching, to be sought after.

NARRATOR 1: She had a friend, a former school-mate at the convent, who was rich and whom she did not like to see any more, because she suffered so much when she came home.

NARRATOR 2: One evening her husband came home with a triumphant air, holding a large envelope in his hand.

HUSBAND: There, there is something for you.

NARRATOR 1: She tore the paper quickly, and drew out a printed card which bore these words:

NARRATOR 2: The Minister of Public Instruction and Madame Georges Rampouneau request the honor of Madame Loisel's company at the palace of the Ministry on Monday evening, January 18th.

NARRATOR 1: Instead of being delighted, as her husband had hoped, she quickly threw the invitation on the table with disdain, murmuring:

WIFE: What do you wish me to do with that?

HUSBAND: Why, my dear, I thought you would be glad. You never go out, and this is such a fine opportunity.

WIFE: And what do you wish me to wear?

HUSBAND: Why, the gown you go to the theatre in. It looks very well to me.

NARRATOR 1: He stopped stupefied, distracted, on seeing that his wife was crying.

HUSBAND: Why, what is the matter?

WIFE: Nothing, only I have no gown, and therefore cannot go to this ball. Give your card to some colleague whose wife is better equipped than I.

HUSBAND: Come, let us see. How much would it cost, a suitable gown, which you could use on other occasions?

NARRATOR 2: She reflected several seconds, making her calculations and wondering also what sum she could ask without drawing on herself an immediate refusal. Finally, she replied:

WIFE: I don't know exactly, but I think I could manage it with four hundred francs.

NARRATOR 1: He turned a trifle pale, for he had been saving just that sum to buy a gun and treat himself to a little hunting trip. However, he said:

HUSBAND: Very well, I will give you four hundred francs. And try to have a pretty gown.

NARRATOR 2: The day of the ball drew near, and Madame Loisel seemed sad, uneasy, anxious. Her husband said to her one evening:

HUSBAND: What is the matter, dear? Come, you have seemed

very strange these last three days.

WIFE: It annoys me not to have jewels, not a single stone. I shall look poverty-stricken. I should almost rather not go at all.

HUSBAND: How silly you are! Go, look up your friend Madame Forestier and ask her to lend you some jewels. You're intimate with her to do that.

WIFE: True enough! I never thought of it.

NARRATOR 1: The next day she went to her friend and told of her distress.

NARRATOR 2: Madame Forestier went to a wardrobe with a glass door, took out a large jewel box, brought it back, opened it, and said to Madame Loisel:

MADAME FORESTIER: Choose, my dear.

NARRATOR 1: She tried on the ornaments before the mirror, hesitated, and suddenly discovered, in a black satin box, a superb diamond necklace, and her heart throbbed with an immoderate desire.

NARRATOR 2: Her hands trembled as she took it. She fastened it around her throat, outside her high-necked waist, and was lost in ecstasy at the sight of herself. Then she asked:

WIFE: Will you lend me this, only this?

MADAME FORESTIER: Why, yes, certainly.

NARRATOR 1: The night of the ball arrived. Madame Loisel made a great success. She was prettier than any other woman present, elegant, graceful, smiling, and intoxicated with joy. All the men looked at her, asked her name, demanded to be introduced.

NARRATOR 2: She danced with rapture, with passion, made drunk by pleasure, forgetting all, in the triumph of her beauty, in the glory of her success.

NARRATOR 1: She left the ball about four o'clock in the morning. Her husband had been sleeping since midnight, in a little deserted anteroom with three other gentlemen whose wives were also enjoying the ball.

NARRATOR 2: He threw over her shoulders the wraps he had brought, the modest wraps of common life, the poverty of which contrasted with the elegance of her ball dress.

NARRATOR 1: She felt this, and wished to escape so as not to be noticed by the other women, who were enveloping themselves in costly furs.

HUSBAND: Wait a minute. You will catch cold outside. I will call a cab.

NARRATOR 2: But she did not listen to him and rapidly descended the stairs. When they reached the street they could not find a carriage, and began to look for one, shouting after the cabmen passing at a distance.

NARRATOR 1: At last they found one of those ancient night cabs which, as if they were ashamed to show their shabbiness during the day, are never seen around Paris until after dark.

NARRATOR 2: The cab took them to their dwelling, and sadly they climbed the stairs to their small apartment.

NARRATOR 1: He reflected that he must be at the Ministry at eight o'clock that morning.

NARRATOR 2: She removed her wraps before the glass so as to see herself one last time in all her glory.

NARRATOR 1: But suddenly she uttered a cry. *(WIFE screams.)*

NARRATOR 2: The necklace was no longer around her neck!

NARRATOR 1: They looked among the folds of her skirt, of her cloak, in her pockets, everywhere, but did not find it. They looked, thunderstruck, at each other. At last, she collapsed on a chair in her ball-dress, without the strength to go to bed; overwhelmed, without fire, without a thought.

NARRATOR 2: Her husband went to the police, to the newspapers, to offer a reward. He even went to the cab companies— everywhere, in fact, where he was urged by the least spark of desperate hope.

WIFE: What are we to do now?

HUSBAND: We must consider how to replace the necklace.

NARRATOR 1: The next day they took the case that had contained the necklace and went to the jeweler, whose name was found within.

NARRATOR 2: He consulted his books.

JEWELER: It is not I, Madame, who sold that necklace. I must simply have furnished the case.

NARRATOR 1: Then they went from jeweler to jeweler, searching for a necklace like the other, both sick with chagrin and anguish.

NARRATOR 2: At last, they found in a shop at the Palais Royale a string of diamonds that seemed, at least to them, exactly like the one they had lost.

NARRATOR 1: It was worth forty thousand francs.

WIFE: We have eighteen thousand francs which your father left us.

HUSBAND: I can borrow the rest.

NARRATOR 2: He did borrow, asking a thousand francs of one, five hundred of another, six louis here, three louis there.

NARRATOR 1: He gave notes, took up ruinous obligations, dealt with usurers and all the race of shady lenders.

NARRATOR 2: He compromised all the rest of his life, and risked his signature without even knowing whether he could honor it.

NARRATOR 1: Frightened by the black misery that was about to befall them, the husband soon went to get the new necklace and placed forty thousand francs upon the jeweler's counter.

NARRATOR 2: When Madame Loisel took back the necklace, Madame Forestier said to her in a chilly manner:

MADAME FORESTIER: You should have returned it sooner. I might have needed it.

NARRATOR 1: Madame Forestier did not open the case.

NARRATOR 2: As her friend had so much feared.

NARRATOR 1: If she had detected the substitution, what would she have thought, what would she have said?

NARRATOR 2: Would she not have taken Madame Loisel for a thief?

NARRATOR 1: Thereafter, Madame Loisel and her husband began to know the horrible existence of the needy.

NARRATOR 2: She, however, bore her part with a sudden heroism.

NARRATOR 1: The dreadful debt must be paid.

NARRATOR 2: She would pay it off.

NARRATOR 1: They dismissed their servant; they changed their lodgings; they rented a garret under the roof.

NARRATOR 2: Every month they met some notes, renewed others, obtained more time. At the end of ten years they had paid—

HUSBAND: Everything.

WIFE: Everything.

NARRATOR 1: Even with the rates of usury and accumulation of compound interest.

NARRATOR 2: But Madame Loisel looked old now. She had become the woman of an impoverished household—strong, and hard, and rough.

NARRATOR 1: With frowsy hair, skirts askew, and red hands, she talked loudly while washing the floor with a great swish of water.

NARRATOR 2: But sometimes, when her husband was at the Ministry office, she sat down near the front window, and thought of that happy evening so long ago; of that ball where she had been so beautiful and so admired. And she thought out loud:

WIFE: What would have happened if I had not lost that necklace?

NARRATOR 1: Who knows?

NARRATOR 2: Who knows?

WIFE: How strange and changeful is life! How little a thing is needed for us to be lost, or to be saved!

NARRATOR 1: But, on Sunday, having gone to take a walk to refresh herself from the labors of the week, she suddenly perceived a woman who was leading a small child.

NARRATOR 2: It was Madame Forestier.

NARRATOR 1: She was still astonishingly young, beautiful, and charming.

NARRATOR 2: Should she speak to her?

NARRATOR 1: Yes, certainly. And now that she had paid in full, she would tell her all about it.

NARRATOR 2: Why not?

WIFE: Good day, Madame Forestier.

MADAME FORESTIER: *(Stammering)* But—Madame—I do not know—You must be mistaken.

WIFE: No. I am Madame Loisel.

MADAME FORESTIER: Oh, my poor dear. How you are changed!

WIFE: Yes. I have had days hard enough since I last saw you, to be sure—days wretched enough—and that because of you!

MADAME FORESTIER: Of me! How so?

WIFE: Do you remember that diamond necklace you lent me to wear at the Ministry ball?

MADAME FORESTIER: Yes, well?

WIFE: I lost it.

MADAME FORESTIER: How can that be? You returned it to me.

WIFE: I returned you another exactly like it. And for this my husband and I have been ten years paying. You can understand that it was not easy for us, us who had nothing. At last it is ended and I am very glad.

MADAME FORESTIER: You say that you bought a necklace of diamonds to replace mine?

WIFE: Yes. You never noticed them! They were very like yours.

MADAME FORESTIER: Oh, my poor dear. Why, my necklace was paste! It was worth, at most, only five hundred francs.

# from "The Ransom of Red Chief" by O. Henry

Here is another classic short story adapted for a classroom performance that is decidedly more humorous in its point of view. "The Ransom of Red Chief," written by Sidney Porter (O. Henry), combines action, excitement, and suspense in building an entertaining story line. The adaptation features several distinct character types and lends itself to the "Literary Character Charades" exercise described in Chapter Five as an imaginative classroom rehearsal technique.

SAM: It looked like a good thing: but wait till I tell you. We were down South, in Alabama—Bill Driscoll and myself—when this kidnapping idea struck us. It was, as Bill afterward expressed it—

BILL: During a moment of temporary mental apparition—

SAM: But we didn't find that out till later. There was a town down there, as flat as a flannel-cake, and called Summit, of course. It contained inhabitants of as undeleterious and self-satisfied a class of peasantry as ever clustered around a Maypole.

BILL: Sam and me had a joint capital of about six hundred dollars, and we needed just two thousand dollars more to pull off a fraudulent town-lot scheme in Western Illinois. We talked it over on the front steps of the hotel. We knew that Summit couldn't get after us with anything stronger than constables and, maybe, some lackadaisical bloodhounds and a diatribe or two in the *Weekly Farmer's Budget.* So, it looked good.

SAM: We selected for our victim the only child of a prominent citizen named Ebenezer Dorset, a stern and tight mortgage holder. The kid was a boy of ten, with freckles and hair the color of the magazine you buy at the newsstand when you want to catch a train. Bill and me figured that Ebenezer would melt down for a ransom of two thousand dollars to a cent. But wait till I tell you.

BILL: About two miles from Summit was a little mountain covered with dense cedar brake. On the rear elevation of this mountain was a cave. There we stored provisions. One evening after sundown, we drove in a buggy past old Dorset's house. The kid was in the street, throwing rocks at a kitten on the opposite fence.

SAM: Bill shouted out—

BILL: Hey, little boy! Would you like to have a bag of candy and a nice ride?

SAM: The boy catches Bill neatly in the eye with a piece of brick.

BILL: That will cost the old man an extra five hundred dollars—

SAM: Says Bill, climbing over the wheel. That boy put up a fight like a welterweight cinnamon bear; but at last we got him down in the bottom of the buggy and drove away. We took him up to the cave, and I hitched the horse in the cedar brake. After dark I drove the buggy to the little village three miles away, where we had hired it, and walked back to the mountain. There was a fire burning behind the big rock at the entrance of the cave, and the boy was watching a pot of boiling coffee, with two buzzard feathers stuck in his red hair. He points a stick at me when I come up and says:

RED CHIEF: Ha! Cursed paleface, do you dare to enter the camp of Red Chief, the terror of the plains?

BILL: He's all right now—

SAM: Says Bill.

BILL: I'm Old Hank, the Trapper, Red Chief's captive, and I'm to be scalped at daybreak. By Geronimo! That kid can sure kick hard!

SAM: Yes, sir, that boy seemed to be having the time of his life. He immediately christened me Snake-Eye, the Spy, and announced that, when his braves returned from the warpath, I was to be burned at the stake at the rising of the sun. Then we had supper, and the kid made a speech something like this:

RED CHIEF: I like this camping out fine! I hate to go to school. Are there any real Indians in these woods? I want some more gravy. What makes your nose so red, Hank? My father has lots of money. Are the stars hot? I don't like girls. Why are oranges round? Have you got beds to sleep on in this cave? Amos Murry has got six toes. How many does it take to make twelve?

SAM: Every few minutes, he would remember that he was a pesky Indian and pick up his stick and tip-toe to the mouth of the cave to let out a war whoop that made Old Hank, the Trapper, shiver. That boy had Bill terrorized from the start, so finally I asked if he would like to go home now.

RED CHIEF: Aw, what for? I don't have any fun at home. I hate to go to school. I like to camp out. You won't take me back home again, Snake-Eye, will you?

SAM: Not right away. We'll stay here in the cave awhile.

RED CHIEF: All right! That'll be fine. I never had such fun in all my life.

BILL: We went to bed about eleven o'clock. We spread down some wide blankets and quilts and put Red Chief between us. He kept us awake for three hours, jumping up and reaching for his rifle and screeching in our ears.

SAM: Just at daybreak, I was awakened by a series of awful screams from Bill. They weren't yells, or howls, or shouts, or whoops, or yawps, such as you'd expect—they were simply indecent, terrifying, humiliating screams, such as women emit when they see ghosts or caterpillars. It's an awful thing to hear a strong, desperate, fat man scream incontinently in a cave at daybreak. I jumped up to see what the matter was. Red Chief was sitting on Bill's chest, with one hand twined in Bill's hair. In the other he had the sharp case-knife we used for slicing bacon;

262

and he was industriously trying to take Bill's scalp, according to the sentence that had been pronounced upon him the evening before. From that moment on Bill's spirit was broken. He laid down on his side of the bed, but he never closed an eye again in sleep. I dozed off for a while, but then I remembered that Red Chief had said I was to be burned at the stake at the rising of the sun. I quickly sat up and lit my pipe and leaned against a rock.

BILL: What are you getting up so soon for, Sam?

SAM: Me? Oh, I got a kind of pain in my shoulder. I thought sitting up would rest it.

BILL: You're a liar! You're afraid. You was to be burned at sunrise, and you was afraid he'd do it. And he would, too, if he could find a match. Ain't it awful, Sam? Do you think anybody will pay out good money to get a little imp like that back home?

SAM: Sure. A rowdy kid like that is just the kind parents dote on. Now, you and the Chief get up and cook breakfast, while I go up on the top of this mountain and reconnoiter.

BILL: O.K., if you say so.

SAM: I went up on the peak of the mountain, expecting to see the village armed with scythes and pitchforks, beating the countryside for the dastardly kidnappers. But there was nobody to be seen. Perhaps, I said to myself, it has not yet been discovered that the wolves have borne away the tender lambkin from the fold. Heaven help the wolves, says I, and went back down the mountain to get breakfast. When I got to the cave I found Bill backed up against the side of it, breathing hard, and the boy threatening to smash him with a rock half as big as a coconut.

BILL: He put a red-hot boiled potato down my back, and then smashed it with his foot! I boxed his ears. Have you got a gun on you, Sam?

RED CHIEF: I'll fix you! No man ever struck Red Chief but what he got paid for it. You better beware!

SAM: I took the rock away from the boy and he took a piece of leather with strings wrapped around it out of his pocket and went outside the cave.

BILL: What's he up to now? You don't think he'll run away, do you, Sam?

SAM: No fear of it. He don't seem to be much of a homebody. But we've got to fix up some plan about the ransom. There don't seem to be much excitement around Summit on account of his disappearance. His folks may think he's spending the night with Aunt Jane or one of the neighbors.

BILL: Well, let's get a message to his father real quick demanding the two thousand dollars for his return.

SAM: Just then, we heard a kind of war whoop such as David might have emitted when he knocked out Goliath. Red Chief had pulled out a slingshot and was whirling it around his head. I dodged and heard a heavy thud and a kind of sigh from Bill, like a horse gives out when you take his saddle off. A rock the size of an egg had caught Bill just behind his left ear. He loosened himself all over and fell in the fire across the frying pan. I pulled him out and poured cold water on his head for about half an hour.

BILL: Sam, do you know who my favorite Bible character is?

SAM: Take it easy. You'll come to your senses presently.

BILL: King Herod.

SAM: Shhh.

BILL: You won't go away again and leave me here alone with him, will you, Sam?

SAM: Shhh.

RED CHIEF: I'll behave, Snake-Eye, if you won't send me home, and if you'll let me play the Scout today.

SAM: I don't know the game. That's for you and Bill to decide. He's your playmate for the day.

BILL: You know, Sam, I've stood by you without batting an eye in earthquakes, fire, and flood—in poker games, police raids, train robberies, and cyclones. I never lost my nerve till we kidnapped that two-legged skyrocket of a kid. He's got me goin'. Please, don't leave me alone with him.

SAM: I'll be back some time this afternoon. You keep the boy amused and quiet till I return. And now, we'll write the letter to old Dorset.

264

BILL: It ain't human for anybody to give up two thousand dollars for that forty-pound chunk of freckled wildcat. I'm willing to take a chance at fifteen hundred dollars. You can charge the difference to me.

SAM: So, to relieve Bill, I agreed, and we collaborated a letter that ran this way:

BILL: Ebenezer Dorset, Esq.:

SAM: We have your boy concealed in a place far from Summit. It is useless for you or the most skillful detectives to attempt to find him. Absolutely the only terms on which you can have him restored to you are these—

BILL: We demand fifteen hundred dollars in large bills for his return; the money to be left at midnight tonight at the same spot and in the same box as your reply—as hereinafter described.

SAM: If you agree to these terms, send your answer in writing by a solitary messenger tonight at half-past eight o'clock. After crossing Owl Creek on the road to Poplar Cove, there are three large trees about a hundred yards apart close to the fence of the wheatfield on the right-hand side. At the bottom of the fence-post opposite the third tree will be found a small pasteboard box. Have the messenger place the answer in this box and return immediately to Summit.

BILL: If you attempt any treachery or fail to comply with our demands stated, you will never see your boy again.

SAM: If you pay the money as demanded, he will be returned to you safe and well within three hours. These terms are final.

BILL: Signed, Two Desperate Men.

RED CHIEF: Aw, Snake-Eye, you said I could play the Scout while you was gone.

SAM: Mr. Bill will play with you. What kind of a game is it?

RED CHIEF: I'm the Scout, and I have to ride to the stockade to warn the settlers that the Indians are coming.

SAM: It sounds harmless to me, Bill.

BILL: All right. What am I to do?

RED CHIEF: You are the hoss. Get down on your hands and knees. How can I ride to the stockade without a hoss?

265

SAM: Loosen up. Keep him interested till we get the scheme going.

BILL: How far is it to the stockade, kid?

RED CHIEF: Ninety miles, and you have to hump yourself to get there on time. Whoa, now!

BILL: For heaven's sake, hurry back, Sam, as soon as you can! I wish we hadn't made the ransom more than a thousand. Say, kid, you quit kicking me or I'll get up and warm you good!

SAM: I walked over to Poplar Cove and sat around the post office and store. I bought some smoking tobacco, referred casually to the price of black-eyed peas, and posted the letter. When I got back to the cave, Bill and the boy were not to be found. In about half an hour, I heard the bushes rustle and Bill waddled out into the clearing. Behind him was the kid, stepping softly like a scout with a broad grin on his face. Bill stopped abruptly, took off his hat, and wiped his face with a handkerchief.

BILL: Sam, I suppose you'll think I'm a renegade, but I couldn't help it. The boy is gone. I sent him home. It's all off. I tried to be faithful to our articles of depredation, but there came a limit.

SAM: What's the trouble, Bill?

BILL: I was rode ninety miles to the stockade, not barring an inch. Then, when the settlers was rescued, I was given oats. Sand ain't a palpable substitute. And then, for an hour, I had to try to explain to him why there was nothin' in holes, how a road can run both ways, and what makes the grass green. I tell you, Sam, a human can only stand so much. On the way back, he kicks my legs black and blue from the knees down; and I've got two or three bites on my hand. So, he's gone. Gone on home. I showed him the road to Summit, and kicked him about eight feet nearer there at one kick. I'm sorry we lose the ransom; but it was either that or Bill Driscoll to the madhouse.

SAM: Bill, there isn't heart disease in your family, is there?

BILL: No. Nothing chronic except malaria and accidents. Why?

SAM: Then you might turn around, and have a look behind you.

BILL: *(Turns, sees the boy, plumps down on the grass and begins to pluck aimlessly at grass and little sticks.)* Hi, Scout ...

SAM: Bill braced up enough to give the kid a weak sort of smile, and promised to play a game of war with him as soon as he felt a little better. But I had another scheme for collecting that ransom. The tree under which the answer was to be left—and the money later on—was close to the road fence with big bare fields on all sides. At half-past eight I was up in that tree, as well hidden as a tree toad, waiting for the messenger to arrive. Exactly on time, a half-grown boy rides up the road on a bicycle, slips a folded piece of paper in the pasteboard box at the foot of the fence posts, and pedals away back toward Summit. I wait a while, slid down the tree, got the note, then slipped along the fence till I struck the woods and was back at the cave in another half an hour. I quickly opened the note, got near the lantern, and read it to Bill. The sum and substance of it was this:

Two Desperate Men,

> Gentlemen, I received your letter today by post, in regard to the ransom you asked for the return of my son. I think you are a little high in your demands, and I hereby make you a counter-proposition, which I am inclined to believe you will accept. You bring Johnny home and pay me two hundred and fifty dollars in cash, and I agree to take him off your hands. You had better come at night, for the neighbors believe he is lost, and I couldn't be responsible for what they would do to anybody they saw bringing him back.

> Very respectfully,

> Ebenezer Dorset

BILL: Sam, what's two hundred and fifty dollars after all? We've got the money. One more night of this kind will send me to a bed in Bedlam. Besides being a thorough gentleman, I think Mr.

267

Dorset made us a very liberal offer. You ain't going to let the chance go, are you?

SAM: To tell you the truth, Bill, this little ewe lamb has somewhat got on my nerves, too. We'll take him home, pay the ransom, and make our get-away.

BILL: Thank you, kindly, Sam.

SAM: We took him home that night. We got him to go by telling him that his father had bought a silver-mounted rifle and a pair of moccasins for him and we were going to hunt bears the next day. It was just twelve o'clock when we knocked at Ebenezer's front door. When the kid found out we were going to leave him at home, he started up a howl like a calliope and fastened himself as tight as a leech to Bill's leg. His father peeled him away gradually, like a porous plaster.

BILL: How long can you hold him?

SAM: His father promised us ten minutes and we were out of there!

BILL: In ten minutes I ran cross the Central, Southern, and Middle Western states and was legging it for the Canadian border!

SAM: As dark as it was, and as good a runner as I am, Bill was a good mile and a half out of Summit before I could catch up with him!

# from "The Unicorn in the Garden" by James Thurber

Here is another short narrative by James Thurber that illustrates a deliciously humorous moral! Much of the subtle humor in "The Unicorn in the Garden," of course, is predicated on the author's rather matter-of-fact treatment of incongruous and preposterous events. There are performance opportunities here for a narrator figure and distinctly individual character voices. Classroom staging should be extrememly simple and the use of Off-stage focus may heighten the desired comic response.

Once upon a sunny morning a man who sat in a breakfast nook looked up from his scrambled eggs to see a white unicorn with a gold horn quietly cropping the roses in the garden. The man went up to the bedroom where his wife was still asleep and woke her. "There's a unicorn in the garden," he said. "Eating roses." She opened one unfriendly eye and looked at him. "The unicorn is a mythical beast," she said, and turned her back on him. The man walked slowly downstairs and out into the garden. The unicorn was still there; he was now browsing among the tulips. "Here, unicorn," said the man, and he pulled up a lily and gave it to him. The unicorn ate it gravely. With a high heart, because there was a unicorn in his garden, the man went upstairs and roused his wife again. "The unicorn," he said, "ate a lily." His wife sat up in bed and looked at him coldly. "You are a booby," she said, "and I am going to have you put in the booby-hatch." The man, who had never liked the words "booby" and "booby-hatch," and who liked them even less on a shining morning when there was a unicorn in the garden, thought for a moment. "We'll see about that," he said. He walked over to the door. "He has a golden horn in the middle of his forehead," he told her. Then he went back to the garden to watch the unicorn; but the unicorn had gone away. The man sat down among the roses and went to sleep.

As soon as the husband had gone out of the house, the wife got up and dressed as fast as she could. She was very excited and there was a gloat in her eye. She telephoned the police and she telephoned a psychiatrist; she told them to hurry to her house and bring a straitjacket. When the police and the psychiatrist arrived they sat down in chairs and looked at her, with great interest. "My husband," she said, "saw a unicorn this morning." The police looked at the psychiatrist and the psychiatrist looked at the police. "He told me it ate a lily," she said. The psychiatrist looked at the police and the police looked at the psychiatrist. "He told me it had a golden horn in the middle of its forehead," she said. At a solemn signal from the psychiatrist, the police leaped from their chairs and seized the wife. They had a hard time subduing her, for she put up a terrific struggle, but they finally subdued her. Just as they got her into the straitjacket, the husband came back into the house.

"Did you tell your wife you saw a unicorn?" asked the police. "Of course not," said the husband. "The unicorn is a mythical beast." "That's all I wanted to know," said the psychiatrist. "Take her away. I'm sorry, sir, but your wife is crazy as a jay bird." So they took her away, cursing and screaming, and shut her up in an institution. The husband lived happily ever after.

Moral: Don't count your boobies until they are hatched.

## Other Fables

There are limitless possibilities to explore fables as thematic programs for classroom performance. Fables are especially valuable texts for beginning performers to initially explore bodily or emotional involvement with literary characters, practice vocal qualities, and experience the dramatic involvement of storytelling that involves moments of suspense, short exchanges of dialog, and sophisticated humor. Here are some examples of other well-known fables suitable for promoting brief, interesting character sketches or for compiling short Readers Theatre classroom performance scripts and skits.

# from Aesop's *Fables*

### "Belling the Cat"

One day the mice held a general council to consider what they might do to protect themselves against their common enemy, the Cat. Some said one thing and some said another, but at last a young mouse stood up and announced that he had a plan which he thought would solve the problem.

"You will all agree," he said, "that our chief danger lies in the unexpected and sly manner in which our enemy comes upon us. Now, if we could receive some warning of her approach, we could easily hide from her. I propose, therefore, that a small bell be obtained and attached by a ribbon to the neck of the Cat. In this way we could always know when she was coming and be able to make our escape."

This proposal was met with great applause, until an old mouse arose and said, "This is all very fine, but who among us is so brave? Who will bell the Cat?" The mice looked at one another in silence and nobody volunteered.

Moral: It is easier to suggest a plan than to carry it out.

### "The Fox and the Woodcutter"

A fox was fleeing. As she fled
A hunter fast behind her sped.
But being wearied, when she spied
An old man cutting wood, she cried,
"By all the gods that keep you well,
Hide me among these trees you fell,
And don't reveal the place, I pray."
He swore that he would not betray
The wily vixen; so she hid,
And then the hunter came to bid
The old man tell him if she'd fled,
Or if she'd hidden there. He said,

271

"I did not see her," but he showed
The place the cunning beast was stowed
By pointing at it with his finger.
But still the hunter did not linger.
He put no faith in leering eye,
But trusting in the words, went by.
Escaped from danger for a while
The fox peeked out with coaxing smile.
The old man said to her, "You owe
Me thanks for saving you, you know."
"Most certainly; for I was there
As witness of your expert care.
But now farewell. And don't forget,
The god of oaths will catch you yet
For saving with your voice and lips
While slaying with your finger tips."

# from Ambrose Bierce's *Fables*

### "The Man of Principle"

During a shower of rain the Keeper of a zoological garden observed a Man of Principle crouching beneath the belly of the ostrich, which had drawn itself up to its full height to sleep.

"Why, my dear sir," said the Keeper, "if you fear to get wet, you'd better creep into the pouch of yonder female kangaroo—the *Saltarix mackintosha*—for if that ostrich wakes up he will kick you to death in a minute."

"I can't help that," the Man of Principle replied, with that lofty scorn of practical considerations distinguishing his species. "He may kick me to death if he wish, but until he does he shall give me shelter from the storm. He has swallowed my umbrella."

### "Religions of Error"

Hearing a sound of strife, a Christian in the Orient asked his Dragoman the cause of it.

"The Buddhists are cutting Mohammedan throats," the Dragoman replied, with oriental composure.

"I did not know," remarked the Christian, with scientific interest, 'that that would make so much noise.'

"The Mohammedans are cutting Buddhist throats, too," added the Dragoman.

"It is astonishing," mused the Christian, "how violent and how general are religious animosities. Everywhere in the world the devotees of each local faith abhor the devotees of every other, and abstain from murder only so long as they dare not commit it. And the strangest thing about it is that all religions are erroneous and mischievous excepting mine. Mine, thank God, is true and benign."

So saying he visibly smugged and went off to telegraph for a brigade of cutthroats to protect Christian interests.

### "Married Woman"

A married woman, whose lover was about to reform by running away, procured a pistol and shot him dead.

"Why did you do that, Madam?" inquired a policeman sauntering by.

"Because," replied the married woman, "he was a wicked man, and had purchased a ticket to Chicago."

"My sister," said an adjacent man of God, solemnly, "you cannot stop the wicked from going to Chicago by killing them."

### "The Ineffective Rooter"

A drunken man was lying in the road with a bleeding nose, upon which he had fallen, when a pig passed that way.

"You wallow fairly well," said the pig, "but my fine fellow, you have much to learn about rooting."

273

# from *Alice in Wonderland* by Lewis Carroll

### "Father William"

"You are old, Father William," the young man said,
    "And your hair has become very white,
And yet you incessantly stand on your head—
    Do you think, at your age, it is right?"

"In my youth," Father William replied to his son,
    "I feared it might injure the brain;
But now that I'm perfectly sure that I have none,
    Why, I do it again and again."

# from "On the Life of Man" by Francis Beaumont

Like to the falling of a star.
Or as the flights of eagles are,
Or like the fresh spring's gaudy hue,
Or silver drops of morning dew,
Or like a wind that chafes the flood,
Or bubbles which on water stood:
Even such is Man, whose borrowed light
Is straight called in and paid tonight.
The wind blows out, the bubble dies,
The spring entombed in autumn lies;
The dew's dried up, the star is shot,
The flight is past—and man forgot.

# from "Amor Vincit Omnia ad Nauseam"
# by John Updike, adapted by Melvin R. White

This amusing John Updike short story, adapted by Melvin R.
White, is based on the familiar nursery rhyme "The Cat and the
Fiddle," but modernized for an imaginative Readers Theatre
classroom performance. Although the adaptation features fanciful
characters like a cat, fiddle, little dog, cow, and moon, the
classroom performance should suggest a highly sophisticated satire
rather than a child's story. The script lends itself to open staging,
suggestive costumes, music, and the use of a dictionary to help
define obscure terms.

## Characters

Narrator:   An enthusiastic storyteller with a mature,
pleasing voice

Cat:   A sophisticatedly "feline" girl, quite sexy of physique
and voice

Fiddle:   The leading man—tall, dark, and handsome

Cow:   Bovine in physique, voice, and personality—
perhaps stupid-sounding

Moon:   A serene and calm lady, probably with a smooth,
contralto voice

Dog:   A cheerful little pixie of a dog, quick of speech and
manner

## Production Note

Although no special attire is necessary, the performers may initially choose to explore elaborate, stylized animal costumes or makeup. The performers may also wish to explore a more subtle interpretation that highlights the personality of the characters rather than the physicality. For example, the Cat might be dressed in a red evening gown, the Fiddle in a three-piece, creme-colored suit, and the Moon in a pale blue jumpsuit. The staging may be as simple as stools and lecterns; as theatrical as platforms, painted backdrop, and sound effects; or as formal as using Off-stage focus to locate the action and the characters.

> *(Brief introductory violin music may introduce the program, perhaps excerpts from "Tales of the Vienna Woods.")*

NARRATOR:  Hey diddle, diddle ...

CAT:  The cat and ...

FIDDLE:  The fiddle ...

COW:  The cow ...

NARRATOR:  Jumped over ...

MOON:  The moon ...

DOG:  The little dog ...

NARRATOR:  Laughed ...

DOG:  *(Laughs.)*

NARRATOR:  To see such sport ...

FIDDLE:  Hey diddle ...?

CAT:  Diddle.

FIDDLE:  You're thinking about God again.

CAT:  I was thinking about *you.*

NARRATOR:  It was true. She had been. The cat had been thinking about the fiddle. She had been thinking about him. He had a long thin stringy neck and a plump brown resinous hollow body. His voice had vibrato.

CAT:  *(Narrating)* Yes. I've been his mistress for four years. It has been ecstatic, but not extremely. You see, I was attracted by his voice.

NARRATOR:  They had met, the Cat and the Fiddle, at a benefit

276

performance given for church mice. A bow had scraped him and he had sung. *(A short violin solo may be inserted here if desired.)* The Cat had gone up afterwards and had rubbed herself against him, and in her whiskers, so decisively parallel, he had recognized something kindred. So he sang to her, and she related to him tales of her previous lovers.

CAT: *(Narrating)* Oh yes, there had been a succession of toms behind the gasworks. They all had terrible voices. They clawed me. They bit me. And slowly I formed an image of a tom who was hairless and toothless, a fragile and lean lover. He would have resonance, yes—but he would be powerless to pounce. I told the Fiddle all this.

FIDDLE: *(Narrating)* It pleased and flattered me. I sang to her. She rubbed against me, and told me of her countless lovers. I did not mind, for now she had chosen me.

NARRATOR: That had been in those days. These were these days. All day the Cat took a small abrasive pleasure in licking the calico fur of her chest while the Fiddle failed to sing but instead leaned in the corner and almost hummed. She looked at him, his shape, his texture, his state of tension.

CAT: *(Narrating)* One of my toms had been made into a tennis racket. Perhaps that had been the attraction. But I needed a larger fate, warmer, kinder, yet more perilous in its dimensions, coarsely infinite yet mottled like me.

NARRATOR: Her vertically slit eyes, hoarding depths of amber, dilated at a shadow memory from her barnyard days as a kitten in the straw. Something large had been often above her. Something smelling of milk. It had mooed.

COW: *(Narrating)* I am only a cow, but I am so in love with the Moon. Throughout the first three quarters I wept solidly, streams and streams. Then the Moon became full. Tears poured down my muzzle in an invincible tide. The full Moon spoke to me.

MOON: You are seeking to purify yourself by giving rein to impossibility.

COW: *(Weeping)* Oh God ... I can't ... I don't ...

MOON: Go on.

COW: *(Very emotional)* When I first saw you, you were new—a sort of weak bent splinter of a sort of nibbled thing. How loathesome, I thought. I think even then I was protecting myself from the truth. I believe even then I deeply knew you were cheese. You began to grow. Mare Serenitatis showed, and one bluish blind mad eye, and the side of your lopsided leprous smile. At first I loved you in spite of your leprosity. Then I loved it because it was part of *you.* Then I loved the leprosity itself, and you because you were the vehicle whereby it was boldly imposed upon the cold night sky. I have never known pain so ungainsayable. I beg you, what ... ?

MOON: Jump.

COW: Jump?

MOON: *Jump.*

COW: *Jump?*

MOON: *Jump!*

NARRATOR: A little dog had been eavesdropping and gave the Cow advice.

DOG: Imagine the Moon as only slightly higher than the Albert Memorial. Or consider the Albert Hall. It is round and deep and vast and many-entranced like a woman's love.

NARRATOR: The Cow was jumping. Splendidly. Galaxies upon diamantine sphere chimed the diatonic music that mesmerized Jerusalem the Golden. Time and space were fooled at their own game. *Ab ovo,* lacto-galactic.

COW: Moon, you are near! You ashy, awful, barren, lunar, luminous. You! Oh, I touched you, dear Moon—just a hint of a ghost of a breath of a touch. But I am now descending, reentering earth's orbit ...

NARRATOR: *(Building toward climax)* The atmosphere sizzled. The Cat's sensitive amber eyes dilated as the shadow from above gathered. She felt the ponderous loved thing smelling of milk and warm above her again.

CAT: Is it to be ... ?

COW: Can't stop. Gravity.

CAT: Oh ... how *right!*

278

NARRATOR: Black ecstasy flattened the Cat. Her ego was, if not eliminated, expanded beyond the bounds of dissatisfaction. She was ever so utterly content. The little Dog laughed to see such sport.

DOG: *(Laughs heartily.)*

FIDDLE: *(Clearing his throat)* Er ... er ... when you laughed like that, I ... er ... *twanged.* Strange to say, I love you insanely.

DOG: Too bad, I love the cow. This face was asleep in me until I saw her jump. What an august uncanny leap that was!

NARRATOR: He was a beagleish Dog. His forepaws, however, had an engaging outward twist. He yapped amorously at the Cow.

DOG: *(Yaps at COW.)*

NARRATOR: Startled, she stepped back into the fiddle. Her glossy hoof fragmented the ruddy wood.

FIDDLE: *(Sobbing)* Thank you ... thank you.

NARRATOR: He had been excessively pampered heretofore. It was bliss to be hurt. And nothing arouses gratitude like an eruption of violence.

FIDDLE: Oh Cow, I love you ... of course I love *you!*

NARRATOR: The Cow became haughty. Her high hot sides made a mist like fog off the Greenwich Reach.

COW: I am sorry, but I have dedicated myself to the memory of the Cat. The Cat has become the angel of death whose abiding iron presence is the destiny of all life to worship. What else is love? Nothing else.

DOG: *(Yowling)* I discover I was confused. It is the Moon I adore, for having permitted itself to be so splendidly jumped. *(Yowls and yowls at the MOON.)*

MOON: *(Beaming)* I love everyone. I shine on just and unjust alike. I give to all the gift of madness. That is my charm. That is my *truth.*

NARRATOR: The Fiddle lived with his wound for a fortnight, as one would live with the shifting shades and fluorescent evanescences of an unduly prolonged sunset. Then ... he found he could sing. He had once sung! He was again singing!

FIDDLE: *(Singing)* "A questo seno, deh! Vieni, idolo mio,
Quanti timori, quante lacrime ..."

279

NARRATOR: Hey diddle diddle ...
CAT: The cat ... and ...
FIDDLE: The fiddle ...
COW: The cow ...
NARRATOR: Jumped over ...
MOON: The moon ...
DOG: The little dog ...
NARRATOR: Laughed ...
DOG: *(Laughs.)*
NARRATOR: To see such sport ...
ALL: And the dish ran away with the spoon!

# from "I'm Herbert" by Robert Woodruff Anderson

This two-person character study appears as the third scene in Robert Woodruff Anderson's popular comedy *You Know I Can't Hear You When the Water's Running*. The characters are mature and the scene is well-marked to encourage a number of inventive interpretations. Staging possibilities may at first appear to be limited because the characters are apparently seated, but the short exchanges of dialog should promote subtle gestures, intimate reactions, and meaningful physical responses.

HERBERT: Baltimore oriole. *(He shifts his glasses, scanning.)* Bobolink. *(Shifts again.)* Rose-breasted grosbeak. *(Shifts again and gets a little excited.)* A black-billed cuckoo. *(He speaks louder.)* Grace, I saw a black-billed cuckoo.
MURIEL: *(Her eyes open)* My name is Muriel, foolish old man.
HERBERT: I know your name is Muriel. That's what I called you.
MURIEL: You called me Grace. Grace was your first wife.
HERBERT: I called you Muriel. You're just hard of hearing and

won't admit it ... Grace ... Grace ... That's what I said!

MURIEL: There! You said it.

HERBERT: What?

MURIEL: Grace ... You called me Grace.

HERBERT: Silly old woman. You call me Harry. But I called you Grace.

MURIEL: Can't you hear yourself?

HERBERT: What?

MURIEL: I said can't you hear yourself?

HERBERT: Of course I can hear myself. It's you that can't hear. I say you call me Harry. Sometimes. Your second husband ... and sometimes George ... your first ...

MURIEL: A hearing aid's a cheap thing ...

HERBERT: See here, Grace ...

MURIEL: I'm Muriel.

HERBERT: You talk about me ... What about you? "Muriel. I'm Muriel."

MURIEL: Cuckoo!

HERBERT: *(He takes up his binoculars.)* Where? I wouldn't call you Grace. Grace was soft and gentle and kind.

MURIEL: Why'd you leave her then?

HERBERT: I didn't. She died.

MURIEL: Mary died. Your first wife. You got sick of Grace and left her and married me.

HERBERT: Left Grace for you?

MURIEL: Yes, you silly old man.

HERBERT: All wrong. Grace was my darling.

MURIEL: She drove you crazy.

HERBERT: My first love.

MURIEL: Mary.

HERBERT: Mary drove me crazy.

MURIEL: She was your first love. You've told me about it often enough. The two of you young colts prancing around in the nude.

HERBERT: Mary?

MURIEL: Yes.

HERBERT: I never saw Mary naked. That was her trouble. Cold woman.

MURIEL: That was Grace.

HERBERT: Grace I saw naked. Oh, how naked! There was never anyone nakeder.

281

MURIEL: You can only be naked. You can't be more or less naked.

HERBERT: You didn't know Grace.

MURIEL: Mary. I did know Grace.

HERBERT: Naked?

MURIEL: Keep a civil tongue in your head.

HERBERT: I never saw you naked.

MURIEL: No, and not likely to. What'd be the point?

HERBERT: Old women forget ... forget the joys of the flesh. Why is that?

MURIEL: I don't forget Bernie.

HERBERT: Who?

MURIEL: Bernie Walters.

HERBERT: Never heard of him.

MURIEL: My second husband. I was married to him when Harry came along ... But Harry went away and then you came along ... a long time after. Platonic marriage. That's what we've had, you and I, George. But it's all right.

HERBERT: Platonic under the willow tree that June?

MURIEL: What willow tree?

HERBERT: Oh, I've been good to you, Mary, for all your carping and your falling off in your old age, because I remember that willow tree. Muriel never knew about it. We were wicked.

MURIEL: If I thought I knew what you were talking about, I'd get mad. But I know you're just babbling. Babbling Bernie ... That's you. Herbert used to say, "How can you listen to him babble?"

HERBERT: I'm Herbert.

MURIEL: If it makes you feel more secure. Go on. Keep reminding yourself.

HERBERT: You called me Bernie.

MURIEL: Oh, sure, sure. And you've never been to Chicago.

HERBERT: I have so. I went there when my daughter died.

MURIEL: Well, I'm glad you admit it.

HERBERT: Why shouldn't I admit it? It's so. You just try to confuse me ... Bernie, Harry, George, Grace, Mary.

MURIEL: You started a long time ago, slipping. Only then you were more honest about it. Very touching. When we went to Florida and you gave me the tickets amd said, "Grace, my mind's slipping, take care of the tickets."

HERBERT: Your name's Muriel.

MURIEL: Yes, yes, lovely. My name's Muriel.

HERBERT: You referred to yourself as "Grace."

MURIEL: *(Sarcastic)* Oh, very likely. Very likely.

HERBERT: You said I gave you the tickets to Florida and said, "Grace, my mind's slipping."

MURIEL: Well, it was.

HERBERT: I've never been to Florida.

MURIEL: Ho-ho. Well, let's not go into it. The pongee suit.

HERBERT: I never owned a pongee suit.

MURIEL: You said it was the same suit you wore when you married Helen, and we had a long discussion about how ironic it was that you were wearing the same suit to run away with me.

HERBERT: Who's Helen?

MURIEL: You were married to her, silly.

HERBERT: I was running away to Florida with you and I was so old my mind was slipping and I couldn't remember the tickets?

MURIEL: Lovely, you're running a lot of things that happened at different times together now. Maybe you should just sit quietly for a while, Harry, till you get straightened out.

HERBERT: My name is Herbert.

MURIEL: That's right. We'll start from there. You're Herbert and I'm Grace.

HERBERT: You're Muriel.

MURIEL: That's right. Now let's just leave it at that now, or you won't sleep tonight.

HERBERT: I always sleep.

MURIEL: A fortune for sleeping pills.

HERBERT: I never had one in my life.

MURIEL: And you've never been to Chicago either, I suppose.

HERBERT: Never. Why should I have gone to Chicago?

MURIEL: Only because our daughter died there and we went to the funeral.

HERBERT: We had no children together.

MURIEL: I think we shouldn't talk any more now. You're getting confused.

HERBERT: You never let me near your lily-white body.

MURIEL: Ho-ho ... and what about that afternoon under the willow tree? I think that's when we conceived Ralph.

HERBERT: Who is Ralph?

MURIEL: Ralph is your stepson. Good God!

HERBERT: I conceived my stepson under the willow tree?

MURIEL: I'd prefer it if we just remained quiet for a while. You can't follow a train of thought for more than a moment ... and it's very tiring trying to jump back and forth with you. Just close your eyes and rest ... Are your eyes hurting you?

HERBERT: No.

MURIEL: That medicine must be very good then.

HERBERT: What medicine?

MURIEL: You see, that's what I mean.

HERBERT: I never had any medicine for my eyes.

MURIEL: Yes, all right. All right. Let's not argue, George.

HERBERT: I'm Harry.

MURIEL: Yes, yes. All right. We'll just hold hands here, and try to doze a little ... and think of happier days ... *(She takes his hand and they close their eyes and rock.)*

HERBERT: *(After a long moment)* Mmmmmm... Venice.

MURIEL: *(Dreamy)* Yes ... Oh, yes ... Wasn't that lovely ... Oh, you were so gallant ... if slightly shocking ... *(She laughs, remembering.)*

HERBERT: The beach ...

MURIEL: The willow tree ...

HERBERT: *(Smiling)* You running around naked ... Oh, lovely ... lovely ...

MURIEL: Yes ... lovely ... *(They go on rocking and smiling, holding hands as the lights dim.)*

# Glossary of Readers Theatre Terms

ARENA: "In-the-round" playing space surrounding the dramatic action on all four sides.

AUDITORY: "Sound" values suggested in a literary text.

BALANCE: Spatial relationship between objects and performers in terms of number, proportion, and weight.

BLACK BOX: Formless staging space that can be adjusted or rearranged in a number of interesting configurations—usually a large, empty room painted black.

BLOCKING: Pictorial composition of performers' movement to create "stage pictures" that illustrate dramatic action in a literary text.

CASE STUDIES: Narratives culled from newspaper accounts and personal histories.

CHAMBER THEATRE: Production that pursues the narrative elements of literature using minimal theatrical devices.

CHARACTER ACTION: Details, individual habits, or traits of characters that surface from an analysis of the literary text.

CHARACTER BIOGRAPHY: Incidents or events that may have happened prior to the story line described in a literary text.

CLIMAX: Highest point in the dramatic action of a literary text.

COLOR: Palette of hues that gives vibrant life and meaning to costumes, lighting, props, and scenic elements in production.

COMBINED FOCI: Mixture of Off-stage and On-stage character focus to achieve a dramatic special effect.

COMPILED SCRIPT: Miscellaneous excerpts of literary and nonliterary materials juxtaposed to explore a selected idea or theme.

COMPLICATION: Obstacles and barriers that provoke conflict or inhibit character realization of specific goals and objectives.

CONNOTATIVE: Implied meaning of words.

CONVENTIONS: Dominant or emergent Readers Theatre practices and principles accepted by the audience as a willing suspension of disbelief.

COUNTER FOCUS: Deliberately avoids a clearly defined point of attention in staging composition and is concerned with the role of *contrast* in visualizing a character's reaction or response to an incident or event.

DENOTATIVE: Dictionary meaning of words.

DENOUEMENT: French term for "unknotting" or untangling of all the loose ends of a story line following the climax.

DESCRIPTIVE ACTION: Provides voice, gesture, and movement of characters from a study of the dialog and description in a literary text.

DIRECT FOCUS: Features a dominant performer in an incident or even by using a diagonal line in blocking to guide audience attention from one performer to another until the dominant performer is identified at apex of the line.

DRAMATIC ACTION: Promotes conflict needed to propel characters into a series of incidents and events described in the literary text.

DRAMATIC SPACE: Literary characters inhabiting a carefully selected, well-defined spatial environment that charges every detail of their interaction with significance.

EMPHASIS: Staging incidents and events that place special importance on isolated, specific dramatic moments.

ENVIRONMENTAL SPACE: Large, open area with a number of separate performance stations, rather than a fixed stage, that encourages the audience to move from place to place and observe multiple incidents or events being performed simultaneously.

EXPOSITION: Background information needed to understand a character's action and situation.

FORM: Shape, silhouette, and outline of the playing area and the performers in the space.

FOUND SPACE: Moves the literary text itself to a locale that suggests the setting described by the author.

FULCRUM: "Balance point" in poetry that begins with forward motion and then moves to counter motion.

INSTINCTIVE ACTION: Spontaneous reactions or responses of a performer that emerge in classroom rehearsal as a result of the habits or traits of literary characters.

INTERIOR MONOLOG: Inventive subconscious or submerged

literary character feelings or thoughts.

MASS: Distribution of the number of performers and their relative spatial weight in the playing area.

MENTAL SYMBOL: Overarching objective of a literary character suggested in an analysis of action, intention, and motivation to achieve a specific desire.

METAPHOR: Implied analogy or comparison which imaginatively identifies one object with another; and invests the first object with qualities usually associated with the second.

MOOD: Emotional attitude of the author toward the subject implied in the atmosphere of the literary text.

OFF-STAGE FOCUS: Placement *out* of the playing space that locates characters, events, or incidents on a straight or angled line slightly above the heads of the audience. A performer's action, business, dialog, reaction, and sight lines are also directed slightly over the heads of the audience; intersecting at a hypothetical point in the center of the audience.

OMNISCIENT: Third-person point of view through whom the story line is told in a text.

OPEN SPACE: Flexible staging area that places performers in the center of the dramatic action, like theatre in-the-round, but which also provides a decorative backdrop or curtains against which the performance is played.

PERFORMANCE VERBS: Encourages performers to respond to the physical movement and vocal quality suggested in the literary text by these action words.

PERSONA: "Second self" of the author through whom the story is told in a literary text.

PERSONAL SIGNATURE: Author's individual word choice, narrative style, use of imagery, and distinctive dialog or language.

PICTURIZATION: Detailed storytelling in staging a literary text using composition, personal gesture, and improvisation to suggest a theatrical interpretation of the author's apparent point of view.

POETIC QUALITY: Term applied to prose to suggest it shares a striking similarity to poetry in terms of its evocative imagery, language, and word choice.

PRODUCTION (STAGING) METAPHOR: Director's artistic expression of the theatrical treatment to be given a literary text in performance, staging, or production.

PROSCENIUM-ARCH: Raised "picture frame" stage through which an audience views a production.

RISING ACTION: Incidents and events that dramatically intensify a character's action or situation.

READING HOUR: Informal, fifteen- to twenty-minute programs with an invited audience that feature original compositions or small-group performance projects.

RHYTHMIC SCHEMES: Recurrent patterns of beat and stress that identify the tempo of a character's spoken language or thought process.

SIMILE: Comparison of two things using "as" or "like."

SPACE STAGE: Defines the dramatic space in terms of lighting to indicate the beginning and ending of incidents or events in a production.

STORY LINE: Sequence of events or incidents that influence character actions and reactions.

SUBTEXT: Hidden meaning that exists beneath the surface of a character's action or spoken lines of dialog.

TABLEAUX: Frozen performer poses.

TAG LINES: Narrative explanations like "he said" or "she said" that indicate the speaker(s) in a literary text.

THEATRICAL IMPULSE: Artistic and dramatic visualization of the actions, attitudes, and emotions of literary characters in classroom performance and production.

THREAD OF ACTION: Sequence of incidents and events that gives the text's story line its continuity and sense of apparent direction.

THRUST: Raised platform in the center of the playing area and audience arranged around three, or occasionally two, sides of the dramatic action.

TONE COLOR: Literary character's implied attitude toward the subject and toward the audience or reader.

WORD PLAY: "Verbal gymnastics," or inventive vocalization of sentences, key words, and phrases that gives the additional dimension to spoken language.

288

# Additional Classroom Performance Resources

Although a number of potential Readers Theatre texts for classroom performance have been recommended for review in each chapter of this book, there is still a wealth of theatrical literature remaining to be reviewed. The broad range of inherently dramatic material that follows is suitable for Readers Theatre adaptations that feature multiple student performers, simple staging, and minimal theatrical accessories like costumes, lights, props, or scenic units. These additional classroom performance resources have been subdivided into convenient categories that draw attention to the variety of literature available for Readers Theatre exploration. Most of the authors or texts mentioned may easily be found in any standard anthology of literature.

Some of the works included here are in the public domain and may be performed without permission from a copyright holder. Most of the works, however, are still under copyright protection. When selecting a work for performance it is suggested that you read the copyright notice appended to the work before performing.

## Biblical Stories

Genesis
Exodus
Judges
Ruth
Job
Psalms
Daniel
Matthew
Mark
Luke
Romans

# Children's Literature

| | |
|---|---|
| Selby Beeler | *Throw Your Tooth on the Roof* |
| Andrew Clements | *Autumn Leaves* |
| Robert Corimer | *I Am the Cheese* |
| Lois Ehlert | *Top Cat* |
| Kenneth Grahame | *The Reluctant Dragon* |
| Norton Juster | *The Phantom Tollbooth* |
| Antoine de Saint-Exupery | *The Little Prince* |
| Shel Silverstein | *The Giving Tree* |
| Bart Vivian | *Imagine* |

# Young Adult Literature

| | |
|---|---|
| Bruce Coville | *Into the Land of the Unicorn* |
| Stephen Crane | *The Red Badge of Courage* |
| Jan Hudson | *Dawn Rider* |
| John F. Kennedy | *Profiles in Courage* |
| Walter Lord | *A Night to Remember* (The *Titanic*) |
| Eve Merriam | *The Inner City Mother Goose* |
| Scott O'Dell | *Sing Down the Moon* |
| Rosa Parks | *Rosa Parks* |
| Shel Silverstein | *Falling Up* |
| Susan Terris | *Nell's Quilt* |
| Elie Wiezel | *Night* |
| Laurence Yep | *Dragon Wings* |

# Folklore and Fairy Tales

Aesop's Fables
Johnny Appleseed
Hans Christian Andersen's Fairy Tales
Paul Bunyan
Davy Crockett
"Mister Fox"
"Little Red Cap"

The Brothers Grimm's Fairy Tales
"Hiawatha"
"The King and Robin Hood's Horny Beastes"
The Pied Piper of Hamelin
"The Fire Bird"

# Diaries

Bartolema de Casas
Anne Frank
*Go Ask Alice*
Thomas Jefferson
Lewis and Clark
Thomas Merton
Samuel Pepys
Saint Perpetua
Sojourner Truth
Virgina Woolf

# Essays

| | |
|---|---|
| Bruce Catton | "Grant and Lee" |
| Ralph Waldo Emerson | "Self Reliance" |
| Mary Ann Ferguson | "The Mother" |
| Langston Hughes | "Salvation" |
| Washington Irving | "Sketchbook" |
| N. Scott Momaday | "The Way to Rainy Mountain" |
| George Orwell | "Shooting an Elephant" |
| Richard Steele | "On Ladies' Dress" |
| Jonathan Swift | "A Modest Proposal" |
| James Thurber | "The Beast in Me and Other Animals" |
| E.B. White | "Once More to the Lake" |

# Letters

Leonardo da Vinci
Amelia Earhart
Martin Luther King, Jr.
Abraham Lincoln
Malcolm X
Richard Nixon
Saint Paul
Sir Walter Raleigh
Will Rogers
George Bernard Shaw
Dylan Thomas
Vincent Van Gogh
Oscar Wilde
William Carlos Williams

# Multicultural

| | |
|---|---|
| Maya Angelou | *I Shall Not Be Moved* |
| Dee Brown | *Bury My Heart at Wounded Knee* |
| Rita Dove | "Thomas and Beulab" |
| Carlos Fuentes | "Old Gringo" |
| Maurice Kenny | *Tekonwatoni: Molly Brant* |
| Maxine Hong Kingston | *The Woman Warrior* |
| N. Scott Momaday | *House Made of Dawn* |
| Toni Morrison | *Jazz* |
| Mildred D. Taylor | *Roll of Thunder, Hear My Cry* |
| Alice Walker | *The Color Purple* |
| John Wideman | *Brothers and Keepers* |

# Non-Dramatic

| | |
|---|---|
| Dave Barry | Syndicated Columnist |
| Erma Bombeck | Popular Humorist |
| Winston Churchill | "An Adress on Dunkirk" |
| William Faulkner | "Nobel Prize Acceptance Speech" |
| Robert Graves | *The Greek Myths* |
| Kathleen H. Hofeller | "Battered Women, Shattered Lives" |
| Jean Kerr | "The Snake Has All the Lines" |
| Jim Murray | Newspaper Editorials |
| Blaise Pascal | "Thoughts" |
| Will Rogers | American Satirist |
| Studs Terkel | *Working* |
| Daniel Webster | "The Union Address" |

# Novels

| | |
|---|---|
| John Barth | *Lost in the Funhouse* |
| Ray Bradbury | *The Martian Chronicles* |
| Truman Capote | *The Grass Harp* |
| Colette | *Gigi* |
| David James Duncan | *The River Why* |
| Ken Kesey | *One Flew Over the Cuckoo's Nest* |
| Carson McCullers | *The Ballad of the Sad Cafe* |
| Alice McDermott | *Charming Billy* |
| Tom Robbins | *Even Cowgirls Get the Blues* |
| Stan Steiner | *La Raza: The Mexican-Americans* |
| Kurt Vonnegut | *Slaughterhouse Five* |
| Tom Wolfe | *The Bonfire of the Vanities* |
| Richard Wright | *Uncle Tom's Children* |

# Playscripts

| | |
|---|---|
| Jean Anouilh | *Antigone* |
| Brian Friel | *Dancing at Lughnasa* |
| David Henry Hwang | *The Sound of a Voice* |
| Tony Kushner | *Angels in America* |
| Cherrie Moraga | *Giving Up the Ghost* |
| Carlos Morton | *The Many Deaths of Danny Rosales* |
| Paul Rudnick | *I Hate Hamlet* |
| Jean Paul Sartre | *No Exit* |
| Neil Simon | *Biloxi Blues* |
| Thornton Wilder | *Our Town* |
| August Wilson | *Fences* |

# Poems  (Long)

| | |
|---|---|
| W. H. Auden | "Miss Gee" |
| William Blake | "Song" |
| Gwendolyn Brooks | "Ballad of Pearl May Lee" |
| Bob Dylan | "Hurricane" |
| Erica Jong | "On the First Night" |
| Audre Lorde | "Dear Toni, Instead of a Letter..." |
| Edna St. Vincent Millay | "Renascence" |
| Sylvia Plath | "Ariel" |
| Anne Sexton | "Transformations" |
| Ntozake Shange | "With No Immediate Cause" |
| William Carlos Williams | "Patterson" |

# Poems  (Short)

| | |
|---|---|
| e.e. cummings | "Spring is like a perhaps hand" |
| Emily Dickinson | "I'm Nobody" |
| Robert Frost | "For Once, Then, Something" |
| Heinrich Heine | "The Loreley" |
| Langston Hughes | "Dream Deferred" |
| Stanley Kunitz | "Open the Gates" |

Sidney Lanier            "A Ballad of Trees and the Master"
Amy Lowell               "A Lady"
Marge Peircy             "Learning To Not Speak"
Theodore Roethke         "Dolor"
Christina Rosetti        "In an Artist's Studio"

# Short Stories

Ray Bradbury             "The Last Martian"
Ernest Hemingway         "The Killers"
James Joyce              "The Boarding House"
Stephen King             "Children of the Corn"
Ring Lardner             "Harmony" and "Haircut"
D. H. Lawrence           "Mother and Daughter"
Paule Marshall           "Brooklyn"
Flannery O'Connor        "A Good Man Is Hard to Find"
Jean Stafford            "At the Zoo"
Eudora Welty             "A Visit of Charity"
Jade Snow Wong           "A Person as Well as a Female"

# Additional Reference Resources

Altenbernd, Lynn. *Anthology: An Introduction to Literature.* New York: Macmillan Publishing Company, 1977.

Arbuthnot, Mary Hill and Dorothy M. Broder. *The Arbuthnot Anthology of Children's Literature.* Glenview, Illinois: Scott, Foresman, 1976.

Bakalar, Nicholas. *Anthology of American Satire.* New York: Meridian Publishing, 1997.

Berger, Arthur. *Anatomy of Humor.* New Brunswick, New Jersey: Transaction Publishers, 1993.

Bogart, Gary. *Short Story Index.* New York: H.W. Wilson Company, 1979.

Chapman, Dorothy Hilton. *Index to Poetry by Black American Women.* Westport, Connecticut: Greenwood Press, 1986.

Cline, Cheryl. *Women's Diaries, Journals, and Letters: An Annotated Bibliography.* New York: Garland, 1989.

Dark, Larry. *Prize Stories 1998: The O. Henry Awards.* New York: Doubleday, 1998.

Elsen, Jonathan and Stuart Troy. *The Novel Reader: Short Fiction, Poetry and Prose in Literature.* New York: Crown Publishers, 1987.

Ferguson, Mary Anne. *Images of Women in Literature.* Boston: Houghton Mifflin Company, 1991.

Garfield, Evelyn Picon. *Women's Fiction from Latin America.* Detroit, Michigan: Wayne State University Press, 1988.

Guy, Patricia. *A Woman's Poetry Index.* Phoenix, Arizona: Oryx, 1985.

Hall, James. *The Realm of Fiction.* New York: McGraw-Hill Book Company, 1970.

Howe, Florence. *An Anthology of Poems by Women.* Garden City, New York: Anchor Press, 1973.

Knowles, Frederic. *A Treasury of Humorous Poetry.* Freeport, New York: Library Press Books, 1952.

Linscott, R. N. *Best American Humorous Short Stories.* New York: Random House, 1945.

Mandelbaum, Allen and Robert Richardson. *Three Centuries of American Poetry.* New York: Bantam, 1999.

Paz, Octavio. *Mexican Poetry: An Anthology.* New York: Grove, 1985.

Pichaske, David. *Beowulf to Beatles and Beyond.* New York: Macmillan Publishing Company, 1981.

Pickering, James. *An Anthology of Short Stories.* New York: Macmillan Publishing Company, 1978.

Randall, Dudley. *Black Poets.* New York: Bantam Books, 1971.

Smith, William James. *Granger's Index to Poetry.* New York: Columbia University Press, 1978.

Walsh, Tom. *Hispanic Anthology.* New York: Gordon Publishers, 1985.

Warren, Robert Penn and Albert Erskine. *Short Story Masterpieces.* New York: Dell Publishing Company, 1954.

# About the Author

Gerald Lee Ratliff is an award-winning author of numerous articles and textbooks in performance approaches to the study of classroom literature. He has held national and international offices as President of the Eastern Communication Association (1993), Theta Alpha Phi (1986), American Association of Arts' Administrators (1998), and Deputy Director General of the (Cambridge, England) International Biographical Centre (1999). He has also served on the advisory boards of the Association for Communication Administration, American Council of Academic Deans, International Arts Association, and Society of Educators and Scholars.

In addition, he was awarded the "Distinguished Service Award" from both the Eastern Communication Association (1993) and Theta Alpha Phi (1992); was selected a Fulbright Scholar to China (1990) and a U.S.A. delegate of the John F. Kennedy Center for the Performing Arts to Russia (1991); elected "Fellow" of the (London) International Schools of Theatre Association (1991); and has received multiple "Outstanding Teacher" awards for pioneering creative approaches to classroom intruction. Currently, he is associated with The State Unversity of New York, College at Potsdam.

# Order Form

**Meriwether Publishing Ltd.**
P.O. Box 7710
Colorado Springs, CO 80933
Telephone: (719) 594-4422
Website: www.meriwetherpublishing.com

*Please send me the following books:*

_____ **Introduction to Readers Theatre #BK-B234** **$16.95**
by Gerald Lee Ratliff
*A guide to classroom performance*

_____ **Mel White's Readers Theatre Anthology** **$15.95**
**#BK-B110**
by Melvin R. White
*28 all-occasion readings for performance and storytelling*

_____ **Readers Theatre in the Middle School** **$12.95**
**and Junior High Classroom #BK-B203**
by Lois Walker
*A guidebook to Readers Theatre for young students*

_____ **Playing Contemporary Scenes #BK-B100** **$16.95**
edited by Gerald Lee Ratliff
*31 famous scenes and how to play them*

_____ **The Theatre Audition Book #BK-B224** **$16.95**
by Gerald Lee Ratliff
*Playing monologs from contemporary, modern,*
*period and classical plays*

_____ **Playing Scenes — A Sourcebook for** **$14.95**
**Performers #BK-B109**
by Gerald Lee Ratliff
*How to play great scenes from modern and classical theatre*

_____ **Theatre Games and Beyond #BK-B217** **$16.95**
by Amiel Schotz
*A creative approach for performers*

These and other fine Meriwether Publishing books are available at
your local bookstore or direct from the publisher. Use the handy
order form on this page.

Name: _____

Organization name: _____

Address: _____

City: _____ State: _____

Zip: _____ Phone: _____
  ❑ **Check Enclosed**
  ❑ **Visa or MasterCard #** _____
                                  *Expiration*
*Signature:* _____ *Date:* _____
      *(required for Visa/MasterCard orders)*

**Colorado residents:** Please add 3% sales tax.
**Shipping:** Include $2.75 for the first book and 50¢ for each additional book ordered.

  ❑ *Please send me a copy of your complete catalog of books and plays.*